STUDIES IN AN INFLATIONARY ECONOMY

STUDIES IN
AN INFLATIONARY
ECONOMY

The United Kingdom
1948 – 1961

BY

F. W. PAISH

LONDON
MACMILLAN & CO LTD
NEW YORK · ST MARTIN'S PRESS
1962

MACMILLAN AND COMPANY LIMITED
St Martin's Street London WC 2
also Bombay Calcutta Madras Melbourne

THE MACMILLAN COMPANY OF CANADA LIMITED
Toronto

ST MARTIN'S PRESS INC
New York

PRINTED IN GREAT BRITAIN

PREFACE

APART from the first and last chapters, which were written in 1960 and 1961 and have not been published before, all the articles and papers which comprise this book were written in the nineteen-fifties. They are all based, directly or indirectly, upon a study of developments in the United Kingdom, though it may be hoped that some of them use methods of exposition or analysis which can be usefully applied in other contexts. The nineteen-fifties are a particularly interesting period in the economic history of the United Kingdom, and it is hoped that these often fumbling attempts at the interpretation of developments whose significance is still not fully understood may be of some interest, both to students of the period and to those interested in techniques for studying the somewhat different problems of the nineteen-sixties.

The seventeen chapters of the book are divided into five groups according to subject. Chapters 1 to 4 are concerned with various aspects of monetary theory, including the determination of interest rates and the Radcliffe Committee's concept of liquidity. The next four chapters discuss developments in the internal economic position of the United Kingdom, with special reference to the problems of inflation and its control. To this group the final chapter of the book provides a postscript. The third group, comprising Chapters 9 to 11, deals with the international economic position of the United Kingdom, especially in the rôle of an exporter of capital. The fourth group, also of three chapters, covers various aspects of business finance, including the London new issue market, the economic functions of the Stock Exchange and the distribution of company profits. Postscripts to Chapters 12 and 14 bring them more nearly up to date. The last group, of two chapters, covers two very dissimilar subjects. Chapter 15, also with postscript, deals with changes since 1938 in the distribution of personal incomes and in the direct taxes on them, while Chapter 16 discusses an economist's view of the functions of industry. The concluding chapter puts forward an explanation of the fluctuations which

v

have occurred in the British economy since the war and examines the economic position as it appeared to exist in September 1961.

One difficulty which has had to be faced in re-printing earlier articles is that the official statistics on which many of them were based have in many cases been revised retrospectively, sometimes very substantially. A particularly awkward development was the double revision of the balance-of-payments estimates, first in April 1961 and again in September. These affected not only the total balance of payments itself and many of its constituent items, but also certain items in the national income estimates. Adjustment for these changes was made particularly difficult by the fact that the revision of the balance-of-payments estimates was carried back only for two or three years, although it is clear that estimates for earlier years must also have been substantially affected. A full revision of the balance-of-payments estimates, carried back at least to 1948, is now urgently needed.

These difficulties have been met in a number of ways. Where revised figures were not available at all, as in Chapters 9 to 11, the only thing to do was to allow the original text and tables to stand, in the hope that the conclusions drawn have not been wholly invalidated. Where, on the other hand, later estimates were available but the original figures were so closely integrated with the text that their amendment would have involved substantial rewriting, footnotes have been added where the conclusions drawn are seriously misleading. Finally, in one or two chapters where the revision of the tables has been possible without much alteration of the text, revised estimates have been substituted for those originally published. Care has been taken to make clear the dates of the sources used, and in some cases it has been possible to refer the reader to revised estimates elsewhere in the book.

A particularly difficult problem arose in Chapter 14, on the distribution of company profits. After the tables had been revised and a postscript added in May 1961, a further substantial revision of the official estimates covering part, but not the whole, of the period under discussion was published in September. In this chapter, therefore, the text and tables in the main article were left without further change, while the new revisions were incorporated in the postscript.

My sincerest thanks are due to various of my colleagues for reading and criticising drafts of one or both of the new chapters, and especially to Professor P. T. Bauer, Professor A. W. Phillips, Professor Lord Robbins, and Professor Sir Dennis Robertson ; also to Mr. R. F. Burch for his comments on the Postscript to Chapter 15. They are, of course, in no way responsible for the shortcomings which remain in these chapters.

F. W. P.

LONDON
January 1962

ACKNOWLEDGMENTS

THE author wishes to acknowledge his indebtedness to the following publications, institutions, and organisations for permission to re-publish the following articles and papers, of which they hold the copyright :

The American Assembly :
Monetary Policy and the Control of the Post-war British Inflation.

The Banker:
Gilt-edged and the Money Supply.
What *is* this Liquidity ?

District Bank Review:
Company Profits and their Distribution since the War.
Progress, Prices, and the Pound.

Economica:
Inflation in the United Kingdom, 1948–57.
The London New Issue Market.

The Economic Journal:
Open and Repressed Inflation.

English, Scottish, and Australian Bank and the University of Queensland :
The Position of the United Kingdom as an Exporter of Capital.

The Institute of Bankers :
The Economic Functions of the Stock Exchange.

Lloyds Bank Review:
Britain's Foreign Investments : The Post-war Record.
The Real Incidence of Personal Taxation.

The London and Cambridge Economic Service and *The Times Review of Industry* :
Saving and Investment in the United Kingdom.

Manchester Statistical Society :
The New Gold Standard.

CONTENTS

CONTENTS

CHAPTER I

A SIMPLIFIED MODEL OF THE MONETARY SYSTEM

I

INTRODUCTION

THE world in which we live is so incredibly complicated that if we are to try to reach any practical conclusions on economic matters we have to make the most drastic simplifications in the picture it presents. While to begin with we probably use other people's simplifications, as time goes on we find that, in attempting to reach practical conclusions, we are making use of simplifications which differ, in greater or less degree, from those used by others. A number of the essays on current affairs included in this volume have been based in this way on my own simplification of the way in which the monetary system works. I have been using this as a basis of thinking for so long that I find it very difficult to remember how much of it I have borrowed from others and how much I have invented for myself. It certainly bears a considerable resemblance to that used by Professor A. W. Phillips in constructing his analogue machine.[1] While, however, I am certainly indebted to Professor Phillips for giving precision to some of my ideas, I think that even before I knew of his work I must have been thinking along the same general lines, for I find no inconsistency between the model here described and my earlier articles, especially the article on ' Cheap Money Policy ' originally published in 1947.[2]

While some idea of the model I have been using could, no doubt, be deduced from its various applications in the following essays, and while in one of them [3] I have set out

[1] See his article on 'Mechanical Models in Economic Dynamics', *Economica*, August 1950.
[2] Originally published in *Economica*, August 1947. Republished in *The Post-war Financial Problem*, 1950.
[3] 'Open and Repressed Inflation' (p. 28). Originally published in the *Economic Journal*, September 1953.

some of its details, I have nowhere yet had the opportunity
of explaining the model as a whole. I do so here in the hope
partly that I may thereby make some of the following essays
more intelligible to those whose approach is different from my
own, and partly that it may prove helpful to some in making
their own appreciations of the real world.

II

Uses of Money

I start by conceptually dividing all the money [1] in existence
in a country at any given moment into two parts. One of
these is held for the purpose of making payments, for purposes
already envisaged, within the foreseeable future. The other is
held as a general store of value, and is not expected to be spent
unless some change takes place either in the particular situation
of the owner or in the general conditions of the system.

In a closed system, where all the money is owned by local
residents, the purposes for which money can be spent can in
turn be divided into two, which may be broadly described as
income transactions and capital transactions. The exact line
drawn between the two depends on the statistical conventions
we accept. On the strictest possible definition, income transactions are confined to those transactions in which the whole
of the money passing is regarded as income by the recipients.
This definition would limit income transactions to payments
for services, either of persons or of their assets, including
wages, salaries, fees, profits, rents, interest, and dividends.
Receipts from the sale of assets (except in so far as they are
payments for the service of selling) are, strictly speaking, never
income, but merely represent a change in assets. Payments
for services are income in the hands of the recipients, regardless
of whether the services are immediately consumed or are used
for the creation of physical objects of greater or less durability.

---

[1] Money is defined as anything which, in the relevant country at the
relevant time, is widely and generally used as a medium of exchange. In
the United Kingdom at the present time it consists of coin, notes, and bank
deposits. Bank deposits include not only current accounts but also deposit
and savings bank accounts with the commercial banks. The two last are
regarded as money which the owners have committed themselves to holding
temporarily idle, like notes in a safe deposit with a time-lock on the door.

III

THE INCOME CIRCULATION

In practice, so strict a definition of an income transaction would be inconvenient. While it is possible to regard the purchase of an ice-cream as a capital transaction, involving a change merely in the form of the buyer's assets but not in their total, we normally regard such purchases of short-lived assets as consumption, rather than as investment in assets with a high rate of depreciation in use. As soon, however, as we regard the purchase of any physical object as consumption, we are faced with an infinite series of possible transactions, within which the line drawn between investment and consumption (that is to say, between a capital transaction and an income transaction) is necessarily arbitrary. In this country the only purchases of physical objects by households which count as capital transactions are purchases of land and houses. All other purchases by ultimate consumers of goods, however durable, are classified as consumption. In other countries the definition of consumption is drawn rather less widely, and purchases of motor-cars and some other durable consumption goods are regarded as capital transactions.

Another type of purchase of physical assets which it is convenient to regard as an income transaction is the purchase of goods by business concerns to maintain their stock-in-trade, although here again the distinction between stock-in-trade and fixed assets becomes arbitrary at the margin. In so far as the cost of stocks bought is equal to the original cost of stocks recently sold, we can visualise a circulation of money entirely within the income account, from consumers to retailers, from retailers to wholesalers, from wholesalers to manufacturers, from manufacturers to suppliers of raw materials, and from all of them to the ultimate income-earners, the suppliers of services, who are also the ultimate consumers. If we bring in the Government, we can also include in the income circulation money paid in taxes and spent by the Government without any long delay; although, if the flow of receipts or payments shows wide seasonal fluctuations, we may have to think of some part of the tax receipts as moving out of the income

circulation for a time and returning to it later. For some
purposes it might be convenient to treat in the same way other
payments showing large seasonal fluctuations, such as payments for annual crops and perhaps for interest and dividends.

As well as moving round and round within the income
circulation, money can both enter it and leave it. If an income-
earner decides not to spend a portion of his current income
on current consumption, that money is regarded as leaving the
income circulation to become at least temporarily idle. If,
on the other hand, he spends on consumption money previously saved, it is transferred out of idle balances back into the
income circulation. Similarly money can be transferred into
the income circulation by spending it on the creation of new
capital goods or by adding to the amount invested in stock-
in-trade, or transferred out of the income circulation by reducing the amount invested in stock-in-trade. These movements
into and out of the income circulation will be discussed in
subsequent sections.

IV
THE CAPITAL CIRCULATION

All payments of money which do not occur in the income
circulation take place in the capital circulation. They include
all purchases of existing fixed assets, all purchases of financial
assets, such as securities, and all loans and repayments of loans.
So long as the money obtained by borrowing, or by the sale of a
security or of an existing fixed asset, is held for the purpose of
re-lending, or for the purchase of a security or of an existing
fixed asset, it remains within the capital circulation. If, however, the proceeds of a loan or a sale are used to finance the
creation of new physical assets, they are transferred to the
income circulation ; while if the borrower or seller does not
expect to use the proceeds for any purpose so long as conditions
(including his own expectations) remain unchanged, they are
transferred to idle balances. Conversely, if the owner of idle
balances decides to invest them, they are transferred, at least
initially, to the capital circulation ; while if he decides to spend
them on consumption, they are transferred to the income
circulation.

V

Money Flows between Circulations

The conceptual system outlined above may be expressed diagramatically as follows :

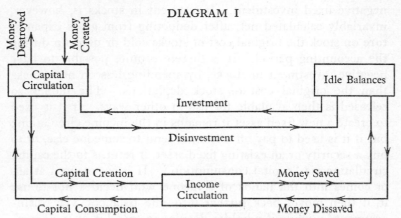

DIAGRAM I

This diagram implies that to divert expenditure from consumption to the creation of new physical assets requires three separate decisions. The first of these is not to spend on consumption the whole of current income. This we call monetary saving, and the money so saved becomes initially idle. The next decision is whether to invest the money saved or to continue to hold it idle. If the decision is to invest, the money is transferred to the capital circulation. It is then necessary to take a further decision, whether to invest in existing assets (including existing physical assets as well as securities and loans) or to use the money to pay for services employed in the construction of new assets. If investment is in existing assets, the money passes round inside the capital circulation until it comes into the hands of someone who either holds it idle, when it is transferred to ' idle balances ', or uses it to pay for the construction of a new asset, when it returns to the income circulation.

It is also possible (though less frequent) for money to flow in the reverse direction. If fixed investment is calculated net, after setting aside enough depreciation to replace the original cost of fixed assets over the period of their working lives, it is possible to carry out what is here called capital consumption by spending less than the aggregate depreciation provisions on creating new fixed assets. If, however, we follow the more usual and generally more convenient practice of calculating fixed investment gross, it is impossible to have negative fixed investment. Investment in stocks is, however, invariably calculated net, after deducting from gross expenditure on stock the original cost of stocks sold or used up during the accounting period. It is therefore quite possible to have negative investment in stocks, by spending less on new stocks than the original cost of stock depletions. The money so released is then available for use in other ways. If it is used to create a new fixed asset it remains in the income circulation ; but if it is used to pay off a loan, to lend to someone else, or to buy a security or an existing fixed asset, it returns to the capital circulation via ' capital consumption '. If it is not used at all, or comes into the hands of someone who decides not to use it, it then moves back further into idle balances, via ' disinvestment ' ; while if a holder decides to spend it on consumption (including the purchase by an individual of any durable consumption good except a house) it moves back again out of idle balances into the income circulation via ' monetary dissaving '.

The three decisions required to move money out of the income account via saving and back into the income account via capital creation (or out of the income account via capital consumption and back via monetary dissaving) are not necessarily separate ones. Money may be saved for a specific purpose, as for instance to repay a debt. In this case it would move at once through idle balances into the capital circulation. Or it may be saved in order to finance the creation of a new capital asset, in which case all three decisions are linked, and the money moves round the whole circle and back into the income circulation again. It is possible, though more difficult, to imagine linked decisions when the money flows in the reverse direction. Thus a shopkeeper might be forced to run down stocks in order to maintain his consumption, in which case the money would be regarded as moving back, via capital consumption, disinvestment, and monetary dissaving, until it reached the income circulation again. The conditions which determine how far the various decisions are independent and how far they are linked will be discussed in a later section.

VI
Changes in the Quantity of Money

In Diagram I provision is also made for the introduction of additional money into the system and for the withdrawal of part of the existing stock of money. In this country money is generally created by borrowing from, or selling an asset to, a bank, and destroyed by repaying a bank debt or by buying an asset from a bank. Newly created money is therefore regarded as being introduced initially into the capital circulation, and money destroyed as being withdrawn from it. Frequently, of course, money is borrowed from a bank for the express purpose of financing the creation of a new capital asset; in this case the decision to borrow the money is linked with a decision to transfer it to the income account via capital creation. It is unlikely that money is often borrowed in order to hold it idle, but there may well be occasions when it is borrowed to finance expenditure on consumption. In this case the decision to borrow the money from the bank is linked with two other decisions, one not to invest it and the second not to hold it idle. Money borrowed from a bank is probably more likely to be transferred to the income circulation by one or other of these channels than is money obtained by the sale of a security to a bank, which is more likely to be used for the purchase of another existing asset and so retained in the capital circulation. A rise in bank deposits caused by a rise in advances is thus more likely to cause an immediate rise in incomes than a corresponding rise in deposits caused by a rise in the banks' holdings of investments, while the latter is more likely to cause a rise in prices of existing assets and lower the rate of interest. The difference between the effects on the rate of rise in money incomes of a rise in bank advances and those of a rise in bank investments is likely to be greatest in times of trade depression, when the creation of new assets tends to be less attractive than the acquisition of existing ones. In these conditions, therefore, new money introduced into the capital circulation is

likely to take a long time to percolate into the income circulation. In times of active trade, on the other hand, when the
creation of new assets is relatively more attractive, this delay
is likely to be shorter, and the difference between the effects
of creating money by a rise in advances and by a rise in bank
investments is likely to be much less marked.

VII

SAVING

The concept of monetary saving, as here defined, is not
the same as that of *ex post* saving, and is more akin to that of
ex ante saving. Money in the income circulation is not regarded as having been saved merely because the recipients of
incomes have not yet had time to spend them all. Net monetary
saving is equal to net capital creation only when the amount
of money flowing out of the income circulation is equal to the
amount flowing in, so that the quantity of money in the income
circulation is unchanged. Monetary saving is therefore equal
to expenditure on capital creation minus the increase (or plus
the decrease) in the quantity of money in the income circulation. As aggregate incomes are assumed to vary in direct proportion to the quantity of money in the income circulation,[1] the
change in aggregate incomes over any given period [2] is equal
to the change in the quantity of money in the income circulation multiplied by the ratio of aggregate incomes for that

[1] This assumption finds some confirmation in the extraordinarily stable
ratio which, in normal peace-time conditions, the quantity of notes and coin
in the hands of the public bears to the national money income. It may be
assumed that notes and coin are used almost wholly in the income circulation, and if we also assume that the quantity of bank deposits included in
the income circulation bears some fairly stable relationship to the quantity
of cash, it follows that the total quantity of money in the income circulation
bears a fairly stable relationship to the national money income.
    The difference between the model here presented and the quantity theory
of money is that the quantity theory assumes that the national money income
varies proportionately with the total quantity of money, and not merely
with that part of it which happens to be included in the income circulation
at the time; or, alternatively, that the quantity of money in the income
circulation forms a constant proportion of the total quantity of money.
    [2] Strictly speaking, over any period which is a whole multiple of the
period in which the national money income is equal to the quantity of money
in the income circulation. In the United Kindgom this period may be of
the order of six weeks or two months. I am indebted to Professor Sir
Dennis Robertson for pointing this out to me.

period to the quantity of money in the income circulation; this is the same thing as the difference between monetary saving and expenditure on capital creation multiplied by the same ratio.

VIII

RATES OF TRANSFER OF MONEY BETWEEN CIRCULATIONS

1. *Volume of Saving.*—Something can now be said about the factors influencing the rates of transfer of money between one circulation and another. Those affecting the level of saving are complex and much disputed. Recent British experience suggests that a rise in money income, even when unaccompanied by a rise in real income, tends to increase both business and (since direct taxation is highly progressive) Government saving. Since business taxes are paid after a considerable delay, much of the increase in business saving takes the form of increases in tax reserves and provisions. It is in business and Government saving, therefore, that the so-called 'forced saving' of inflation makes its appearance. Part of this increase is likely to be offset by a fall in personal saving, but since many people neither own capital nor save, a faster rise in prices than in personal incomes after tax forces them to reduce consumption. In the longer run, of course, as more and more people come to anticipate further rises in prices, it takes larger and larger increases in money incomes and prices to maintain the proportion of national income saved. In the end the assumption that aggregate incomes are a constant multiple of the quantity of money in the income circulation breaks down, the velocity of circulation rises without limit, and ultimately money becomes unacceptable. But if the initial rise in prices is moderate, and especially if it is occasionally interrupted, the process of breakdown may be a very long one.

On the other hand, a rise in money incomes, when accompanied by a rapid rise in real personal income, seems to stimulate not only business and Government saving but also personal saving. In the United Kingdom there is a very marked contrast between the years before 1952, when real personal incomes after tax were almost stationary and personal savings were negligible, and the subsequent years, when real

personal incomes after tax rose by an average of over 2 per
cent a year per head and about a fifth of the increase was saved.

Even more disputable are the effects on saving of changes
in the rate of interest. The existence of other and probably
more powerful factors make it difficult to draw any clear conclusions from the historical evidence, and we are obliged to
fall back on *a priori* reasoning. On the one hand, it is possible
to take the view that if the income which people can expect to
obtain by investing their new savings is increased, saving
becomes more attractive and people do more of it. On the
other hand, if we take the view that a main motive for personal
saving is the desire to prevent, or reduce the risk of, a future
fall in the standard of living, it is possible to reach the opposite
conclusion. A rise in the rate of interest means that more
consumption is obtainable in the future at the cost of a given
sacrifice in the present. If, therefore, an individual's level of
saving is already adjusted to providing the desired amount of
consumption equalisation through time, he is likely to divide
the benefits of a higher rate of interest between the present and
the future, increasing his consumption in the present by
saving less, but still saving enough to give some increase of
consumption in the future.

The effects of a rise in the rate of interest on business and
Government saving are also doubtful. On the whole it seems
likely that the increased cost, and possibly difficulty, of raising
money in the market will cause companies to distribute less
in dividends and plough more back to reserve (though it is
possible that some companies, which need to raise money in
the market in any case, may raise dividends in order to prevent
a decline in the market value of their shares). On the other
hand, any increase in business saving may well be offset by
a fall in Government saving as the result of higher interest
charges on short-term debt, certainly within the financial year,
and possibly over a longer period if the Government hesitates
to raise taxes.

2. *Investment.*—About the other movements of money
between the different circulations (that is, between idle balances
and the capital circulation and between the capital circulation
and the income circulation) it is possible to speak more
definitely. Decisions about transfers between idle balances

and the capital circulation can be said to depend on two factors : (1) the amount of income which is expected to be forgone as the result of holding a given quantity of money idle instead of using it to buy an existing asset ; and (2) the amount of money which people are prepared to hold idle at each level of income sacrifice. If the choice is assumed to be between holding money idle and buying fixed interest securities, we can call the first of these factors the rate of interest and the second the liquidity preference schedule. Frequently, of course, the alternative to holding money idle is the purchase, not of fixed interest securities, but of existing physical assets or ordinary shares. We can, however, assume that, in a free market, the expected yields on different types of assets, allowing for differences in risk and liquidity, as well as in distribution of income over time, will tend to become equated. We can therefore regard changes in the yields on fixed interest securities as evidence of similar changes in the expected yields on all types of existing assets. The greater is this rise in the income expected from the use of a given sum to buy an existing asset, the greater is the cost of holding money idle, and the larger is the amount of money we should expect to see transferred from idle balances to the capital circulation.

3. *Capital Creation.*—Decisions about the transfer of money from the capital circulation to the income circulation also depend on two factors. One is the relationship between market prices of existing assets and the income expected to be derived from their ownership, and the other is the relationship between the cost of creating new physical assets and the income expected to be subsequently derived from their possession. Whenever the expected yield on existing assets falls relatively to the yield expected from the creation and ownership of new assets, we should expect a shift from the purchase of existing assets to the creation of new ones, a rise in capital creation and an increase in the net transfer of money from the capital circulation to the income circulation.

It should be noted that, although for convenience we may speak of ' the rate of interest ', the validity of the statement that a rise in prices of existing assets tends to stimulate the creation of capital does not depend on the existence of any system of contractual payments, or indeed of any money payments for the services of assets. In a system where there are only two kinds of assets, money and physical objects, and where physical assets render services only to their direct owners, a rise in prices of existing assets relatively to the cost of constructing new ones will still have the effects of stimulating the construction of new assets, causing a net transfer of money from the capital circulation to the income circulation, and raising the level of money incomes.

IX

PRICES OF EXISTING ASSETS

Any increase in the quantity of money in the capital circulation tends to raise prices of existing assets, while a net withdrawal of money, either into idle balances or into the income circulation, tends to lower them. A convenient assumption to make is that the aggregate market value of all marketable assets varies proportionately with the quantity of money in the capital circulation. This assumption carries two implications. One is that, if the quantity of money in the capital circulation is unchanged, an increase in the supply of marketable assets depresses the aggregate value of those previously in existence. The other is that, again with an unchanged quantity of money in the capital circulation, a rise in the prices of any one class of asset will depress the aggregate value of all other classes. Thus an increase in the demand for ordinary shares, caused by more optimistic expectations about their future yields, will bring about a rise in their prices but a fall in those of other assets, including fixed interest securities. This is, of course, merely the process through which market forces equate the expected yields of different classes of assets.[1]

X

SAVING AND INTEREST RATES

While the effects of a change of interest rates on the level of saving are largely indeterminate, the effects of a spontaneous

---

[1] In fact, the quantity of money in the capital circulation cannot remain unchanged, unless there is a simultaneous shift in the liquidity preference schedule, since the rise in interest rates will draw in more money from idle balances. It cannot, however, draw in enough to prevent some rise in interest rates, since without some rise in rates none would be drawn in.

change in the rate of saving on the level of interest rates are also
by no means certain ; all that can be said is that the normal
effect of a rise in saving is to lower it and of a fall in saving
to raise it. This is for three reasons. The first is that, unless
the whole of the money saved is retained in idle balances, some
part of it will pass into the capital circulation and increase the
demand for existing assets. The second reason is that a rise
in the proportion of incomes saved tends to reduce the level
of money incomes, initially of incomes derived from the production and sale of consumer goods and services. If the
decline in the yield of assets employed in producing consumption goods is expected to be prolonged, investors may
be deterred from moving money from the capital circulation
to the income circulation in order to finance capital creation.
Thus to the effect of the extra money entering the capital
circulation from saving is added that of a reduction in the
quantity of money leaving it. The quantity of money in the
capital circulation is thus doubly reinforced, and asset values
as a whole will rise further. If at the same time the expectation
of reduced yields on some physical assets, or on titles to them,
causes prices of these assets to rise less than the average of all
assets, or to fall, prices of other assets, including fixed interest
claims, will rise by more than the average and the current
yield on fixed interest securities will be still further reduced.

These effects, however, while normal, cannot be regarded
as inevitable. If owners of physical assets regard the fall in
the incomes derived from them as purely temporary, they may
not reduce their investment plans at all — indeed, they may
regard the release of scarce resources from the production of
consumer goods as providing a good opportunity for implement-
ing them. In this case the flow of money from the capital
circulation to the income circulation will not be checked.
Again, an increase in monetary saving may be accompanied
by, or even give rise to, an increase in liquidity preference, so
that the whole, or more than the whole, of the extra money
saved may be added to idle balances. It is unlikely an increase
in liquidity preference would in fact coincide with the maintenance of capital creation; but it is quite possible for the increase
in liquidity preference to be so great that it would absorb
not only the whole of the increase in saving but also the whole,

or more than the whole, of any reduction in new capital creation. Thus the reduction in the inflow of money into the capital circulation from idle balances might be greater than the reduction in the outflow of money from the capital circulation to the income circulation, so that the quantity of money in the capital circulation, and the aggregate value of assets, would both fall. In extreme cases, the fall in asset values might extend, not only to physical assets and claims to them, but also to fixed interest securities. This seems to be what happens when the initial stages of a business recession are accompanied by a severe financial crisis.

XI
LIMITATIONS OF THE MODEL

The highly simplified model of the monetary system outlined above omits, of course, many of the factors which have to be taken into account in assessing an actual situation. In particular, since it describes only monetary phenomena, it has no direct information to give about changes in real, as opposed to money, incomes. All we can do is to guess that, unless we start from a position of heavy unemployment of both labour and capital, a continued rise in money incomes of more than a few per cent a year will almost certainly outstrip the rise in output and be accompanied by rising prices. Again, since our model says nothing about population changes, it gives no direct information about changes in income per head. Nor, since it deals in aggregates, does it show changes in the distribution of incomes inside the income circulation or in the relative prices of assets inside the capital circulation. It further assumes that there is only one kind of money, and cannot therefore be used directly in the discussion of problems arising from the existence of multiple forms of money.

XII
APPLICATIONS OF THE MODEL

1. *Controls on Inflation.*—In spite, however, of these and other limitations, I have found the model useful for a number of purposes. It is, for instance, helpful in classifying the

various official controls on the use of money which have been applied at various times, especially since 1939. All attempts to check inflation must have the objective of slowing down the rise in money incomes — that is to say, of restricting the flow of money into the income circulation. Direct attempts to do this must take one or more of four general forms : measures designed to increase the proportion of income saved, such as restrictions on consumption and larger budget surpluses ; to decrease the amount dissaved, as by restrictions on hire-purchase finance ; to restrict (the amount of money spent on) certain forms of capital creation, as by the control of building licences ; and, more rarely, to promote capital consumption, as by the enforcement of maximum prices, which prevent retailers from defending their stocks, together with restrictions on production, which prevent them from replenishing them.

Indirect measures for keeping money out of the income circulation are of two main kinds : those which attempt to restrict the total quantity of money, and so the quantity of money in the capital circulation ; and those which restrict freedom of borrowing and investment, in the hope of keeping money out of the hands of people who would want to use it for the finance of consumption, or for the creation of assets which are officially regarded as unnecessary or undesirable. The former type of measure tends to reduce prices of all assets, raise interest rates, check capital creation, and promote a flow of money out of idle balances ; the latter, if successful, makes money unobtainable by some would-be borrowers and more plentiful for the rest. It therefore tends to keep market rates of interest down and promotes the retention of money in idle balances. It is, however, very difficult to make effective ; there are many ways in which money can leak from those for whom it is plentiful to those for whom it has been made artificially scarce.

2. *Cheap Money Policies.*—Besides its usefulness for purposes of classification, there are some actual problems on which the model, with all its limitations, can throw useful light. Let us take the example of a government which, in order to reduce the cost of servicing the national debt, wishes to bring down interest rates. It can always do this by creating sufficient

new money and using it for the redemption or purchase of Government debt. This introduces new money into the capital circulation and drives down interest rates. Not all the new money, however, will stay in the capital circulation. On the one hand, the fall in interest rates reduces the cost of holding money idle and encourages an increase in idle balances;[1] on the other, the rise in prices of existing assets makes the construction of new assets relatively more attractive, and more money will be transferred to the income circulation to finance increased capital creation. How much money will move in each direction will depend largely on the state of trade. In a severe trade depression, when prices of existing physical assets are often well below their cost of replacement, it may take a large rise in prices of second-hand capital goods to have much effect on the production of new ones. In this case the effects of the increase in the quantity of money will be mainly a fall in interest rates and a rise in idle balances, while the effect on incomes will be slow. If, on the other hand, prices of existing physical assets are already up to or above the cost of constructing new ones, as is the case during a boom, expenditure on new construction will be rapidly stimulated, much of the new money will move rapidly into the income circulation, and the effects of the increase in the quantity money will be seen rather in higher incomes than in lower interest rates.

The effect of a rise in incomes on output and prices will, of course, also depend on the state of trade. If there are large unemployed resources, the effect of the rise in money incomes will be to expand output, so that real income rises along with money incomes, and the rise in prices, if any, is small. Unfortunately, conditions in which rapidly rising money incomes are matched by rising output are also those in which money created to repay Government debt is least likely to move into the income circulation; and those in which a rise in incomes is most likely to lead to higher prices are also those in which the creation of money is most likely to lead rapidly

---

[1] The transfer of money out of the capital account into idle balances may be smaller, or even negative, if the effect of the fall in interest rates is to make investors believe that interest rates will fall further, or even that rates will remain low for a very long time. Such a change in expectations may shift the position of the whole liquidity preference function. Such a shift is most likely to occur in a time of trade depression.

to higher incomes. In periods of heavy unemployment, therefore, the creation of even large amounts of additional money for the repayment of Government debt is unlikely to raise incomes at all quickly, although once incomes have begun to rise the existence of large quantities of idle money may make it difficult to prevent the rise from going too fast and too far. On the other hand, an attempt to force down interest rates in a period of full employment is likely to be frustrated by the rapid transfer of money out of the capital circulation into the income circulation (leading in turn to rising prices), unless controls can be made sufficiently effective to keep the money artificially penned up in the capital circulation and idle balances. While such controls may be effective for limited periods, especially in time of war or other national crisis, it is unlikely that they can be successfully enforced for long periods in a democratic country in peace-time.

XIII
Uses of the Model as a Framework

1. *Changes in Wage Rates.*—Even when a particular problem involves factors not included in the model described above, it often provides a useful framework to which the extra factors can be added. Three examples are given below, each concerned with a different circulation.

In the income circulation, the model itself makes no assumptions about the way in which incomes are distributed or how changes in aggregate incomes affect different classes of income receivers. The easiest assumption to make, which may often be a reasonably close approximation to reality, is that all classes of incomes rise or fall proportionately. If we make this assumption, it follows that a rise in aggregate incomes, however caused, will increase the aggregate incomes received from the ownership of existing assets. If we further assume that expectations about the yields on newly created assets depend upon recent yields on existing assets, a rise in aggregate incomes will encourage new capital creation and promote a further rise in incomes. On these two assumptions, a trade depression can be cured by an enforced rise in wage rates, provided that the rise is initially financed by some additional net movement of money, however small, into the income circulation.

If, however, the assumption that all classes of incomes move together does not hold, we may find that a rise in wages, so far from curing the depression, makes it worse. If part of the rise in wages is, or is expected to be, paid for out of a fall in incomes derived from the ownership of assets, the effect of a rise in wages, even if it results in an initial increase in aggregate incomes, is not to increase the expected yield from the ownership of new assets but to reduce it. The resulting discouragement to the creation of new capital may well, in course of time, reduce the inflow of money to the income circulation by more than the payment of higher wages has increased it, so that in the long run not only aggregate incomes, but also the aggregate incomes of wage-earners, may fall back below the initial level. There is therefore no general answer to the question whether raising or lowering wage rates is more likely to remedy unemployment; it depends on which assumptions are relevant to any particular situation.

2. *Deposit Accounts.*—Our second example relates to idle balances. One institutional factor which tends to increase the willingness to hold money idle is the payment of interest on idle balances. In the United Kingdom, for instance, the banks pay a rate of interest on deposits on which their owners undertake to give seven days' notice of withdrawal. Not all idle balances, of course, are on deposit account. Many holders of idle balances do not trouble to shift them from current to deposit account, especially when interest rates are low. Nevertheless, the raising of the rate of interest paid on even a part of idle balances must tend to check the flow of money from idle balances to the capital circulation, slow down the rise in the velocity of circulation, and increase the effect on market rates of interest of any given reduction in the quantity of money.

If this is so, there would seem to be serious disadvantages attached to the system, which exists in many countries, of allowing banks to hold smaller cash reserves against deposit accounts than against current accounts. When in these countries a rise in deposit rates causes the transfer of already idle balances from current account to deposit account, the banks can increase the total of all deposits held on the basis of a given cash reserve. The effects of an initial restriction of the banks' cash reserves on market rates of interest and indirectly on the rate of rise in incomes are thereby weakened. Conversely, the effects of an expansion of the commercial banks' cash reserves in order to bring down interest rates and expand incomes are likewise weakened, since part of the additional cash reserves will be absorbed in providing additional backing for the money transferred from deposit account to current account as the result of the fall in the rate paid on deposit. Thus the effectiveness of monetary policy is reduced in both directions.

3. *Funding Operations.*—The third example of the way our model can be used as a framework for the investigation of more complex problems is taken from the capital circulation. All future incomes derived from the ownership of earning assets can be divided into two parts: the expected money income and the (usually negative) imputed income arising from the uncertainty with which the expectation is held. The only case in which the future income is exactly known is when money is safely invested at a fixed rate of interest to be repaid on exactly the date on which it is required to meet a known need. If the security matures before the date on which it is needed, it is impossible to foretell the rate of interest that will be earned for the remainder of the period; if it matures after the date on which the money is needed, it is impossible to foretell the price it will fetch when sold and therefore its average yield to completion of sale. Different investors will have different demands for investments of different maturities, and relative prices of securities with different maturities can be affected by changes in the relative importance of different classes of investors or in the volumes of securities with different maturity dates.

Let us now examine the effect of a large change in the relative volumes of long-dated and short-dated securities, due to a large-scale funding operation by the Government. Let us assume that the Government borrows a large amount of money from the public on long-term and pays off short-term securities, also held by the public. Prices of long-dated securities will fall and their yields rise, while prices of short-dated securities will rise and their yields fall. Since yields will have fallen on those securities which are the closest substitutes for money, the opportunity cost of holding money idle will

fall and former holders of short-dated securities will hold part
of the proceeds in idle balances. Even though at the other end
of the scale some former holders of short-dated securities will
be induced by the higher long-term rates to re-invest in long-
dated securities, the net effect of the operation will be to cause
some money to shift out of the capital account into idle
balances and to raise the general level of interest rates. That
this is the logical effect of a funding policy is perhaps even
more apparent if we look at it another way. Even though the
Government has not altered its cash holdings, it has increased
the general liquidity of its position by converting short-term
liabilities into long-term.[1] At the same time, it has induced a
corresponding fall in the liquidity of the public by bringing
about a corresponding change in its assets. In order to restore
its liquidity to its former level, the non-government sector must
now hold a larger proportion of its total assets in the form of
money, and will therefore transfer money out of the capital
circulation into idle balances. Although the non-government
sector is only trying to maintain its previous standard of
liquidity, it has increased its demand to hold money, while
the Government has increased its general liquidity although its
demand to hold money is unchanged. For the system as a
whole there has been an increase in liquidity preference, in the
conventionally restricted meaning of the term, even though
there has been no increase in the real liquidity preference of
the people holding the additional idle balances.

XIV
LINKED DECISIONS

We are now in a position to return to the discussion of how
far decisions to move money from one circulation to another
are independent of each other and how far they are inter-
linked. The conditions which seem most to favour the independence of decisions are those in which savings are made
voluntarily by individuals for the general purpose of providing
security and increasing their future incomes. In these conditions, it would appear that three separate decisions must be

---

[1] For a fuller discussion of this point see 'British Floating Debt Policy'
(*Economica*, August 1940), republished in *The Post-war Financial Problem.*

taken : two of them, about how much is saved and how much is invested, by the saver ; and the third, about whether to use the money for the acquisition of existing assets or the creation of new ones, usually by the person or institution who has sold existing assets to, or borrowed money from, the original saver. The existence of institutional borrowers, such as savings banks and building societies, which provide highly liquid assets in exchange for money, probably greatly reduces the proportion of these strictly personal savings which is held idle.[1]

There is less independence of decisions when personal savings are made, not entirely voluntarily, but to permit the fulfilment of previous contracts, such as payments of life-insurance premiums or repayments of debts to building societies. Here there are direct links between the act of saving and the movement of the money saved into the capital circulation, although the decision about transferring the money back to the income circulation in order to finance capital creation remains a separate one. Even between saving and transfer to the capital circulation the link is not invariable, for contractual payments may be made, not out of new saving, but by the release of money from idle balances, out of the proceeds of the sale of assets, or from new borrowings.

In business enterprises where ownership is separated from control there is a considerable, though perhaps not very high, probability that the links will extend all the way from saving to the return of the money to the income circulation through capital creation. The links may originate in either direction : companies may be induced to undertake more capital creation because they have been able to make more savings ; or they may restrict dividends and save more because they have capital creation to finance. The links, however, do not always exist. Companies often refrain from increasing dividends by the full increase in their distributable profits, even when they do not need the extra saving to finance capital creation ; and they finance a substantial part of their capital creation by the issue of new securities.

[1] The number of linked decisions by private individuals would be considerably increased if we included with capital goods durable consumption goods other than houses. If such goods are regarded as investments, a switch of buying from non-durable to durable consumption goods becomes a series of linked decisions to save and invest in new physical assets.

The links between saving and capital creation are probably closest in business enterprises where ownership and control are in the same hands. Such enterprises, whether incorporated or not, often find it difficult to obtain much long-term capital from outside, while those controlling the business stand to gain very directly from its expansion. They therefore have the strongest incentives to plough back as large a proportion of profits as possible in order to finance the expansion of their productive assets.

It seems probable that in recent years the closeness of the direct links between saving and capital formation has been somewhat diminished. The sharp rise in personal saving which has occurred since 1952 must mean that a larger proportion of saving is subject to a free choice of how it will be invested, either by the savers or by the institutions to which it is transferred. One effect of this is seen in the great increase in new capital issues by companies.

A type of saving, which since 1948 has become very important and for which the links with capital creation are small, or even negative, is Government saving. To-day the size of the ' above-the-line ' budget surplus is often determined, not by the volume of public investment but by the Government's desire to restrict or expand the level of total demand. To a smaller extent, public investment is varied for the same purpose. Thus a rise in the budget surplus may well coincide with a reduction in public investment and vice versa. While a rise in money incomes, when accompanied by a corresponding rise in real incomes, may cause Government saving and Government capital creation to increase together, a rise in money incomes without a corresponding rise in real incomes is likely to bring more Government saving and less Government investment; conversely, a fall in money incomes, or even a slower rise in money incomes than in productive capacity, is likely to induce less Government saving and more Government investment.

XV

INTERNATIONAL TRADE

So far we have been discussing the monetary system of a closed economy. If we open the economy to trading and financial relationships with other countries, some part of the stock of local money will probably come into the possession of foreigners. These foreign-owned balances will be augmented by transfers from the income circulation in payment for imports, and depleted by transfers to the income circulation in payment for exports, when both types of payment are made in local money. Foreign-owned money balances may also be increased by the transfer from the capital circulation of money borrowed or the proceeds of securities sold there by foreigners, and reduced by transfers to the capital circulation of money invested there by foreigners or used for the repayment of debt. Transfers to the income circulation in payment for the creation of local physical assets are regarded as taking place via the capital circulation. Foreign-owned balances, so far as the rest of the system is concerned, thus resemble idle balances, except that they are fed from the income circulation through payments for imports, instead of by saving, and depleted by payments for exports, instead of by dissaving.

Besides being replenished by payments for imports and by local borrowing, foreign-owned money balances can be expanded out of the proceeds of the sale of foreign money to the local monetary authorities. Such transactions (unless deliberately offset) have the effect of increasing the total quantity of local money in existence. Similarly, if foreign-owned balances are used to buy foreign money from the authorities, they are cancelled. Money created or destroyed in this way is regarded as being introduced directly into foreign-owned balances or withdrawn directly from them. The effect of introducing foreign balances to our system is shown in Diagram II.

Even if no foreign balances are transferred abroad (that is to say, are cancelled by being used to buy foreign money from the monetary authorities), an adverse balance of payments on current account reduces the quantity of money in the income circulation and the aggregate incomes of local residents; similarly, a favourable balance of payments increases the quantity of money in the income circulation and expands incomes. In addition, there will probably be secondary effects on incomes of changes in saving and capital creation, induced by the initial change in incomes.

B

It is unlikely that the whole of any excess of payments for imports over payments for exports will remain permanently in the form of foreign-owned money balances, or that an excess of payments for exports will be met wholly out of money balances. It is much more likely that much or all of an increase in foreign-owned balances will be invested or used to repay debts, while a decrease will probably be made good by borrowing or the sale of assets. The effect of such transfers between

DIAGRAM II

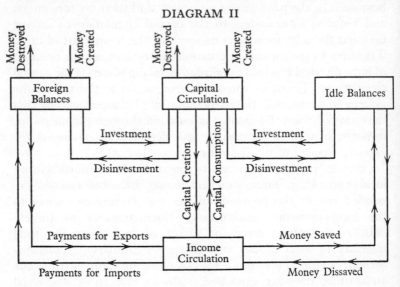

foreign-owned balances and the capital circulation will be to diminish, but not wholly to offset, the effects on incomes of a balance-of-payments surplus or deficit. If an initial increase in foreign balances is transferred to the capital circulation for investment, it will tend to raise asset prices, lower the rate of interest, and stimulate capital creation; while if a fall in foreign-owned balances is made good by borrowing or selling assets, the resultant rise in interest rates will tend to check capital creation. The interest rate changes will not, however, do more than partially reverse the initial changes in income; for the effect on capital creation continues only so long as the change in interest rates is maintained, and this can persist only so long as the quantity of money in the income circulation is lower (or higher) than it was originally.

The extent to which transfers between foreign-owned money balances and the capital circulation offset the initial changes in incomes depends partly on the maturity dates of the securities bought or sold by foreigners. Generally speaking, the longer-dated are the securities bought or sold, the greater effect are changes in their yields likely to have on the volume of capital creation. Further, long-dated securities are less perfect substitutes for cash than short-dated securities, and changes in their yields tend to have smaller effects on the volume of idle balances. Where balance-of-payments surpluses or deficits are covered entirely by foreign transactions in the local long-term capital market, it may not take any large change in saving or capital creation to maintain a position of equilibrium which, if not permanent, may last for many years.

While in general the investment of foreign-owned balances will cause a fall in interest rates, it is possible, in the special conditions [1] which exist in the United Kingdom, for it to have the opposite effect. If the foreign balances consist of deposits with the clearing banks, if the investment is in Treasury or other bills, and if the clearing banks' liquid assets ratios are near their minima, the investment of foreign-owned balances may cause the banks' liquid asset ratios to fall below their desired levels. This will compel the banks to sell securities, thus both reducing deposits and driving up long-term interest rates. In this case, therefore, the investment of foreign-owned balances may reduce the quantity of money, force up interest rates, check capital creation, and reinforce the fall in incomes caused by the initial adverse balance of payments. Conversely, if a favourable balance of payments forces foreigners to sell bills, the effects of the resultant increase in the banks' liquid assets ratio may reinforce the initial rise in incomes.

Whether the local money which foreigners obtain by selling foreign money or gold to the monetary authorities represents an addition to the total stock of money, or merely a redistribution of the existing stock, depends on the types of institution that exist and the policies they follow. If the foreign money

---

[1] In particular, the obligation on the banks to hold a rigid minimum ratio of liquid assets to deposits, the high proportion of Treasury bills among the banks' liquid assets, the high proportion of the total issue of Treasury bills held by the banks, and the inelasticity of the demand by other holders for Treasury bills.

is sold to a commercial bank, the increase in the bank's assets will be accompanied by an equal rise in its deposits. There is also the possibility that the bank will regard the foreign money as a liquid asset, and feel justified in expanding its other assets on the basis of its higher liquidity ratio. In this case the rise in bank deposits will be greater than the increase in foreign-owned deposits, the quantity of money held by local residents in the capital circulation will rise and interest rates will fall. If the foreign money is sold to a central bank, the potential expansion in the stock of locally-held money is even greater, for the central bank may feel justified in permitting a more than equal expansion of its own assets and liabilities, and the increase in central bank liabilities may permit a more than equal expansion in commercial bank assets and liabilities. If the sales of foreign money by foreigners are necessitated by an excess of exports over imports, the direct effect of the favourable balance of payments in raising incomes will be reinforced by an increase in the quantity of locally-owned money in the capital circulation and a fall in interest rates, while the direct effects on incomes of an adverse balance of payments will be reinforced by a reduction in the quantity of money in the capital circulation and a rise in interest rates. Thus whereas the effects on incomes of a favourable balance of payments will usually be partially offset if foreigners replenish their money balances by sales of securities on the capital market, they will be reinforced if they replenish them by sales of foreign money or gold to the banks.

This difference creates a lack of symmetry in the effects of balance of payments surpluses and deficits between countries which regard foreign currencies as liquid assets and those which do not. If a country which holds its reserves in foreign money (a 'customer' country) has a favourable balance of payments with the country whose money constitutes its reserves (the 'banker' country), the effects on incomes in the banker country are equal to the initial fall caused by the transfer of money from the income circulation to foreign-owned balances, minus the effects of lower interest rates caused by the transfer of money from foreign balances to the capital circulation. In the customer country, on the other hand, the immediate rise in incomes will be reinforced by lower interest rates induced by the rise in the liquidity of the banking system. Thus the rise in incomes in the customer country will be greater than the fall in the banker country, and aggregate incomes in both countries taken together will rise. Conversely, if it is the banker country which has the favourable balance, its rise in incomes will be partly offset, and the fall in incomes in the customer country reinforced, by a rise in interest rates in both countries. Thus if customer countries have favourable balances of payments with banker countries, incomes in the world as a whole are likely to be rising faster than if banker countries have favourable balances with customer countries.[1]

[1] On this point see also 'Banking Policy and the Balance of International Payments' (*Economica*, November 1936, republished in *The Post-war Financial Problem*) and 'Open and Repressed Inflation' (*Economic Journal*, September 1953, republished in this volume.)

CHAPTER 2

OPEN AND REPRESSED INFLATION [1]

I

INTRODUCTION

ONE of the first essays I was set to write as an undergraduate at Cambridge was on whether economics is a science or an art. I do not think I can have written a very good essay, for I am sure that I had then not the slightest idea of what the question was really about. But the older I get the surer I become that economics, or at least applied economics, is much more an art than a science. The element of personal idiosyncrasy resides not so much in the effort to discern causal relationships between given phenomena, for much of this is a branch of logic or even of mathematics, as in the selection of phenomena which we choose to regard as significant. In the world to-day there are over 2000 million persons, each with many sets of different relationships with other persons. Out of this enormous welter of many thousands of millions of partially related variables, with both the variables themselves and their relationships changing continuously, the applied economist has to select two or three (or if he is a mathematician perhaps six or even a dozen), between which he has to assume relationships which are reasonably stable; and he has to select these variables in such a way that, for the particular period and purpose that he has in mind, he can ignore the effects of all the millions of others and draw practical conclusions only from the few he has selected. Nor can he assume that the same choice of factors will remain relevant for long, even for the same type of problem. Old factors lose part of their relevance and new ones grow in significance, so that, even if by some miracle we are originally right in our choice of factors, we soon begin to

[1] Presidential Address to Section F of the British Association, delivered at its meeting in Liverpool, September 1953. Published in the *Economic Journal*, September 1953.

drift into error unless we continuously revise our choice of relevant data.

Is it then to be wondered at that economists are notoriously better able to foretell the past than the future ? And is it any wonder that a dozen different economists, surveying the seething, shimmering, continually changing complex of factors which constitutes our world, should each select a different combination of factors that seem to them of prime significance, just as a dozen different artists may see a dozen different significant patterns in the same landscape ?

The highly simplified model which every applied economist, like every other human being, constructs for himself as an aid to the understanding of an infinitely complex real world, is therefore an inevitably subjective creation, often inappropriate to others even for the limited purposes for which it was designed. Speaking for myself, I often think I find it easier to understand the real world, infinitely complicated though it is, than the simplifications of some of my colleagues whose models are not the same as mine, just as, say, Sir Alfred Munnings seems to find it difficult to understand the simplifications of Picasso, and perhaps vice versa.

Thus in putting before you to-day my own simplified model, devised for the particular purpose of examining problems of monetary inflation in Britain during the recent past, I cannot expect that everyone, or be sure that anyone, will find it useful. All that I can claim is that this is a way that I myself have found a useful one of looking at the world, and I am not altogether without hope that there may be some of my listeners who may find it useful too.

What do we mean when we use the word 'inflation' ? For some people it is merely a condition in which prices rise rapidly for a considerable time ; but this definition is not only too wide but is also couched in terms of symptoms rather than of causes. For me, inflation is essentially a monetary pheno-menon, whereas a rise in prices can be caused by a fall in physical output as well as by changes originating on the monetary side. Nor for me is a rise in prices the essential characteristic of an inflation, although it is a normal symptom of it. I prefer to relate the phenomenon of an inflation to a rise in money incomes rather than in prices, and to define it in the first place as a condition in which money incomes, almost entirely personal money incomes,[1] show a persistent increase. This is still, however, not a sufficient definition, for a rise in personal money incomes, accompanied by a corresponding or faster increase in the quantity of things to buy, so that prices do not rise, is not ordinarily called an inflation. We must therefore add to our definition that personal money incomes must not only be rising, but must be rising faster than personal real incomes.

While this definition is formally satisfactory, not all the conditions to which it might apply would be regarded as undesirable. Even in the depths of a trade depression, with many factors of production unemployed, a recovery in output will very possibly be accompanied by a somewhat more rapid rise in money incomes and by some rise in prices; but a rise of, say, 50 per cent in money incomes accompanied by a rise of 49 per cent in real incomes would be regarded by most people as a desirable step towards recovery, and would probably be classified, to use the jargon of the recent past, as ' reflation ' rather than ' inflation '. At the other extreme, even in an active boom with very few unemployed factors, a further rise in money incomes might very well (though by no means necessarily) be accompanied by some slight rise in real incomes; but in such conditions a rise of 50 per cent in money incomes would undoubtedly be regarded as undesirably inflationary, even if it were accompanied by, say, a 1 per cent rise in real incomes. How large a rise in real incomes would have to accompany a given rise in money incomes to make the inflation desirable is necessarily a subjective judgment, depending often on the personal circumstances of the observer; but in general it can be said that, especially when there are few unemployed factors, the faster money incomes rise the less likely will it be that real incomes will rise sufficiently to compensate for the disadvantages of inflation in the destruction of money savings, the arbitrary redistribution of wealth and income, and the distortion of the economic and often the corruption of the political system.

[1] For completeness we should also include money received by the Government from the sale of services of Government property and used by it for the direct purchase of goods and services; but the amount involved is so small — in the United Kingdom about 2 per cent of the gross national product — that for our present purpose it can be safely ignored.

While for me the essential element of an inflation is a rise in personal money incomes, its essential cause is that collectively the community overspends its income. If we like, we can divide expenditure into two rather arbitrarily defined parts, and call one consumption and the other investment. We can also, if we like, divide income into two parts, one part allocated to expenditure on consumption and the other called saving. Since the part of income allocated to consumption is by definition the same as the amount spent on consumption, any excess of expenditure over income is equal to the excess of investment over saving. Under present conditions, however, I am not sure that the alternative way of looking at the matter is not equally valid. Often to-day the first charge on income is not consumption expenditure but contractual saving. Many income receivers first set aside the money for the insurance, for the contribution to the pension fund, for the repayment of the mortgage to the building society and for the hire-purchase payments, and only after they have made provision for these can they devote the rest to current consumption. If a man then overspends his income, is it not at least as true to say that he is spending on consumption more than he has left after providing for investment as that he is investing more than he saves? Perhaps the reason that we look at the phenomenon from the second of these points of view rather than from the first is that we have a familiar word for the margin of income left after providing for current consumption — we call it saving — while we have no such word for the margin left after providing for current investment.

In any case, for my purposes to-day it will be more convenient to look at the relationship between total income and expenditure rather than that between part of income and part of expenditure. But to look at the relationship between income and expenditure we shall have to extend still further the range of transactions we have to take into consideration. The expenditure we meet out of income is not gross but net expenditure — total expenditure minus all receipts which are not regarded as income. For my present purpose I want to take account not only of payments made out of income but of all payments, however financed; I can therefore modify my definition of the cause of inflation from an excess of expenditure over income to an excess of total money payments over total money receipts.

This definition, of course, at once brings us up against the difficulty that, since every payment immediately results in a corresponding receipt, receipts and payments are always equal. I think, however, that we can overcome this conceptual difficulty if we think of receipts as occurring, not quite simultaneously with payments, but an instant later. We can then get a lack of identity between payments and *previous* receipts ; for while every payment automatically creates a receipt, every receipt does not create a payment. Clearly this lack of identity between payments and previous receipts must relate to some fairly short period of time ; the information that payments had been greater than previous receipts over the whole of the last fifty years would give us no guidance about the way money incomes were changing at the present moment. For this reason I have divided time up into a series of short periods of, say, one week or one month each. The first monetary transactions of each period consist of the receipt of the personal incomes which have been paid at the end of the previous period ; the last transactions of each period are the payments of the amounts which will constitute the personal incomes of the next period. (For the purpose of this discussion, personal incomes are defined as all receipts of money by persons which the recipients consider they can spend on current consumption, however defined, without consuming capital.)

For all other transactions, both receipts and payments fall within the same income period. (This enables us, if we want to, to net out all non-income transactions, and makes the difference between expenditure and income the same as the difference between total payments and total previous receipts within any income period.) These other transactions include all payments to persons other than those which are regarded as income by the recipients, and all payments of every kind to businesses and governments. There is a little difficulty in the treatment of payments to proprietors of sole businesses : we must think of these as separating their personal accounts from those of the business, and paying themselves salaries out of their receipts only at the end of each income period.

Now let me try to describe my own particular picture of the

monetary system. Most pictures of this sort represent as a circular flow a limited type of monetary transactions — those relating to the national income — over a given period, usually a year. They thus omit not only the whole range of non-income transactions, but are unable to indicate changes through time in the volume and direction of the various flows ; and it is just these changes which for our present purpose we are most interested in watching. My own approach is rather different. Conceptually, I follow the life history of each separate unit of money, observing the circumstances of its creation and disappearance, as well as of its changes of ownership as it passes from bank account to bank account or from pocket to pocket, and even keeping an eye on it when it lies dormant for a period in the same ownership. It is quite possible thus mentally to trace the life history of a unit of money without recourse to visual aids ; but I think that my exposition may be made easier with the help of diagrams, and I have therefore constructed a visual model.

In this model, every unit of money traces for itself a separate line through time, rather as if it were making a recording on a barograph. Ideally, the units should be pounds, or even pence ; but as a diagram containing even 6000 million lines would be a little awkward to handle, we must content ourselves with much larger units — say, of £100 million or so — and even with these we shall have room for only a fraction of the total.

So long as money is held in the same ownership, it is represented by a dotted horizontal line, running from left to right through time :

Every now and then a given unit of money changes hands. The change of ownership will involve a payment by one party and a receipt by the other ; let us show payments by squares and receipts by circles. As every payment necessarily involves a receipt, we will link payments and receipts together by solid lines :

We must now proceed to distinguish the different types of accounts into and out of which payments are made. The simplest model which will be useful for our purpose must distinguish five different types of accounts : personal income accounts; personal capital accounts; business accounts; government accounts; and accounts *of* (not, of course, *with*) banks. These distinctions could, and perhaps for some purposes should, be multiplied almost without limit. For some purposes, for instance, it might be convenient to distinguish payments to retailers from payments to wholesalers or manufacturers; for others, payments to makers of consumption goods from payments to makers of capital goods; and for others again, payments for long-term fixed-interest securities from payments for short-term securities, or for shares, or for various types of physical assets. But for our purpose to-day these five categories will suffice. Here is our notation :

	Personal		Business	Government	Banks
	Income	Capital			
Payments	■	□	⊟	⊞	⊠
Receipts	●	○	⊖	⊕	⊗

While a payment is automatically and immediately linked to a receipt, the delay between a receipt and a payment may be of indefinite length. When, however, a payment is ultimately made, it must be made out of the same account as that which earlier received the money. The only change in notation between receipt and payment occurs when a person saves part of his income or dissaves part of his capital, and thus converts an income balance into a balance on capital account, or vice versa.

E.g., persons receive wages from businesses, save them and lend them to the Government.

Now let us trace a simple series of monetary transfers through a single income period :

1.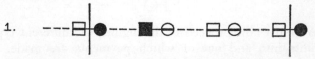

An interpretation of this might be : Persons receive incomes from businesses at the beginning of a period, and spend them on consumption goods. Retailers replace their stocks by buying from manufacturers, who pay out wages for the creation of new goods. These wages form the personal incomes for the next period.

Now let us introduce the Government :

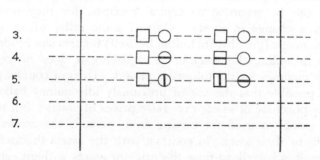

e.g. the Government collects from retailers half the personal incomes spent on consumption goods, perhaps by means of purchase taxes, and uses the money to buy goods from manufacturers who pay wages in order to make more.

Meanwhile, other units of money are lying idle, or are being used for the purchase and sale of assets and titles, or for loans and repayments :

In line 3 a person buys assets, say securities, from another person, who buys from a third, who holds the money over the end of the period ; in line 4, a person buys securities from a business, which buys others from a person ; and in line 5 a person lends money to the Government, which uses it to buy an asset from a business. Lines 6 and 7 are idle balances.

The total quantity of money is found by counting the number of lines (in this case 7), the total turnover of money is found by counting the number of transactions (in this case 13), while the total of personal incomes is two.

II
OPEN INFLATION

Let us now turn, with the aid of this model, to an examination of the phenomena connected with a changing level of money incomes. On the definitions given here, the rise in the total of money incomes from one income period to the next is identical with the amount by which payments for the period exceed receipts for the same period. There are two ways in which a man can pay out during any period more than he has received in the same period. One is by spending a stock of money which he has carried over from a previous period. This expenditure will, of course, not necessarily generate increased incomes; as we have seen, if he uses his money for a capital transaction, and if the recipient either holds the money or uses it for another capital transaction, and so on, the money will eventually be carried over to the next period without giving rise to increased incomes. All receipts other than those by persons for the services of themselves or of their assets can be regarded as capital receipts, for they involve merely a change in assets. Only if some seller of an asset pays someone (possibly including himself) for services rendered either in selling the asset or in replacing it does he create money incomes for the following period. It is, of course, perfectly possible that the use of previously idle money balances for the purchase of assets may raise prices of assets; but until more money is used for buying from persons the *services* of persons or their assets, in contrast with the assets themselves, the result is merely to raise the price of assets without raising the price of services, or, in other words, to lower the rate of interest.

Sooner or later, of course, the rise in prices of existing assets will begin to induce an increase in the demand for new ones, thus increasing the amount of money paid for the services employed in creating them. In times of acute depression, however, when prices of existing assets, and especially of durable assets, may stand well below their replacement cost, there may be a considerable delay before the increase in demand for existing durable assets is reflected in increased orders for new ones, or before holders of excessive stocks are induced by their decrease to increase their replacement orders. In times of active trade, on the other hand, when prices of existing assets are already fully up to parity with those of new ones, a rise in expenditure on buying assets is more likely to be reflected rapidly in a rise in payments for new assets and in incomes :

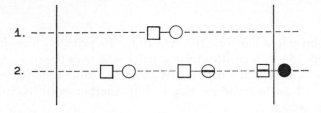

Of the two instances of the activation of personal idle balances shown above, the first results merely in a change in the ownership of an asset, say a house, while in the second the seller replaces the house by buying from a speculative builder, who pays out the money in incomes for building new ones.

A second way in which it might be possible for a person to pay out more money than he had received during the same period would be to make it. As a general practice, the manufacture of money is rightly frowned on by the authorities. There are, however, certain institutions in a modern system which have this privilege. Exactly what these institutions are varies from country to country, but everywhere the power of creating additional money lies with some combination of the commercial banks, the central bank and the Government. For convenience, we shall call these collectively 'the banks', and we shall define banks as those institutions whose debts are widely and generally used as money. The banks can, therefore, create money simply by getting into debt, which they normally do by adding to their assets, usually by making a loan or buying securities. Conversely, whenever they reduce their liabilities, usually as the result of selling securities or having loans repaid, they cancel some of the money already in existence. In our model, we therefore show no connection between the receipt of money by the banks and its reissue;

the money is destroyed by its receipt and created afresh when
it is reissued :

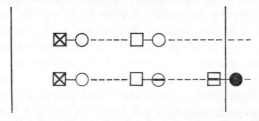

This might illustrate the activation of a privately owned idle
balance to buy securities from a seller who uses the proceeds to
pay off a debt to the banks. At about the same time the banks
make a loan to someone else to buy another security from a
private seller.

It should be noted that neither the creation of new money
by the banks nor their destruction of old money has any necessary effect on incomes. For instance, the creation of money by
means of a bank loan to finance the purchase of an existing
house has no immediate effect on incomes, except perhaps of
house-agents. Only if the borrower, or one of a series of
sellers of existing houses, uses the money to pay for services
rendered in building a new one will the rise in the quantity of
money be reflected in a rise in incomes :

Of these two instances, the first represents a bank loan spent
on buying an existing house from a private owner. In the
second, the borrower buys a house from a speculative builder,
who uses the proceeds to finance the building of others.

Now let us begin to use our model to look at the genesis
and development of an inflationary movement. If idle balances
are large (and in practice they are probably several times larger
than those being used in income transactions), it would be quite
possible for a very considerable rise in money incomes to take

place without any increase in the total quantity of money in existence. Sooner or later, however (and probably sooner unless something had occurred greatly to alter the money-using habits of the population), the rising level of incomes, of activity in the markets for assets and probably of asset prices would absorb the quantity of idle balances that their owners were willing to activate. Further rises in incomes could then occur only by diverting money from the capital circulation, thus bringing about a fall in the demand for assets, a fall in their prices relatively to those of services and a rise in interest rates, and ultimately a check to the rise in the demand for services to create new assets :

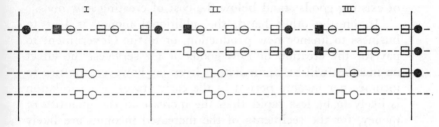

In the above illustration the total number of units of money is four throughout. In the first period one of these is used to pay incomes, one is idle and two are in use for asset transactions. In the second period the idle balance is activated and used for an income payment, thus doubling the level of incomes. In the third period incomes can be raised further only by diverting one unit of money from the market for assets, thus leaving, in period IV, only one unit in the asset market instead of two, reducing the demand for assets and raising the rate of interest.

It should be noted that if the idle balance had first been activated into the capital circulation, the initial effect would have been to raise prices of assets relatively to those of services and lower the rate of interest. In that case the rate of interest would not have risen above its original level until not only this unit but another as well had been diverted from the capital circulation to the income circulation.

While the increase in incomes induced by an activation of idle balances, though possibly large, is at any rate finite, the increase caused by an increase in the quantity of money is potentially infinite. Like the activation of idle balances, an

increase in the quantity of money is not inflationary until it
begins to augment personal incomes. So long as its effects
are confined to the demand for existing assets, it merely lowers
the rate of interest. The speed with which a rise in the quantity
of money will be reflected in incomes will depend partly on
the way the extra money is created and partly on the economic
climate of the period. If, for instance, money is created (as
in 1932) by the banks' purchases of securities on the market,
or by Government borrowing from the banks to finance the
repayment of securities or the purchase of existing assets,
the effects may well be confined for a considerable time to the
capital circulation and the rate of interest, especially when prices
of existing goods stand below the cost of creating new ones.

If, on the other hand, the additional money is lent to
business to finance new production, or to the Government to
pay for the creation of new goods or for services, the effect
on incomes will be immediate. Even so, however, the rise in
incomes per income period in the early stages of an inflation
is likely to be less rapid than the increase in the quantity of
money, for the recipients of the increased incomes are likely
to save a part of them and so transfer money back to the capital
circulation. This is particularly likely to happen when the
rise in money incomes is accompanied by a substantial rise in
real incomes; but it may well happen for a time when real
incomes are not rising or are even falling. In a country which
has not experienced a major inflation within living memory,
income receivers may for a time be deterred from buying
goods, especially durable goods, by the belief that they are
unduly ' expensive ', and that in due course prices will return
to a more ' normal ' level. The movements of money in the
early stages of an inflation may therefore look something like
this :

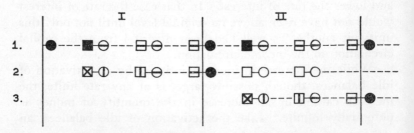

In this illustration the Government has caused the banks to create for its use an extra unit of money in each of periods I and II, but one of the new units has been diverted to the capital circulation, so that incomes per period have risen by only one unit. If the unit diverted had been used to buy new Government securities instead of an existing asset, the Government would not have needed to borrow at all from the banks in period II.

This early stage of an inflation is a temporary one. If the inflation is at all rapid, as it proceeds the expectation that prices will rise further will become increasingly general, and income receivers will not only cease to save but will begin to activate idle balances in order to accelerate their purchases, especially of durable consumption goods ; at the same time both income receivers and businesses will endeavour to supplement their existing balances by borrowing from the banks. Incomes will then begin to rise faster than the quantity of money and faster still than Government borrowings from the banks :

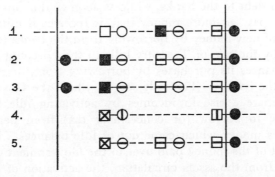

In this illustration, Government borrowings from the banks during the period have risen by one unit, but the total quantity of money has risen by two units, and, thanks to the activation of idle balances, incomes by three units.

As the existence of the inflation becomes more and more obvious to more and more people, so do the activation of idle balances increase and money incomes rise progressively faster than the quantity of money. In the last stages of the inflation the whole model collapses, for the income period itself is shortened and wages are paid more and more frequently, first, perhaps, twice weekly, then daily and then twice a day, while income receivers rush to spend their money the moment they receive it. When this happens, however much new money is created, its aggregate value falls faster and faster towards zero until it disappears altogether. At the last the use of the existing money is abandoned, and until a new money which commands confidence can be introduced, the economy reverts either to barter or to the use of some commodity as a substitute for money.

Theoretically, a rise in money incomes leading to an inflation could be caused by the activation of money in, or the creation of money for, any one of the three sectors into which we have divided our economy. There is, however, a technical reason why an expansion of incomes generated by the British Government (though not by all) will nearly always arise through the creation of new money rather than by the activation of existing balances. The reason is that the British Government never carries any appreciable quantity of idle balances. As soon as these tend to accumulate, they are used to pay off debt to the banks, while as soon as the Government begins to pay out more money than it receives it initiates the creation of new money by borrowing from the banks (or, more strictly, by the sale of Treasury bills to the Discount Market, which finances its purchases by borrowing from, or re-selling bills to, the banks). The only way in which the Government could initiate a rise in incomes by activating idle balances would be to borrow (or conceivably tax) from persons or businesses money which came out of idle balances. If, however, part of the money paid over to the Government came, as is likely, from the assets circulation, the activation of balances would be accompanied by some rise in interest rates and fall in asset prices, which would in turn ultimately tend to check the rise in incomes.

A rise in incomes originating in the two non-government sectors, on the other hand, is likely to begin with the activation of balances and to be supported by an increase in the quantity of money only when it has gone a certain distance. A rise in money incomes is, however, likely to develop into a major inflation only if it is fed by an expansion in the quantity of money for the benefit of the Government, partly because the Government is the only one of the three which combines the rôles of borrower and monetary authority. Of the other two sectors, a rise in money incomes is probably more likely to develop into an inflation by reason of an increase in the quantity of money for the benefit of the business sector (as in the United Kingdom in 1919–20) than for the personal sector, though personal borrowing for purposes of stock-exchange speculation might conceivably provide an exception, and an increase in bank loans for the finance of hire-purchase agreements could certainly at least contribute to an inflation.

There is one further way in which an increase in money incomes could originate, though it would be unlikely to develop into a major inflation. Hitherto we have discussed our economy as if it were a closed system. In an open system, with trade relations with other economies, a rise in incomes can be initiated by a favourable balance of payments. The exact way in which the extra money passes into the income circulation will depend on the institutional arrangements in force. The simplest case is where two economies share a common currency (as in Great Britain and Northern Ireland, or, to a considerable extent, Great Britain and Eire). In this case actual money is directly transferred from the country with the adverse balance to the country with the favourable balance of payments. Unless the excess exports are from unreplaced stocks, the imported money will rapidly pass into the incomes of the exporting country (B), while if the excess imports are substitutes for home-produced goods, the diversion of purchases will bring about a corresponding fall in incomes in the importing country (A):

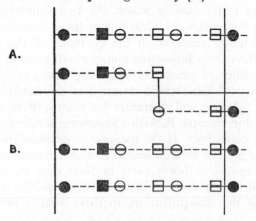

These changes in incomes will in due course tend to reduce
A's imports from B and to increase B's imports from A, and so
to restore the balance of payments and to check the rise in
incomes in B. If, however, the excess imports are in satisfaction of an additional demand, due perhaps to the activation of
idle balances, the rise in incomes in the exporting country may
not be matched by a fall in the importing country, and there
may be a net expansion in incomes in the two countries taken
together :

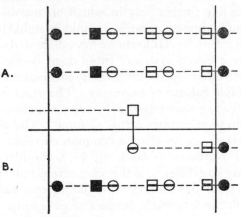

In this case, equilibrium will be restored mainly as the
result of a rise in B's imports, though if A's demand for B's
exports is elastic, A's payments for imports may also decline
if B's export prices rise.

A more usual case is where the two countries have independent currencies. Unless one of these countries holds its
foreign-exchange reserves in the currency of the other, the
banks of the excess importing country will have to finance its
adverse balance of payments by selling assets (either gold or
the currency of some third country) to the banks of the net
exporter. Money will therefore be destroyed in country A
and created in country B, with a symmetrical effect on incomes
in the two countries. If the increase or decrease in the banks'
holdings of gold or foreign exchange also increases or decreases
their willingness to hold assets in their own currencies, the
quantity of money created in B and destroyed in A may be a
multiple of the disequilibrium in their balance of payments,

though if policies on both sides are symmetrical, there will still be no net change in the incomes of both countries taken together.

A more complicated position arises where country A finances its import surplus by raising a long-term loan in country B. This is likely both to draw some money out of the capital circulation of B and to activate some idle balances. It will thus tend to raise both incomes and interest rates in B, while if, as is probable, the import surplus represents a net addition to expenditure in A there will be no fall in incomes there. Indeed, if, as is frequently the case, the loan is raised in advance and is spent partly within A, its transfer to A will involve the creation by the banks of additional money there and will induce a rise in incomes which will ultimately bring about an import surplus.

Perhaps most interesting of all is the case where one country keeps its foreign-exchange reserves in the currency of the other, but not vice versa. This relationship, which may be typified by that between the United Kingdom and other members of the sterling area, almost inevitably leads to an asymmetrical result. If, for instance, the United Kingdom has an adverse balance of payments with New Zealand, United Kingdom pounds will be sold to the New Zealand banks in exchange for the New Zealand pounds which the United Kingdom importers need to pay their debts in New Zealand. Thus the quantity of New Zealand money and incomes in New Zealand rise, while if their larger holdings of United Kingdom pounds cause the New Zealand banks to be more willing to acquire New Zealand assets, the quantity of New Zealand money, and probably New Zealand incomes, will rise still more. What, however, the effect in the United Kingdom will be will depend partly on the way in which the New Zealand banks hold their sterling. If they hold it in United Kingdom money, it will mean that part of the money in circulation will be diverted into idle balances.

In this case, incomes in the United Kingdom will probably fall, though it is unlikely that the fall will be intensified by a reduction in the willingness of United Kingdom banks to hold United Kingdom assets. It is likely, however, that the New Zealand banks will wish to keep part of their increased sterling

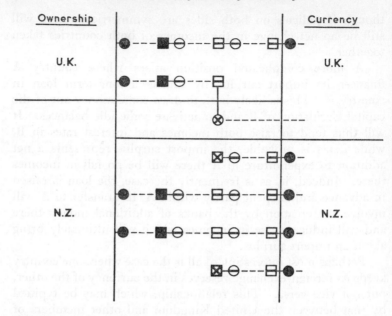

balances in the form of earning assets, and that they will therefore wish to invest at least a part of them.   Thus some at
least of the United Kingdom pounds withdrawn from the
income circulation will not become permanently idle but will
be transferred to the United Kingdom capital circulation, thus
reducing interest rates, expanding the demand for assets and
tending to maintain incomes.   Thus, both because there will
often be a multiple effect on the quantity of money in New
Zealand but not in the United Kingdom, and because of the
effect on United Kingdom interest rates, the rise in incomes in
New Zealand is likely to be larger than the fall in incomes
in the United Kingdom, and there will probably be a net
expansion in incomes in the two countries taken together.

When it is New Zealand that has the adverse balance, the
asymmetry works in the opposite direction.   The effect of
falling sterling balances in decreasing New Zealand incomes is
likely to be larger than in increasing United Kingdom incomes,
so that the incomes of both countries combined is likely to fall.
It is for this reason that when 'customer' countries are enjoying
favourable balances of payments, incomes in the world as a
whole tend to rise, while when their balances are unfavourable

Ownership   Currency

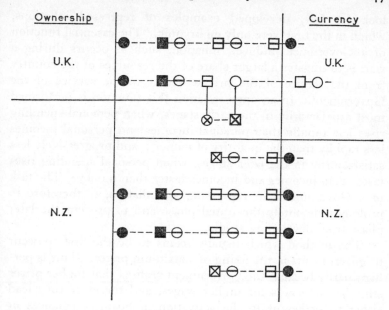

U.K.   U.K.

N.Z.   N.Z.

world incomes tend to fall. Thus an expansion of credit and incomes in a banker country tends to spread to all its customer countries and to continue until it is checked by the development of an adverse balance of payments between the whole group and the rest of the world. If there were a single banker country in the world, with all other countries keeping their reserves of foreign exchange in its currency — a relationship not so very different from that between the United States and the rest of the world at the present time — an inflation in that one country would tend to generate an inflation throughout the world, with no automatic tendency towards a reversal; while the effects of an inflation in any customer country would be largely local and, in the absence of continual currency depreciation, would in due course be checked by the depletion of that country's reserves of foreign exchange.

III

REPRESSED INFLATION

Whereas the First World War provided some classic examples of open inflation, it is to the second that we must look for fully developed examples of repressed inflations, which in the first were only embryonic. The essential function of a Government-induced inflation, such as occurs during a war, is to transfer a larger share of the resources of the country from the service of the private sector to the service of the Government. In an open inflation this function is performed most satisfactorily in the early stages, when personal spending rises less rapidly than personal incomes and personal incomes less rapidly than the quantity of money; and progressively less satisfactorily in the later stages, when personal spending rises faster than incomes and incomes faster than money. The task of a Government, in repressing an inflation, is therefore to prolong indefinitely the initial phase and to prevent the later phase from developing at all.

The method which usually seems to be the first to occur to governments is the fixing of maximum prices. This is perhaps partly because the Government realises that higher prices stimulate demands for higher wages, and therefore they lead either to strikes or to the activation of business balances or business borrowing from the banks in order to pay them. But it is perhaps also partly because governments tend to treat symptoms rather than causes, and rising prices are the most obvious and unpopular symptom of an inflation.

The fixing of maximum prices of consumption goods, at a time when the Government is raising prices of services and incomes by bidding factors away from the service of the private sector with newly created money, tends to have a double effect: to reduce the quantity produced and to increase the quantity consumed. In point of fact, however, the British Government never seems to have relied for reducing the quantity of goods and services supplied to the private sector on making their production unprofitable. It seems to have preferred to restrict output by restricting supplies of materials and labour, or by direct limitation of the amounts or types of goods allowed to be produced. For such output as was still permitted prices seem to have been fixed at a level which made production of that amount quite adequately profitable, even though these prices were still well below those which would have equated demand with the reduced supply.

On the side of demand, the fixing of maximum prices slows

down the rise in personal incomes in three different ways. In the first place, by reducing the pressure for higher wages under the threat of strikes, it reduces the tendency for the money created for the use of the Government to be supplemented by money activated or created for the use of businesses. Secondly, it makes it impossible for retailers and wholesalers to protect their stocks by raising prices, while their full replenishment is prevented by direct controls. Thus in the early stages of price control the increased demands of consumers can be satisfied for a time out of depletion of stocks. During this period, part of the money paid by consumers remains immobilised in the hands of retailers and wholesalers, to be held idle or lent to the Government instead of being spent on the creation of new goods and of personal incomes :

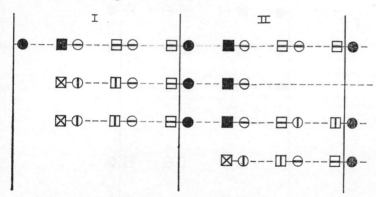

In this illustration, the Government in period I borrows two units of money from the banks and pays them over to manufacturers, who pay them out in wages, thus creating two additional units of incomes in period II. In period II, both these extra units are spent on consumption goods, but the retailers are prevented from spending them on replenishing their stocks. One of the units is held idle, thus enabling the Government to borrow from the banks and spend an additional unit without raising incomes further ; the other is invested in newly-issued government securities. Thus in period II the Government retains control of the additional resources it attracted in period I without raising incomes above the level of three units.

This stage of the repression of an inflation by price controls is of limited duration. Once stocks are fully depleted, consumers begin to be unable to find means of spending the whole of their incomes, at least on things which they prefer to the possibility of spending savings at some future date on things they want more. When this stage is reached, the excess incomes begin to accumulate in the hands of persons rather than of businesses. If these lend them to the Government, the diversion of the control over resources is achieved directly. If they hold them idle or pass them round in the capital circulation, the Government can cause the banks to create more money to take their place without raising incomes :

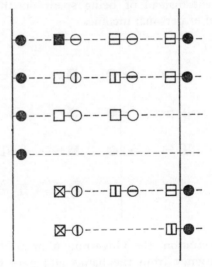

Of these four units of personal income, three are diverted to Government use. One is lent to the Government by persons, one is diverted to the personal capital circulation, no doubt raising prices and reducing interest rates there, and one is held idle. The two last units are replaced by new money borrowed from the banks. Personal incomes remain unchanged.

The supplementation of price control by a system of rationing makes no fundamental difference to this process, for though it distributes consumption goods differently between consumers, it does not change the aggregate amount that can be spent on them. It does, however, make the system of

controls more politically acceptable, greatly reduces the scope
for favouritism in the distribution of scarce supplies and probably also reduces the incentive to break the law. Adjusted by
rationing to appear at least superficially equitable, and supplemented by controls over capital construction and the distribution of producers' goods, these methods of price control
appear to operate as reasonably successful repressers of inflation
so long as a war actually continues.

One possible method of checking demand, which seems to
have considerable merit in principle, but which never seems to
have been tried in practice, is rationing *without* price control.
If, for instance, every consumer were given coupons to the face
value of, say, £1 per week which, together with money to the
same value, would have to be surrendered in payment for
certain classes of goods, the maximum total weekly demand
for these classes of goods would be limited to as many pounds
as there were consumers. If demand for one of the classes of
goods rose, that for the others would necessarily fall; or if
demand for all classes rose in one part of the country, it would
necessarily fall elsewhere. If prices of these goods were then
allowed to rise and fall freely in accordance with changes in
demand, the variations in prices between products or between
areas would greatly facilitate adjustments in the distribution
both of resources between different products and of products
between different areas.

Whatever the precise method of its implementation, and
however successful it is in restraining inflation during the war,
a policy of limiting expenditure by means of direct controls
leaves a very difficult situation when the war comes to an end.
Since both consumers and businesses have been prevented from
spending as large a part of their monetary receipts as they
would have wished, they have been obliged to accumulate
either idle balances or Government securities in excess of their
desires. At the same time, much of the expenditure prevented
in war-time, especially on the replacement or repair of assets,
is merely postponed. The difficulty of the situation is still
further increased if, as in Britain, many of the Government
securities issued and obligations incurred during the war are
repayable on demand or short notice, so that their owners have
the power at any time to force the Government to create

additional money in order to meet its obligations to repay. Thus, even though the Government itself rapidly ceases to rely on the creation of new money for the finance of a deficit, there are present all the potentialities of a renewed and accelerated inflation through the activation of excess idle balances or the enforced creation of new money to make repayments of Government debt.

In face of this potential inflation, the Government has the choice of a number of possible policies, alone or in combination. One of these is to continue the methods of direct control of demand that have been in force during the war. Unfortunately, such controls seem to operate much less satisfactorily in peace-time than in time of war. As soon as the stimulus of the common danger and the single objective is removed, income earners and businesses become progressively less willing to produce and trade in order to obtain money which they cannot spend on what they want to buy; thus production is checked, and more of what is produced tends either to be consumed by its producers or bartered directly for other goods. At the last, if rigid controls are enforced indefinitely, the use of legal-tender money may be abandoned entirely over large sectors of the economy in favour of barter or the use of some kind of commodity money ; and the final stage of a repressed inflation may thus be not dissimilar to that of an open inflation.

Even if the policy of control is not carried to the point of this ultimate breakdown, the effect of partial controls are in their own way almost equally unsatisfactory. If, for instance, as is often the case, controls are more effectively enforced over demand for essentials than for non-essentials, the resources released by the fall in defence expenditure tend to be absorbed in supplying less essential, rather than more essential needs, whether at home or for exports. Further, with the loss of war-time incentives and the release of much enterprise and initiative from the armed forces, the control laws become increasingly difficult to enforce and breaches of them increasingly frequent. Unless the Government is prepared to use more resources for enforcement than it can well afford and more drastic methods of enforcement than public opinion is likely to tolerate, the continuation of war-time physical controls over expenditure cannot be relied upon by themselves to do more than create a breathing-space during which methods can be devised for eliminating, rather than merely continuing to frustrate, the potential excesses of demand.

One drastic method for eliminating excess demand, which has been widely used on the Continent, is the compulsory writing-down of the values of money and money-claims. This forcible decrease in money and money-claims can be applied, if so desired, in different proportions to different types of holdings or even of holders. If the decreases are sufficiently drastic, and if the Government itself can subsequently so order its finances as to avoid the necessity of re-creating an excessive quantity of money, such a policy can solve at a blow the problem of potential excess demand, though probably only at the cost of much hardship, injustice, and perhaps unrest.

If the Government is not prepared to contemplate so drastic a solution of the problem of excessive liquidity in the private sector, it must rely on other methods. One way in which it could destroy some of the money and money assets created during the war would be to develop a very large budget surplus and use it for paying off debt, including debt to the banks. A similar effect could be achieved by means of a very large special tax on capital. It is true that any very large budget surplus, whether or not achieved by means of a formal capital levy, would in fact be paid largely out of idle balances and the assets circulation. If, however, the greater part of the money withdrawn from the assets circulation were simultaneously returned to it by Government repayments or purchases of Government securities held by the public, and only a small part, together with the payments out of idle balances, were used to destroy money by paying off debt to the banks, the reduction in the public's surplus of money and money assets could be achieved without directly affecting the rate of interest; for any reduction in the quantity of money in the assets circulation would be offset by the reduction in the quantity of assets to buy with it. Indeed, if the whole of the money withdrawn from the assets circulation were returned to it, rates of interest would tend to fall.

In such a situation, it would probably be better to obtain the surplus with which to pay off debt by a once-for-all capital levy than by very heavy taxes imposed on income, as being less likely to deter effort or divert it to forms less liable to tax. The fact that the payments were made out of idle balances or the assets circulation would not matter, for the purpose of the operation would be to remove the excess of liquidity and so to prevent an unwanted further rise in money incomes rather than to reduce money incomes below the existing level. The position is thus very different from that in which a Government uses taxes paid out of capital for making income-creating payments ; in this case, the effects of the Government's financial operations are on balance inflationary, though less inflationary than if it made income-creating payments out of newly created money borrowed from the banks. It is thus not high taxation as such which tends to be inflationary but the use of such taxation for making income-creating payments ; and it is on Government expenditure rather than on taxation that the emphasis should be laid if it is feared that the payment of taxes out of capital is having inflationary effects.

Even if the Government cannot see its way to an actual reduction in the public's holdings of money and money assets, there are still two ways in which it can limit their inflationary effects while gradually removing direct controls. The first of these is to find alternative ways of limiting income-forming expenditure without raising interest rates. If, for instance, it were possible to persuade persons to spend considerably less than their incomes and so to transfer large amounts of money from the income circulation to the assets circulation or to idle balances, the effect of business transfers of money into the income circulation in the process of replacing physical assets depleted during the war would be counteracted. Unfortunately, the shortage of personal physical assets, the excess of money and money assets already owned by persons and the redistribution of incomes due to the heavy taxation necessitated by continued heavy Government expenditure combined to reduce personal saving in Britain after the war to a very low level ; and the devoted workers of the National Savings Movement may be congratulated on their achievement in preventing a much larger consumption of war-time personal saving than has in fact occurred.

A more successful method of keeping down personal-consumption expenditure has been the restraining of wage increases in the face of rising prices. By this means, wages have been kept generally below the equilibrium level, business profits (before tax) at above the equilibrium level, and incidentally un-employment at a level lower than has probably been achieved ever before over so long a period. A very large part of these business savings has been drained off by high business taxes, and much of the rest retained for the replenishment of business assets, more for the reason of business needs than because of the Government's discouragement of increases in dividends. It would not be far wrong to say that, at least until quite recently, all Governments in Britain since the war have used businesses as a kind of involuntary tax-collecting agent, rather as King John is said to have used the money-lenders of his time.

A third possibility is for the Government itself to impose personal taxes of a type likely to be paid out of income, in excess of its own income-creating payments. While in the years from 1948 to 1951 the Government seems to have had total income-destroying receipts (including the proceeds of foreign aid) substantially in excess of its own income-creating payments, a very large part of these receipts was derived from the excep-tional profits obtained by businesses. Indeed, the attempt to secure a much larger tax yield at the direct expense of personal incomes would probably have encountered serious economic and political difficulties.

Throughout the period since 1947, the Government has supplemented its efforts to divert money out of the income circulation with efforts to restrict the total quantity of money, or at any rate to keep its rate of increase below that of the real national income. With a constant quantity of money, the amount of money in the income circulation can be increased only by depleting idle balances and the assets circulation. Incomes can therefore continue to rise for a time, but the rise will sooner or later be checked when the rise in the income circulation and the fall in the assets circulation and in idle balances have restored their relationship to equilibrium. The increasing depletion of the assets circulation will bring with it a rise in interest rates, the extent of which will depend on the success of the Government's efforts, referred to above, to return money from the income to the assets circulation. The

c

more successful the Government is in restraining the income-creating expenditure of persons, the greater the proportion of the national resources which can be made available for the increase of physical assets held by businesses or the Government, and the more rapid will probably be the rise in the real national income. But there is no doubt that, if the Government is willing to face the effects on asset accumulation of a sufficiently high rate of interest, an inflation can always be brought to an end simply by action to ensure that the quantity of money does not rise further.

There is one question which still remains to be answered: Do we really want the gradual inflation of recent years to be brought to an end? Hitherto it has been possible to maintain an abnormally high level of employment by ensuring that the rise in money wages lags sufficiently far behind the rise in selling prices to ensure that the demand for labour, in most occupations and in most places, is in excess of the supply. If the inflation ends and prices cease to rise, wages will tend to catch up, gross profits will return to normal, the excess demand for labour will disappear and unemployment will rise. On the other hand, if even creeping inflation continues here after it has ceased in most of the rest of the world, we may expect more balance-of-payments crises and probably further depreciations of the currency.

There seem to be only two possible solutions to the problem of reconciling the present level of employment with the absence of inflation. One is the permanent pegging of wage rates at below an equilibrium level, either by self-denying decisions of the trades unions (if they can get their members to follow them) or by Government regulation; and even if either of these courses should prove possible, they would involve further difficulties in securing and maintaining a desirable distribution of labour between places and occupations. The only other conceivable solution seems to be a continual increase in real output per person employed, so that money wages could continue to rise, without raising costs of production, though always just a little later than when most employers could afford to pay them. Even this, of course, would not prevent a high degree of unemployment in the event of a serious fall in world demand for our exports, or renewed inflation and balance-of-payments crises if our rising production was offset by a continual worsening of our terms of trade, so that the real national income failed to rise. Nevertheless it seems to offer a chance, perhaps the only real chance, of reconciling full employment with a continued absence of inflation. Let us hope that conditions at home and abroad will enable us to turn this theoretical possibility into an actual achievement.

CHAPTER 3

GILT-EDGED AND THE MONEY SUPPLY [1]

DURING the past forty years the long-term rate of interest, as represented by the yield on $2\frac{1}{2}$ per cent Consols, has fluctuated widely, from a maximum of over $5\frac{1}{2}$ per cent at the end of 1920 to $2\frac{1}{2}$ per cent at the end of 1946 and back again to $5\frac{1}{2}$ per cent in the autumn of 1957. Even if we smooth out temporary movements by the use of annual averages, the fluctuations range from $5\frac{1}{4}$ per cent in 1920 and 1921 to 2·6 per cent in 1946 and back to 5 per cent in 1957 and 1958. This article attempts to find an explanation of these movements.

In the table are set out estimates of net national money income for the years 1921 to 1957 (and a provisional estimate for 1958), together with annual average totals of net clearing bank deposits and note circulation and the average yield on $2\frac{1}{2}$ per cent Consols. From these we observe that falls in the yield on Consols are usually associated either with falls in national income (1921–22 and 1929–32) or with rapid rises in the total of bank deposits (1932–33 and 1943–46); whereas rises in the yield on Consols generally occur in periods when national income is rising rapidly while bank deposits are rising more slowly or not at all (1936–39, 1948–52, and 1954–57). When both bank deposits and national income are stationary or changing at similar rates, the yield on Consols also tends to remain steady (1924–28 and 1957–58). There is therefore some prima facie evidence that rises in national money income and falls in bank deposits both tend to cause rises in long-term interest rates, while falls in national income and rises in bank deposits both cause falls in long-term rates. In view of this, it would seem that the operative factor may not be the absolute change in either, but the relationship between the two. Chart I has therefore been prepared to compare (as a time series) changes in the percentage ratio of net clearing bank deposits to net national income with changes in the yield

[1] Published in *The Banker*, January 1959.

Net Money National Income (£m.)*	Quantity of Money (£m.) Clearing Bank Net Deposits†	Quantity of Money (£m.) Note Circulation	Quantity of Money (£m.) Total	Note Circulation as Percentage of National Income	Clearing Bank Deposits as Percentage of National Income	Yield on 2½% Consols
1921	4,460	1764	437	2201	9·8	39·5	5·2
1922	3,856	1730	400	2130	10·4	44·9	4·4
1923	3,844	1629	388	2017	10·1	42·3	4·3
1924	3,919	1622	391	2013	10·0	41·4	4·4
1925	3,980	1610	383	1993	9·6	40·4	4·4
1926	3,914	1615	375	1990	9·6	41·2	4·6
1927	4,145	1661	373	2034	9·0	40·1	4·6
1928	4,154	1709	372	2081	9·0	41·1	4·5
1929	4,178	1743	362	2105	8·7	41·7	4·6
1930	3,957	1747	359	2106	9·1	44·1	4·5
1931	3,666	1711	355	2066	9·7	46·7	4·4
1932	3,568	1745	360	2105	10·1	48·9	3·7
1933	3,728	1906	371	2277	9·9	51·1	3·4
1934	3,881	1830	379	2209	9·8	47·2	3·1
1935	4,109	1947	395	2342	9·6	47·4	2·9
1936	4,388	2156	431	2587	9·8	49·1	2·9
1937	4,750	2220	480	2700	10·1	46·7	3·3
1938	4,816	2213	486	2699	10·1	46·0	3·4
1939	5,160	2175	507	2682	9·8	42·2	3·7
1940	6,120	2408	575	2983	9·4	39·4	3·4
1941	7,080	2849	651	3500	9·2	40·3	3·1
1942	7,800	3145	807	3952	10·3	40·3	3·0
1943	8,300	3544	966	4510	11·6	42·7	3·1
1944	8,500	4012	1136	5148	13·4	47·2	3·1
1945	8,480	4541	1284	5825	15·1	53·6	2·9
1946	8,000	4922	1358	6280	17·0	61·5	2·6
1947	8,500	5454	1384	6838	16·3	64·6	2·8
1948	9,507	5703	1254	6957	13·2	60·0	3·2
1949	10,157	5761	1269	7030	12·5	56·7	3·3
1950	10,675	5800	1287	7087	12·0	54·3	3·5
1951	11,692	5918	1342	7260	11·5	50·6	3·8
1952	12,692	5844	1435	7279	11·3	46·0	4·2
1953	13,547	6012	1532	7544	11·3	44·4	4·1
1954	14,504	6225	1630	7855	11·2	42·9	3·8
1955	15,325	6171	1760	7931	11·5	40·3	4·2
1956	16,604	5998	1875	7873	11·3	36·1	4·7
1957	17,604	6122	1967	8089	11·2	34·8	5·0
1958‡	18,200	6330	2025	8355	11·1	34·8	5·0

* Source: A. R. Prest, *Economic Journal*, March 1948 and 1958 National Income Blue Book. Figures revised to 1961 appear in Table 1 of Chapter 8.
† Source: London and Cambridge Economic Bulletin, annual average. These figures differ slightly from those published in the regular series in *The Banker* since they are calculated by excluding not only the items in course of 'collection' of all banks but also the intra-bank 'transit' items of Lloyds Bank.
‡ Estimates.

on 2½ per cent Consols. For purposes of comparison, the
ratio of the note circulation to national income is also included.

It is obvious from this chart that there is a very marked
inverse correlation between the bank deposits/national income
ratio and the yield on Consols : the yield on Consols generally
rises when the ratio of bank deposits to national income falls,
and vice versa. There are, however, few, if any, signs of any
similar relationship between the rate of interest and the ratio
of the note circulation to national income. Apart from the
exceptional rise in the note circulation during the later years
of the war (which may have been due to a certain desire for
anonymity by some holders of money in a period of strict
price controls), the note circulation/national income ratio
remains remarkably constant over long periods, between the
wars at an average level of rather under 10 per cent, and since
1951 at rather over 11 per cent. The rise in the ratio since
before the war may be due in part to the fact that the smallest
size of note remains 10s., which is the equivalent of less than
4s. in 1938, so that notes may have taken over some of the
functions of silver ; and perhaps in part to the redistribution
of income away from the cheque-using classes.

While, however, the ratio of deposits to national income in
most years moves inversely to the rate of interest, there are
occasional years (1933–34, 1939–40, 1946–47, and 1952–54) in
which both curves move in the same direction. Further, while
similar ratios are frequently accompanied by similar rates of
interest, even when the years concerned are separated by long
periods of time (*e.g.* 1925 and 1955), other years with similar
ratios have very different interest rates (*e.g.* 1931 and 1935, or
1925 and 1941) and years with similar interest rates have very
different ratios (*e.g.* 1935 and 1947, or 1940 and 1949). In the
hope of throwing light on the reasons both for the correlations
and for the exceptions to the general rule, the same figures
have been expressed in Chart II as a 'scatter' diagram. In
this the yield on Consols in each year is plotted against the
ratio of bank deposits to national income in the same year,
the resulting point being marked with the date. When this is
done, it becomes clear that the points form two distinct series,
one for the years 1921–33 and 1947–57, and the other for the
years 1934–46. The trend in each series can then be displayed

CHART I

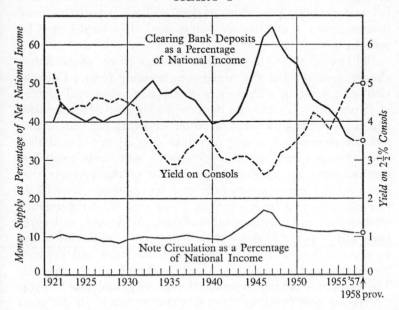

CHART II

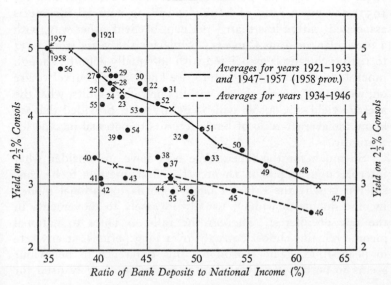

by averaging. Taking the upper and lower series separately, average positions have been calculated for all those points that fall within each 5 per cent 'bracket' of bank deposits/national income ratio; these average points have then been joined by straight lines.

The result of joining up these average points gives us two almost straight lines, the higher one running from a Consols' yield of 5 per cent with a ratio of deposits to national income of 37 per cent to a yield of 3 per cent with a ratio of 62 per cent, and the other from a yield of rather under $3\frac{1}{2}$ per cent with a ratio of 40 per cent to one of rather over $2\frac{1}{2}$ per cent with a ratio of 62 per cent. Both series give a reasonably small dispersion about the average curves. Out of the 24 years that comprise the upper series only one (1954) shows a yield on Consols diverging by more than $\frac{1}{2}$ per cent from the average relationship, and only four others (1921, 1933, 1955, and 1956) show a divergence of more than $\frac{1}{4}$ per cent; while out of the 13 years in the lower series, none shows as much as $\frac{1}{2}$ per cent divergence, and only two (1939 and 1942) more than $\frac{1}{4}$ per cent. The two series nowhere overlap, though 1939 lies close to 1954.

We are now faced with the fact that in nearly all the years from 1921 to 1933 and again from 1947 to 1957 (or, indeed, 1958, the provisional point for which coincides with that for 1957) any given ratio of bank deposits to national income is associated, within less than $\frac{1}{4}$ per cent of yield either way, with a particular yield on Consols; while for the years from 1934 to 1946 each ratio is associated with an equally definite, though much lower yield. If, therefore, we know which curve we are on, we can tell, nearly always within fairly close limits, what the average yield of Consols will be in any year, provided that we know the average ratio of bank deposits to national income for that year.

So much for the facts. We now have to consider what interpretation to put on them. The first question to be considered is why the ratio of bank deposits to national money income fluctuates widely, usually inversely to movements in the rate of interest, whereas the ratio of notes to national income remains almost constant over long periods, at any rate in peace-time. The reason for this difference in behaviour seems to be that the two sorts of money are largely used for different purposes. The examination of this difference leads us to the heart of the problem not only of the behaviour of the note circulation but also of the relationships between bank deposits, national income, and the rate of interest. This calls for some precision in definitions.

It is probably true to say that, in this country and in peace-time, notes are used almost entirely for current 'income-creating' expenditures and are rarely used for capital expenditures, while nearly all capital transactions are paid for by the transfer of bank deposits, usually by cheque. 'Income' transactions may be defined as those concerned with payments for services, either of persons or of their assets, together with purchases of goods which are rapidly replaced by the sellers by newly-created goods and so lead quickly to payments for services. In contrast to these income-creating expenditures are capital transactions, in which money is lent, or used for buying titles to assets or to money, or for buying existing physical assets that are not automatically replaced by newly-created ones. Such transactions do not create incomes (except the incomes of those who provide the service of facilitating sales), but merely result in the exchange of money for some other asset.

If more money is introduced into the income circulation (*i.e.* is spent for income-creating purposes), it tends to raise the price of services, both of persons and of their assets, while if more money is introduced into the capital circulation (*i.e.* is made available for the purchase of capital assets — for instance, when the banks buy gilt-edged from the public), it tends to raise the price of assets. Where the assets take the form of fixed interest securities, this rise in their prices lowers current yields and the long-term rate of interest. Thus changes in the quantity of money in the income circulation are reflected in changes in the total of incomes, while changes in the quantity of money in the capital circulation are reflected in inverse changes in the rate of interest. While some part of bank deposits forms part of the income circulation, and, like notes, probably fluctuates in absolute amount proportionately with incomes, a large and probably the greater part is held in the capital circulation, either as an investment itself or to finance capital transactions. It is therefore only the fluctuations in

C2

this second part that directly affect interest rates.

While we can thus account for two of the facts disclosed by the statistical analysis — the fact that the total of the note circulation normally forms an almost constant proportion of national income, and that the rate of interest tends to move inversely with the total of bank deposits — we have not yet provided any explanation why the rate of interest also tends to move in the same direction as the national income. For this relationship there seem to be two main reasons. In the first place, when incomes rise, the total of bank deposits in the income circulation rises with them. If the total of all bank deposits is unchanged, the amount left in the capital circulation is diminished. The result is therefore the same as that of a reduction in total deposits with incomes unchanged.

Secondly, and probably more important, a rise in incomes usually alters the relative values of different types of assets dealt in in the capital circulation. A rise in the general level of money incomes normally includes a rise in the incomes (monetary or imputed) derived from the ownership both of physical assets and of titles to ownership of them, such as ordinary shares. This rise in the incomes derived from physical assets and from titles to them increases the attractiveness of owning such assets, while there is no corresponding increase in the attractiveness of owning fixed interest securities. There is therefore a tendency for owners of fixed interest securities to sell them and buy physical assets or titles to physical assets. Prices of fixed interest securities therefore fall and long-term interest rates rise. Still more important on many occasions is the effect on expectations of a past rise in the incomes derived from physical assets and equities. If, because of past rises, incomes derived from the ownership of physical assets and equities are expected to rise further in the future, prices of these assets will continue to rise, often to a level where the yield, on the basis of past incomes, is below what it was before the rise in incomes began, while prices of fixed interest securities continue to fall and the market yield on them to rise.

During this process it is likely that the aggregate value of all assets, after deducting the fall in the price of fixed interest securities, will show a net rise. This is possible because, as the rate of interest rises, the cost of holding money idle becomes heavier, so that money is released from idle balances and the velocity of circulation rises. This rise in velocity, however, is obtained only at the cost of rising interest rates. Unless, therefore, the quantity of bank deposits is increased, their continuing absorption into the income circulation will force the rate of interest continually higher until it overtakes the rise in expectations, checks investment, and brings the expansionary process to an end.

Just as it is possible to force interest rates up by reducing the quantity of bank deposits when national income is stable, or by preventing a rise in bank deposits when national income is rising, so we can bring down the rate of interest by increasing the quantity of bank deposits when money incomes are stable, or can accelerate a decline in rates when incomes are falling. The duration of the lower level of interest rates so achieved will depend on how rapidly the lower rates stimulate investment, and, possibly, consumption. In conditions of active trade and business optimism, the lower rate of interest is likely to be rapidly reflected in a rise in investment, in payments for services, and in national money income. Unless, therefore, the rise in incomes is checked by some other development, such as an increase in voluntary saving or in the over-all budget surplus, further creations of bank deposits will be necessary to hold the rate of interest down to the level established by their initial rise. These, in turn, will bring a further rise in incomes, until the rate of increase exceeds that of output, so that inflation develops and prices rise. In conditions of trade depression, on the other hand, the rapidity with which lower interest rates will stimulate either investment or consumption is likely to be less, and their effect, at least for a time, may merely be to slow down the rate of fall in incomes. Even when incomes do begin to rise again, the existence of unemployed labour and capital is likely to ensure that for some time, and perhaps indefinitely, the rise in incomes is matched by a rise in output.

The only way in which a 'cheap money policy' can be made consistent with the absence of inflation in a period of full employment is through a drastic and effective system of controls over investment and consumption. While such a system may be practicable for a considerable time in special conditions, such as a war, it does not seem possible, in a democratic country and in peace-time, to make it effective for long, if only because few people will be willing for long to work and sell in exchange for money that they have no early expectation of being allowed to spend.

We have now been able to provide some at least of the reasons why a rise in national money income should have an effect on the long-term rate of interest similar to that of a reduction in bank deposits, and a fall in national income an effect similar to that of a rise in bank deposits. If, therefore, deposits and national income rise together, the two movements tend to cancel out each other's effects on the rate of interest and to leave it unchanged. We therefore have the possibility of a schedule of interest rates that will vary with the ratio of bank deposits to national income, rather than with the absolute changes in either. We have thus gone some way towards explaining the regularity of either one of the two series in Chart II, but we have still to explain why there are two series instead of one, and the causes of the switch from one series to the other.

CHANGES IN INVESTORS' EXPECTATIONS

For these explanations we have to look for the causes, not of movements of interest rates 'along' or in accordance with each schedule, but of shifts in the schedules themselves. The easiest way to start this search is to look for some factor that is present in the whole of one series and is absent from the whole of the other. This factor can hardly be the state of business activity, for both the lower series (1934–46) and the upper series (1921–33 and 1947–57) contain years of severe depression and of over-full employment. Nor can it be the level of short-term interest rates, for low short-term rates did not disappear in 1947, but continued into the second half of 1951. On the whole, the most likely factor, which seems to have been present in the years 1934 to 1946 and absent from the remainder, is a belief in the permanence of low long-term interest rates.

If the possibility of any large fall in prices of long-term fixed interest securities is excluded from investors' calculations, such securities become very much better substitutes for money

than if there is a real possibility of their future loss of value.
When investors believe that the risk of serious capital depreciation is negligible, the proportion of their assets that they wish
to hold in money at any given level of interest rates is reduced
and the velocity of circulation is correspondingly increased.
If, therefore, investors can be induced to acquire such a belief,
it is reasonable to expect a revision of the whole relationship
between the deposits/national income ratio and the long-term
rate of interest; while a later loss of the belief could be expected
to give rise to a similar shift in the whole schedule in the
reverse direction. What is surprising, however, is that, with all
the changes that had taken place in the size and composition
of the national debt, in the distribution of income and capital,
and in many other circumstances, the shift of schedule in 1947
should have brought it so exactly back into line with that
ruling in the 1920s. It can only be surmised that in some way
these other factors cancelled one another out, leaving similar
changes in expectations to produce similar results.

This explanation of the major shifts of schedule in 1934
and 1947 also throws light on the minor divergences within
each schedule. The fall in the rate of interest in 1934, which
occurred in spite of a sharp fall in the ratio of deposits to
national income, followed two years in which the rate of interest
had been steeply forced down by rapidly rising ratios. In other
words, it took two years of cheap money policy, in a time of
acute trade depression and after the abandonment of the gold
standard, to convince investors that cheap money was really
here to stay. Again, in the years 1936–39, the normal effects
on interest rates of a sharp rise in national income, with bank
deposits almost stationary, seem to have been reinforced by
doubts about the future level of rates, no doubt caused by
growing fears of war. When, however, war actually came and
it was found that, with modern powers of control, wars and
high interest rates were no longer synonymous, interest rates
fell back again, even though at first national income continued
to rise faster than deposits. Only in 1947, when it was realised
that, in peace-time and under conditions of full employment,
the controls could no longer be relied on to prevent money
leaking into the income circulation, was confidence in the
permanence of cheap money lost.

The movements of the long-term rate in the years 1952–54 present an interesting comparison with those of 1931–34. In both periods a balance-of-payments crisis had recently passed and short-term interest rates had fallen sharply. But whereas in 1931–34 it took two years of rising deposits/national income ratios to convince investors that cheap money would continue, in 1952–54 it took no more than a slowing-down of the fall in the ratio. This difference may have been due to the fact that the period 1931–34 followed many years of high interest rates, whereas in 1953 it may have been possible to believe that the rising rates of the preceding six years had been a mere aberration in the new order of things. Whatever the reasons for them, the expectations of 1953–54 were disappointed. This disappointment may be one of the reasons why 1958, which also has seen the (even more emphatic) passing of a balance-of-payments crisis, a sharp fall in short-term rates of interest, and, in addition, a definite slackening of excess demand and a rise in bank deposits about proportional to the rise in incomes, seems likely to show an average yield on Consols just about as high as 1957. It looks very much as if any attempt in the near future to shift the liquidity preference schedule downwards by persuading people that lower long-term rates of interest are likely to come and remain will encounter considerable psychological resistance from the investing public.

WHAT HOPES OF LOWER RATES IN 1959?

If it is true that the Government can no longer expect to bring down long-term interest rates by inducing a shift in the liquidity preference schedule, it follows that the only way of bringing about a permanent fall in rates is by allowing them to move 'along' the schedule : that is to say, by increasing the ratio of bank deposits to national income. In the absence of a substantial fall in money incomes (which, it may be surmised, no modern government would willingly tolerate) the increase in the total of bank deposits needed to bring about a fall of even one-half of one per cent in the long-term rate would be very considerable. If we assume a rise in national money income of 3 per cent from 1958 to 1959 (a rise that might be just compatible with stability of prices), this would bring net national income up from £17,600 millions in 1957 and an estimated £18,200 millions in 1958 to about £18,700 millions in 1959. If the schedule we are assumed to follow is the general average trend of the upper schedule in Chart II, to reduce the yield on Consols from 5 to 4½ per cent by the end of 1959 would require a rise in the net deposits/net national income ratio from 35 per cent to about 40 per cent. If, instead, we assume that the schedule follows the steeper slope of the years 1954–58, the ratio consistent with a 4½ per cent yield on Consols would be about 38 per cent. Even if we assume the schedule follows a path parallel to that recorded for the years 1931–33, the ratio required would still be over 37 per cent. On the first assumption, in order to reduce the Consols' yield to 4½ per cent by the year-end, the increase needed in deposits above the present level would be about £1100 millions during the next twelve months, on the second assumption about £700 millions, and even on the third well over £500 millions.

In view of the recent Government policy of endeavouring to stimulate demand by measures other than lower long-term interest rates, and of the political need to leave something in hand for reduction of taxation in the budget, it seems unlikely that bank deposits will be allowed to rise as rapidly as even the smallest of the (large) rates of growth indicated above. Indeed, it may well be that any increases that occur will do no more than keep pace with the rise in national money income. If so, the ratio of bank deposits to national income will remain at what would in earlier years have been regarded as the crisis level of 35 per cent, and the investing public may have time to get used to the idea that a yield of 5 per cent on long-dated British Government securities is no longer exceptional.

CHAPTER 4

WHAT *IS* THIS LIQUIDITY?[1]

THIS article is concerned primarily with the central issue of principle that runs through the Radcliffe Committee's analysis, and shapes many of its conclusions, on monetary policy. There are, however, some other major aspects, selected from the many, that cannot be passed over without comment.

It has first to be acknowledged that in its descriptive sections the Report provides a clear and very useful statement of existing knowledge, together with a good deal of new information on matters, such as the changes in the amount and distribution of national debt in non-official hands, about which it has hitherto been possible only to guess. About the recommendations on the relationship between the Bank and the Treasury, which I should imagine would give rise to more disagreement than almost anything else in the Report, I am not competent to speak; but I have every hope that the recommendations for more factual and other information about the operations of the monetary authorities will meet with enthusiastic support from everyone — subject, perhaps, to the regrettable exception of the monetary authorities themselves.

The main recommendations on policy hold out no hopes of easy and general solutions, and to some may appear largely negative. I am, however, profoundly grateful to the Committee for two recommendations of the greatest importance. The first is that 'the authorities should not aim at complete stability of interest rates, but should take a view as to what the long-term economic situation demands and be prepared by all the means in their power to influence markets in the required direction' (498),[2] and that a continuation of 'moderately high bond rates' is appropriate to the situation likely to exist in the early 1960s (571 to 577). One reason that the Committee

[1] Published in *The Banker*, October 1959.
[2] Numbers in brackets refer to paragraphs of the Radcliffe Committee Report.

gives for the latter view merits particular emphasis : 'the belief that a well-spread portfolio of equities gives the investor the chance to share in the benefits of economic growth' (574).

This belief springs directly from the expectation that no government will in future allow any really substantial amount of unemployment to appear, even temporarily. So long as a large proportion of employment remains in the private sector, this means that business profits will have to be allowed (or induced) to rise more or less in step with national money income. Even with stable prices, it may be expected that national money income will rise by an average of at least 2 per cent and perhaps 3 per cent a year. If dividends, which still absorb an unusually low proportion of company earnings, rise proportionally with profits, an investor with a 'well-spread portfolio of equities' can look forward to an average rise of 2 per cent or 3 per cent a year in his investment income and, with stable interest rates, in the capital value of his securities. The removal of the fears of a major trade depression also removes the main reason which in the past has kept the yield on sound equities above the long-term gilt-edged rate, and the investor is now given the choice between securities which offer a stable income and, at best, stable capital values and others which offer incomes and capital values rising by 2 per cent or 3 per cent a year. It would not be unreasonable to prefer equities even when they offer a current yield appreciably below that obtainable on long-dated government securities. But the yield on equities cannot stand too far below what companies can hope to earn on new investments, or a rush of new issues will either pull equity prices down again or give rise to excess demand and inflation. If therefore it is to offset the attractions of capital appreciation (even if subject to tax), the yield on fixed interest securities is likely to remain high.

The other finding of the Report for which I am particularly grateful is that the cheapest way out of its difficulties for a country with over £3000 millions of short-term foreign debts and an inadequate gold reserve is to behave in such a manner that the owners of the debts retain the confidence that they will be able to get their money whenever they want it. The best way to retain this confidence is to maintain a sufficiently large favourable balance of payments on current account. 'We regard the right course of action as one calculated to add to the reserves or reduce liabilities out of a current surplus sufficiently large to leave room also for long-term investment abroad' (662).

The parts of the Report that I find less enlightening than I had hoped come mainly in the analysis of the way the system operates. At several points I have found myself wishing that the Committee had taken its analysis further and made it more precise.

A matter of which a fuller analysis would have been particularly welcome is the Committee's concept of what constitutes a change in the liquidity of the system. The Report repeatedly insists that 'the factor which monetary policy should seek to influence or control is something that reaches beyond the "supply of money". It is nothing less than the state of liquidity of the whole economy' (981). But we are nowhere given any clear definition of just what is meant by 'the state of liquidity of the whole economy', and an attempt has therefore to be made to deduce it from the various references scattered through the Report.

The Committee is, of course, on unassailable ground in refusing to limit the concept of changes in liquidity to changes in the supply of money. Much misunderstanding would have been avoided if the phrase 'liquidity preference' had never been given a purely monetary connotation. In the full meaning of the term, liquidity preference can be exercised not only through the amount of money held, but also through an infinite number of variations in the forms and proportions not only of non-monetary assets but also of liabilities. But whether a given change in the form of non-monetary assets or liabilities, or in the institutional facilities through which they can be marketed or pledged, does or does not increase or decrease the state of liquidity of the economy can still be decided by a monetary test. If there is an increase in non-monetary liquidity in either of these qualitative ways, a given standard of total liquidity can be achieved with a smaller holding of money, while a decrease in non-monetary liquidity requires an increased holding of money if the same standard of over-all liquidity is to be maintained. Thus an increase in non-monetary liquidity will cause a decrease in liquidity preference, in the conventional sense, while a decrease in non-monetary liquidity will increase it. An increase in non-monetary liquidity therefore has the same effect as an increase in the quantity of money, since the money set free by the increase in non-monetary liquidity is made available for additional expenditure on assets, thus bringing down the rate of interest, or on services, thus raising national money income.

CONFLICTING DEFINITIONS

The effects of changes in the form of assets and liabilities, and of developments in the markets dealing in them, upon the demand for money at given levels of national income and interest rates (or, to put the same thing another way, upon the level of interest rates at given ratios of money supply to national income) may very well have great importance over long periods. Over shorter periods, however, it seems probable that they have a much smaller effect on the level of interest rates, not only than changes in the money/national income ratio (which, as the Committee shows (in 478), has fluctuated from just over 50 per cent in 1930 to nearly 80 per cent in 1947 and back to about 43 per cent in 1958), but also than other non-monetary changes in liquidity. Of these by far the most important seem to have been changes in expectations about the future stability of interest rates, which may cause wide variations in the acceptability of fixed interest securities as substitutes for money as a store of value. The Committee itself provides evidence of the importance of these expectations in its argument for rejecting the policy of stabilising long-term interest rates, on the ground, among others, that it would mean the 'monetisation' of the whole national debt (494). Their importance is also emphasised in a contrary argument, that wider fluctuations in yields on bonds are undesirable on the ground that various financial institutions would find government bonds less satisfactory substitutes for money (491) — in other words, such fluctuations would mean the 'de-monetisation' of the national debt. (It is difficult to reconcile these two paragraphs, unless we take the view that whatever degree of monetisation the national debt has achieved at any particular moment should necessarily be maintained.)

That the Committee attaches much greater importance than

seems justified by the foregoing analysis to short-term changes in assets and in market institutions suggests that it may be using a definition of liquidity that differs from the one used above. This impression is supported by the fact that the Report seems to attribute increases in non-monetary liquidity not only to changes in the *form* and *marketability* of assets, but also to changes in their *quantity* (*e.g.* 478). Now while we can be certain of the direction (though not the amount) of the changes in the demand for money that will follow changes in the form and marketability of existing non-monetary assets, there is no such certainty about the effects on the demand for money of the creation of new assets. This is because, while all assets (not merely financial assets, as the Committee seems to suggest) are to a greater or less extent substitutes for money as a store of value, they are complementary to money in its capacity as a medium of exchange. While, therefore, all assets possess some degree of 'moneyness' in the former capacity, it is usually possible, at any given time and in any given country, to draw a fairly sharp line between those assets which are widely and generally used in the payment of debts, and those which are not. As a medium of exchange money provides a service that is unique, and the demand for that service is increased by, among other causes, an increase in the quantity of non-monetary assets (since that will tend to increase the turnover in the markets for such assets).

If, therefore, new assets are created, there are two opposing results on the demand for money. The new assets provide substitutes, the closeness of which depends upon their form, for money in its capacity as a store of value. But they also tend to increase the demand for money in its capacity as a medium of exchange. Which effect will prove the stronger, and whether the net effect is to increase or decrease the aggregate demand for money at unchanged levels of interest rates and incomes, it is not possible to predict. The closer the substitutes that the new assets provide for money as a store of value, the more likely it is that the fall in the demand for money as a store of value will be greater than the rise in the demand for it as a medium of exchange, and that the net effect will be an increase in over-all liquidity. But there can be no certainty.

The fact that the Committee regards it as axiomatic that an

increase in the volume of financial assets brings an increase in liquidity suggests that it has in mind a definition of liquidity different from that given above. The best word I can find for what I think they mean is 'unsqueezability'. If a man is owed a debt that is repayable in the near future, or owns assets that can be easily sold or pawned, it is difficult to stop him getting hold of money. If the quantity of money is fixed, the resultant new demand for money competes with existing ones, and tends to drive up the rate of interest. This in turn induces some release of money from idle balances, and allows the velocity of circulation to rise.[1] If the supply of money is limited, everyone with saleable or pledgeable assets can join in the competition for the available supply of funds, including the money newly released from idle balances, and those who are prepared to pay most for them get them. Often the successful bidders intend to use the money for purposes which the Government does not regard as of high priority; but the wider the distribution of assets, and therefore of creditworthiness, and the more perfect the organisation of the capital market, the more difficult it is to prevent people getting hold of money and using it as they want to.

The difficulties of the authorities in controlling the use of resources in the economy are greatly increased when the owners of assets can not only assert a claim to a share in the use of existing money, but can force an expansion in its quantity. This power has long existed for a limited group of holders of a particular kind of assets. The right of the discount market to borrow unlimited amounts of money from the Bank of England has made it impossible for the Bank to prevent the discount houses, and through them the clearing banks, from obtaining as much cash as they want; all the Bank can do is to make it more expensive to turn non-cash assets into cash by raising Bank Rate. Since the immense rise in the size of the Government redeemable debt, this power of obliging the authorities to convert non-money assets into money has been extended from the discount market to the general public.

---

[1] The Report says (footnote 1, p. 133) that the velocity of circulation can be regarded as dragging interest rates up with it. This is surely to reverse cause and effect. It is the rise in interest rates, caused by an excess of demand for loans over supply at existing rates, that induces some holders to release idle balances and so brings an increase in velocity.

Anyone holding Government securities due for repayment can force the Government to provide him with money simply by declining to renew his loan ; and if the Government wishes to avoid borrowing from the banks and so creating more money it must offer to holders of existing balances interest rates high enough to persuade them to release them. In these circumstances, any attempt by the Government to limit the use of money by the public by making it generally scarce results merely in the attempted squeeze being passed straight back to the Government; and, apart from physical controls, the Government's only defence is to offer sufficiently high interest rates to induce either existing borrowers to cut down their demands or holders of idle balances to release them. On this definition, therefore, a rise in the volume of Government debt increases the liquidity of the non-Government sector even though it may also increase (and probably has increased) the aggregate demand for money at given levels of interest rates and national income.

The great vulnerability of the Government to counter-pressure, from those who seek to escape from a shortage of money by declining to renew maturing Government loans, fully justifies the Committee's views about the impossibility of the Government's standing aside from monetary decisions, and about the importance for the economy of the way the national debt is managed. It is also possible to understand, if not necessarily to agree with, its proposals that, in conditions of emergency, the Government should take steps to shield itself from the efforts of the private sector to 'squeeze back' at it, by direct controls over capital issues and consumer credit (524, 984), and by requiring the banks to hold a minimum proportion of their assets in the form of Government obligations of all types, including securities (527). (The Committee calls this a maximum ratio of advances to deposits, but it comes to the same thing.)

IMPORTANCE OF MONEY SUPPLY

It is, however, difficult to believe that, even on the definition of liquidity that the Committee seems to adopt, over short and medium periods changes in the quantity, form, or market-

ability of non-monetary assets held by the public are comparable in their effects with those caused by changes in the
money/national income ratio or (more rarely) by major changes
in expectations about the future level of interest rates. After
all, the last great increase in the ratio of Government debt to
national income occurred during the First World War (as the
Committee shows, the rise in the quantity of Government
debt in non-official hands since before the Second World War
has hardly kept pace with the rise in national income); while
the only two major changes in the form of the debt during the
past forty years occurred during the heavy funding of short-
term bonds in the 1920s and with the great expansion of short-
and medium-term debt during the Second World War. While,
therefore, changes in non-monetary liquidity, as apparently
defined by the Committee, may be of great importance in
comparing conditions to-day with those of twenty-five or fifty
years ago, they are almost certainly of minor importance in
considering changes from month to month and from year to
year. It is therefore difficult to understand the Committee's
determination to discuss monetary problems in terms of over-
all liquidity, which is not measurable, instead of in terms of the
quantity of money (or rather, of the money/national income
ratio), which is.

It is also difficult to understand why the Committee, because
changes in the quantity of money exercise their effects mainly
through changes in interest rates, should discuss the results of
official purchases or sales of Government securities so largely
in terms of their impact effect on interest rates and so little
in terms of their effects on the quantity of money. After all,
the ability of the Government to avoid borrowing from the
banks on Treasury bills is the clearest evidence that it has been
able to withstand a 'squeeze-back' by the private sector.

The Committee is less hampered than might have been
expected by its expressed refusal to consider effects of changes
in the quantity of money rather than in general liquidity for
the reason that, where really necessary, it sometimes does talk
about the quantity of money, though often under some dis-
guise. Thus in its discussion (490) of the difficulty of attempting to control the economy by large and sudden reversals of
the long-term rate of interest, it says that 'the Bank of England

is the ultimate source of *liquidity* and can name its price for every maturity in which it chooses to trade' and 'when it wants to reverse the operation it has to pour out cash in exchange for bonds, and this glut of *liquidity* is likely to be a great embarrassment in the future' (my italics). In both sentences, for 'liquidity' read 'money'. There are, however, other occasions when the Report's conclusions may very well have been influenced by the Committee's analytical approach. There is, for instance, the rather puzzling recommendation that local authorities should revert to the practice of borrowing from the Treasury rather than from the public, partly on the ground that by borrowing so largely on short-term they have been acting 'clean contrary to the funding policy of the monetary authorities' (597). But there is surely a world of difference between a short-term local authority loan from the public and an increase in the Treasury bill holdings of the banks. An increase in the Treasury bill issue is inflationary mainly in so far as it adds to the liquid assets of the banks and to the total of bank deposits. An increase in Treasury bills held entirely by the public (the banks' customers) is only slightly more inflationary than an issue of securities.

Another verdict in the Report that might have been different with a different approach to liquidity is that on the usefulness of monetary measures in dealing with temporary outbreaks of excess demand, presumably as the result of fluctuations in the demand for stocks. The Committee argues, in my opinion rightly, that a long-term tendency towards an excessive level of fixed investment can appropriately be dealt with by a restriction of liquidity (in practice, of bank deposits) in the hands of the public and a rise in long-term interest rates. But it feels that in dealing with temporary fluctuations in demand it would be undesirable to attempt to use wide fluctuations in long-term rates, while it considers that small fluctuations in long-term rates, or any fluctuations in short-term rates, would have little or no effect (488, 489). In reaching this conclusion, the Committee may be underestimating the effects of even small movements in long-term rates *provided that they are regarded as temporary*, and provided that they are accompanied by much larger movements of shorter-term rates. If a rise in long-term rates is confidently expected to be reversed in six

months' time, people requiring long-term finance will look at
the changes in capital values rather than at current rates. If
by postponing the issue or sale of a security an extra 5 per cent
can be realised on its price, there is quite a substantial incentive
to postpone the sale or issue, even though a 5 per cent change
in the price of a long-dated 5 per cent bond represents a change
of little more than ¼ per cent in its yield to maturity. The
postponement of the issue or sale will, however, have no effect
on expenditure if the gap can be bridged by a short-term
loan ; but the would-be investor will not seek such a bridge
if the cost is enough to offset the advantages of postponing
the long-term borrowing. For a six months' loan this cost
would have to be about 10 per cent above the normal level,
or perhaps 15 per cent in all. A similar result would, of course,
be achieved if borrowers, unable to obtain additional facilities
from their usual sources, were obliged (as the Committee suggests is sometimes the case) to borrow elsewhere at much
higher rates. If it is generally believed that long-term rates of
interest are likely in future to show only small fluctuations at
round about the existing level, there seems no reason why
quite small fluctuations in long-term rates, accompanied by
much wider movements in short-term rates, should not exercise
a very appreciable effect on postponing expenditures — and
since, by definition, the difficulties are temporary, it is postponement rather than cancellation that is desirable.

In conclusion, it may be noted that there is one recommendation in the Report which, if adopted on a large scale,
might well do more to increase the liquidity of the system than
many of the other factors to which the Committee draws
attention. This is the institution of a 'giro' system, possibly
by the Post Office in co-operation with the banks, which would
accept interest-free deposits, to be freely transferable to other
'giro' accounts throughout the country on the instructions,
usually written, of the owner. Although part of the rise in
'giro' accounts would no doubt be offset by a reduction in
existing forms of money, the final effect would almost certainly
be a net addition to the existing stock of media of exchange ;
and if this addition turned out to be large, its effect would be
equivalent to that of the creation of a large additional amount
of existing types of money.

CHAPTER 5

SAVING AND INVESTMENT
IN THE UNITED KINGDOM [1]

THE foreign exchange crisis of August and September, which
was largely the result of the weakness of the United Kingdom's
international capital position, should not be allowed wholly
to divert attention from the very encouraging developments
which have taken place during the last few years in both the
size and the use of the country's real income. If we divide the
ten years from 1946 to 1956 into two equal parts, we find that
the rise in total production was slightly larger in the first half,
when it rose by 15 per cent, than in the second, when it rose
by 14 per cent. Between 1949 and 1951, however, the rise in
production was largely offset by the worsening of the terms of
trade, while in 1952 and 1953 it was supplemented by their
improvement, with the result that the rise in the real national
income between 1951 and 1956, at 18 per cent, was more than
half as large again as the rise of 11 per cent between 1946 and
1951. The rise in the rate of increase per head of population
was even larger, from 8 per cent between 1946 and 1951 to
16 per cent between 1951 and 1956. If we can trust the link
between 1938 and post-war years, it would seem that it is
only since 1951 that the real national income per head of
population has been appreciably higher than before the war.

Almost as encouraging as the accelerated rise in real
national income between 1952 and 1956 are the changes in the
uses to which it has been put. So far from inflationary pressure
being caused by a rise in the proportion devoted to personal
consumption, this proportion has fallen almost continuously,
from 75 per cent in 1947 to 71 per cent in 1951 and to under
67 per cent in 1956. While the proportion of real national
income still devoted to current personal consumption is no
doubt higher than in some countries — in Russia it is reputed
to be under 50 per cent — it is almost certainly lower than in

[1] Published in the *London and Cambridge Bulletin*, December 1957.

any peace-time year since 1914, and probably for many years before that.

In the first two years after the war the proportion of real national income taken by the public authorities' expenditure on goods and services fell sharply; but from 1948 to 1952 it rose again, mainly for purposes of defence, and absorbed nearly the whole of the resources released by the fall in the proportion used for personal consumption. Since 1952, however, the

TABLE I

GROSS REAL NATIONAL PRODUCT AND GROSS
REAL NATIONAL INCOME IN THE
UNITED KINGDOM
1946–56 (1938 = 100)

	Total		Per Head of Population	
	Production	National Income	Production	National Income
1946	103·0	96·4	99·5	93·0
1947	103·7	96·9	99·2	92·7
1948	107·0	100·6	101·8	95·7
1949	110·9	104·4	105·1	99·0
1950	113·9	106·3	107·6	100·3
1951	118·2	107·2	111·2	100·8
1952	118·6	109·0	111·1	102·0
1953	123·2	114·2	115·2	106·6
1954	127·9	118·9	119·2	110·8
1955	132·7	123·2	123·4	114·4
1956	134·5	126·2	124·6	117·0
1957 (estimated)	137·2	129·4	126·6	119·4

stabilisation of public expenditure in real terms has caused it to absorb a falling proportion of a rising real income, and this fall, together with the continued fall in the proportion devoted to personal consumption, has enabled the proportion saved to rise sharply. This rise in the proportion saved of a rapidly rising real national income has brought an increase in the absolute level of real saving far greater than even the most optimistic observer of a few years ago would have dared to prophesy. In gross saving (saving plus depreciation) the estimated rise, at 1948 market prices, is from £1710 millions in 1951 and £1735 millions in 1952 to £2627 millions in 1956, or by over 50 per cent. The rise in net saving, after deducting the estimated cost of making good the consumption of fixed capital, is even more remarkable — from £712 millions in 1952 to £1448 millions in 1956, or by over 100 per cent. The 1956 ratio of net saving to net national income was nearly 11 per cent, which was certainly much greater than in any inter-war year, and not immensely below the net 13 per cent or 14 per cent believed to have been saved in 1913, when the distribution of income was very different.

The main source of the recent rise in real saving has been the even more remarkable recovery in personal saving. Between 1947 and 1951 gross personal saving was very small and net personal saving probably substantially negative. In 1952 it rose very sharply and unexpectedly, rose further in 1953, fell back a little in 1954, and then rose sharply again in 1955 and still more in 1956. The generally accepted explanation of the 1952 rise is that it marked the end of spending involuntary war-time savings and of restoring depleted household stocks of durable consumption goods; but this explanation is hardly adequate to cover the rises in 1955 and 1956. We can account for about a third of the 1956 rise by the restrictions on hire purchase. A partial explanation of the rest may be that, in 1952 as well as in 1955–56, even a slight hint of disinflation and of some reduction in the security of future individual incomes was sufficient to cause a significant number of consumers to postpone part of their expenditure, especially on durable goods.

If in the years before 1952 anything like this rise in personal and total saving had been foreseen, most observers would have expected that it would be fully adequate to eliminate inflationary pressure and to release sufficient resources to create a favourable balance of payments large enough to remove for ever any threat to the stability of sterling. Yet, in the event, the past three years have seen a severe renewal of inflationary pressure and the development of a balance-of-payments crisis hardly less serious than that of 1951–52. The basic cause of the return of financial difficulties in spite of the phenomenal rise in the level of saving is the almost equally large rise which has taken place since 1952 in the level of domestic fixed investment, first in the form of new houses and later of industrial and other investment.

| | Consumers' Expenditure | | | | Public Authorities' Expenditure on Goods and Services | | | Saving and Depreciation | | | Gross Nationl Income | |
| | | Percentage of | | | | Percentage of | | | Percentage of | | | |
	£m.	National Income	1948	1948 per Head of Population	£m.	National Income	1948	£m.	National Income	1948	£m.	Percentage of 1948
1938	8,564	73·3	101·1	106·2	1750	15·0	99·3	1373	11·7	89·8	11,687	99·2
1946	8,245	73·1	97·3	98·7	2589	23·0	147·0	438	3·9	28·6	11,272	95·8
1947	8,519	75·2	100·5	101·0	1773	15·7	100·6	1030	9·1	67·5	11,322	96·3
1948	8,471	72·0	100·0	100·0	1761	15·0	100·0	1529	13·0	100·0	11,761	100·0
1949	8,616	70·6	101·7	101·0	1915	15·7	108·7	1672	13·7	109·3	12,203	103·7
1950	8,825	71·0	104·2	103·3	1899	15·3	107·9	1705	13·7	111·5	12,429	105·6
1951	8,780	71·1	103·6	102·4	2048	16·3	116·2	1710	13·6	111·9	12,538	106·5
1952	8,731	68·6	103·0	101·3	2267	17·8	128·8	1735	13·6	113·4	12,733	108·3
1953	9,099	68·1	107·3	105·4	2306	17·3	131·0	1952	14·6	127·6	13,357	113·5
1954	9,503	68·4	112·4	110·1	2287	16·4	130·0	2112	15·2	138·2	13,902	118·2
1955	9,796	68·0	115·7	113·0	2255	15·7	128·0	2354	16·3	153·9	14,405	122·4
1956	9,847	66·7	116·3	113·1	2285	15·5	129·9	2627	17·8	171·8	14,759	125·4
1957 (est.)	10,100	66·8	119·2	115·3	2250	14·9	127·8	2780	18·2	180·0	15,130	128·4

	£m.	Per cent of Gross National Income	Price Index (1948 = 100)
Consumers' expenditure	13,409	65·0	136
Public authorities' expenditure on goods and services	3,498	17·0	153
Saving and depreciation	3,704	18·0	141
Gross national income	20,611	100·0	140

Note: The proportion of national income devoted to personal consumption is higher, and the proportion devoted to public authorities' expenditure on goods and services lower, at 1948 prices than at current prices, as the result of an exceptionally large rise in the price index for goods and services bought by public authorities. Figures for 1956 at current prices are as follows:

By far the greater part of this increase in fixed investment occurred in the private sector and, especially for net investment, in new houses and other types of building. Much of the rise may well have been due to an uprush of previously frustrated demand released by the relaxation of direct controls. While the release of this demand has undoubtedly increased the difficulty of restraining inflation, the fact that it is no longer suppressed means at least that inflationary pressure is now no greater than appears on the surface and that there are no longer hidden forces waiting their chance to erupt.

Until 1955 the rise in fixed investment almost exactly paralleled the rise in saving, so that, after making allowance for changes in grants from abroad and in errors and omissions, the surplus in real terms of saving over fixed investment at home was no larger in 1955 than it had been in 1952, and only slightly larger than in 1951. Meanwhile there appeared a new development which emphasised the inadequacy of this margin. The two other forms of investment which have to be financed out of the surplus of saving over fixed investment are (1) investment in increasing the volume of stocks and (2) investment abroad (which, if we include increases in gold stocks with foreign investment, is identical with the balance of payments on current account). Since the war the annual rise in the volume of stocks has averaged about 2 per cent or about two-thirds the average rise of 3 per cent in total production; but the rise in stocks has occurred very intermittently. The usual pattern is for a year of heavy stock increase to be followed by several years of lower accumulation. In the years of heavy stock increase — 1947, 1951, and 1955 — the investment in stocks has absorbed more than the whole of the margin of savings over fixed investment, so that the balance of payments has been adverse ; while, in the years of low stock accumulation, the balance of payments has usually been enough to finance long-term capital exports without drawing on the gold reserve.

While, however, the immediate cause of three out of the four post-war sterling crises (that of 1949 was an affair mainly for the rest of the sterling area) was an exceptional rise in the volume of stocks, the underlying cause has been the continuously inadequate margin of saving over fixed investment. Without the imposition of exchange controls on capital transfers to

TABLE III
SOURCES OF SAVING IN THE UNITED KINGDOM
(£m. at 1948 Prices)

	Persons and Unincorporated Businesses	Companies and Public Corporations	Tax Reserves	Public Authorities	Total Savings and Depreciation	Depreciation of Fixed Assets	Total Net Saving
1938 (partly estimated)	650	863	52	− 192	1373	835	538
1946	358	534	− 42	− 412	438	..	..
1947	164	424	264	178	1030	..	..
1948	30	745	182	572	1529	889	640
1949	124	861	24	663	1672	921	751
1950	90	894	128	593	1705	958	747
1951	91	697	436	486	1710	999	711
1952	547	864	− 23	347	1735	1023	712
1953	656	1059	− 30	267	1952	1062	890
1954	553	1210	104	245	2112	1107	1005
1955	749	1216	− 15	404	2354	1157	1197
1956	1041	1143	111	332	2627	1179	1448
1957 (estimated)	..	..	..	..	2780	1210	1570

the rest of the sterling area, it does not seem possible to keep exports of long-term capital much below £150 millions a year at current prices even in times of severe financial stringency, and as soon as that stringency is relaxed they are likely to rise to £200 millions a year or more. In addition, it will be necessary to provide in the coming years for the repayment of the £200 millions borrowed last December from the International Monetary Fund and of the £89 millions borrowed from the Export-Import Bank, the gradual liquidation of the £125 millions of debt owed to the European Payments Union, the continued payment of £38 millions a year in reduction of the 1946 North American Loans, and almost certainly for some net repayment of sterling balances, especially, perhaps, those held by the former colonies which have recently become independent states.   It is also urgently necessary to build up the gold reserve to a level which will make sterling less vulnerable than it is now to the assaults of foreign speculators. To secure all these objectives a favourable balance of payments averaging £400 millions a year at present prices would be hardly adequate. If we add to this an investment in additional stocks at the average rate of £170 millions a year (2 per cent of £8500 millions), we reach a total for the required margin of saving over domestic fixed investment of something like £600 millions at present prices, or over £400 millions a year at 1948 prices. Only with a margin of this magnitude shall we be able to regard fluctuations in the level of stock accumulation and in long-term foreign investment with even moderate equanimity.

The year 1956 saw a very substantial advance towards this objective.   One effect of the check to consumers' demand was to reduce the growth of total production to under $1\frac{1}{2}$ per cent, or barely half the average annual increase, but an improvement in the terms of trade brought the rise in real national income up to nearly $2\frac{1}{2}$ per cent, or not far below the post-war average. Real personal incomes after tax rose by over 3 per cent, but personal consumption by only $\frac{1}{2}$ per cent, so that personal saving, and with it total saving, recorded the sharp increase noted above.   Meanwhile tighter money and higher rates of interest were gradually checking the uprush of fixed investment, with the result that the margin of saving over fixed investment nearly doubled, from £171 millions at 1948 prices

TABLE IV

GROSS DOMESTIC FIXED CAPITAL FORMATION IN THE UNITED KINGDOM

(£m. at 1948 Prices)

	Vehicles, Ships, and Aircraft			Plant and Machinery			New Dwellings			Other Building, etc.			Total		
	Private Sector	Public Sector	Total	Private Sector	Public Sector	Total	Private Sector	Public Sector	Total	Private Sector	Public Sector	Total	Private Sector	Public Sector	Total
1938	..	..	205	..	..	402	..	..	474	..	..	478	1086	473	1559
1946	..	..	..	..	..	..	..	..	..	..	..	..	..	..	1058
1947	..	..	292	..	..	398	..	..	356	..	..	258	..	..	1304
1948	211	55	266	355	135	490	45	292	337	153	182	337	764	666	1430
1949	211	75	286	356	181	537	54	276	330	188	222	410	809	754	1563
1950	183	70	253	393	209	602	50	273	323	218	245	463	844	797	1641
1951	164	56	220	382	277	659	49	267	316	188	264	452	783	864	1647
1952	161	49	210	337	287	624	77	300	377	175	285	460	750	921	1671
1953	185	56	241	326	306	632	133	360	493	177	306	483	821	1028	1849
1954	204	52	256	375	320	695	185	334	519	214	311	525	978	1017	1995
1955	223	64	287	435	332	767	212	267	479	281	310	591	1151	973	2124
1956	236	84	320	462	322	784	227	242	469	328	333	661	1253	981	2234
1957 (est.)	..	..	..	..	..	..	..	..	..	..	..	..	..	..	2300

to £335 millions. This is the highest level recorded since the war, and has been approached only once, in 1948, when domestic savings were supplemented by heavy receipts of Marshall Aid. Although stock accumulation in 1956, while smaller than in 1955, remained well above the average level, the balance of payments recovered to about the same level (in real terms) as those of 1952 and 1954 (when stock accumulation was small), and would probably have been large enough to relieve the strain on sterling had not political events precipitated heavy withdrawals of sterling balances, mainly by countries outside the sterling area.

ESTIMATES FOR 1957

The recent rise in the level of industrial production encourages the expectation that the rise in total production will be found to be rather larger than that recorded in 1956 — perhaps 2 per cent as against less than $1\frac{1}{2}$ per cent last year. The recent improvement in the terms of trade may add another $\frac{1}{2}$ per cent to this, giving a total rise of $2\frac{1}{2}$ per cent in real national income, or about the same as from 1955 to 1956. It seems likely that personal consumption, after its check last year, has risen appreciably in 1957, perhaps by more than in proportion to the rise in real national income ; but expenditure by public authorities on goods and services, at 1948 prices, is likely to have fallen below the 1956 level by at least last year's expenditure on Suez. The proportion of real national income saved has therefore probably risen again. Only part of the further rise in saving seems to have been absorbed by the now slackening rise in fixed investment so that (unless there is a large change in 'errors and omissions') the margin of saving over fixed investment seems to have widened perceptibly further. The whole, or almost the whole, of this increased margin seems, however, to have been absorbed by an increase in the rate of stock accumulation, and the balance-of-payments surplus has probably been not very different from that of 1956.

OUTLOOK FOR 1958

While this year's improvement in the balance of payments, if any, has probably been small, a very substantial improvement

TABLE V
GROSS AND NET FIXED DOMESTIC CAPITAL FORMATION IN THE UNITED KINGDOM
(£m. at 1948 Prices)

	Vehicles, Ships, and Aircraft			Plant and Machinery			New Dwellings			Other Building, etc.			Total		
	Gross	Depr.	Net	Gross	Depr.	Net	Gross	Depr.	Net	Gross	Depr.	Net	Gross	Depr.	Net
1938	205	159	46	402	268	134	474	142	332	478	266	212	1559	835	724
1946	..	..	..	..	..	..	..	..	..	..	..	..	1058	..	..
1947	292	..	..	398	..	..	356	..	..	258	..	..	1304	..	..
1948	266	135	131	490	308	182	337	170	167	337	276	61	1430	889	541
1949	286	144	142	537	323	214	330	173	157	410	281	129	1563	921	642
1950	253	156	97	602	340	262	323	176	147	463	286	177	1641	958	683
1951	220	168	52	659	360	299	316	178	138	452	293	159	1647	999	648
1952	210	178	32	624	377	247	377	181	196	460	287	173	1671	1023	648
1953	241	191	50	632	396	236	493	186	307	483	289	194	1849	1062	787
1954	256	205	51	695	416	279	519	190	329	525	296	229	1995	1107	888
1955	287	222	65	767	437	330	479	191	288	591	307	284	2124	1157	967
1956	320	234	86	784	454	330	469	185	284	661	306	355	2234	1179	1055
1957 (est.)	..	..	..	..	..	..	..	..	..	..	..	..	2300	1210	1090

seems at least possible in 1958. Given the continuation of present policies, it seems probable that fixed investment will level off, while it is difficult to believe that the volume of stocks will show an unusually large rise for the fourth year in succession. The stabilisation of total fixed investment at the present high level is not inconsistent with a continued rise in industrial fixed investment, since investment in new houses, to judge from the number under construction, is likely to fall further in 1958. If plans for a reduction in defence expenditure are fulfilled, public authorities' expenditure on goods and services will again be reduced, while it would not be surprising if next year's rise in personal consumption was only moderate. If all these expectations are fulfilled, the vital question to ask is how far the resources so released by the limitation of home demand would be absorbed in expanding the favourable balance of payments and how far their non-employment would result in a fall, or a check to the rise, of production and real national income. The answer depends largely upon how far we may expect the maintenance of active business conditions in the rest of the world. While some loss of potential output is a very probable concomitant of any diversion of resources to foreign investment which is induced by a restriction of home demand, it is believed that, in so open an economy as that of the United Kingdom, the loss of output would be relatively small so long as a high level of business activity was maintained in the rest of the world. In these conditions, it seems likely that a large part of the resources released by the restriction of home demand would be rapidly diverted to expanding exports, and that, with imports limited by the restriction of demand, the improvement in the balance of payments might be so large as to justify a fairly early relaxation of credit restrictions.

If we make the opposite assumption, that the world is about to enter on a major depression, then any unemployment of resources caused by present checks on domestic demand would be quite insignificant compared with that inevitably caused by a major fall in the volume of exports. If this should happen, no doubt urgent steps would be taken in all countries to restore demand. It is to be hoped that these efforts would not, as in the early 1930s, be directed exclusively to the re-expansion of domestic demand, but that at least equal energy

TABLE VI

SOURCES AND USES OF INVESTIBLE FUNDS IN THE UNITED KINGDOM

(£m. at 1948 Prices)

	Investible Funds				Gross Domestic Fixed Capital Formation	Surplus available for Stock Accumulation and Foreign Investment	Use of Surplus	
	Gross Saving	Capital Grants and Transfers from Abroad	Errors and Omissions	Total Investible Funds			Physical Increase in Stocks	Net Foreign Investment
1938	1373	—	—	1373	1559	− 186	—	− 186
1946	438	173	—	608	1058	− 447	− 58	− 389
1947	1030	172	—	1202	1304	− 102	+ 356	− 458
1948	1529	234	− 19	1744	1430	+ 314	+ 175	+ 139
1949	1672	186	− 50	1808	1563	+ 245	+ 63	+ 182
1950	1705	159	− 22	1842	1641	+ 201	− 188	+ 389
1951	1710	66	+ 20	1796	1647	+ 149	+ 400	− 251
1952	1735	27	+ 86	1848	1671	+ 177	+ 5	+ 172
1953	1952	21	+112	2085	1849	+ 236	+ 95	+ 141
1954	2112	9	+ 83	2204	1995	+ 209	+ 35	+ 174
1955	2354	10	− 69	2295	2124	+ 171	+ 230	− 59
1956	2627	10	− 68	2569	2234	+ 335	+ 165	+ 170
1957 (estimated)	2780	10	(− 60)	2730	2300	+ 430	+ 260	+ 170

would be devoted to co-operative measures for the re-expansion of international trade.

A third possibility, more likely than the second of these and perhaps than the first, is that the check to British home demand will coincide with a small and temporary decline in business activity in the rest of the world. This would make it more difficult to transfer resources from production for domestic use to production for export without a considerable rise in unemployment. It would, however, probably be more in the long-run interests of the country to facilitate the transfer of resources to export production by more liberal foreign credits and other measures to maintain the level of export demand than to re-expand home demand and allow exports to fall to a level below that which will be needed again after the temporary recession.

NOTE ON THE CONSTRUCTION OF THE TABLES [1]

TABLE I.—Production, 1946 to 1956: N.I. and E., 1957 Table 11.   1938: Author's estimate.
    Real National Income: See Table II.
TABLE II.—Consumer's Expenditure: N.I. and E., 1957, Table 20.
    Public Authorities' Expenditure on Goods and Services: 1946 to 1956: N.I. and E., 1957, Table 11.   1938: Author's estimate.
    Savings and Depreciation: See Table VI.
    Real National Income: Total of above.   It thus consists of the aggregate of all expenditures at 1948 market prices including expenditures on fixed capital formation, increased stocks, and foreign investment deflated at price indexes appropriate to each type of expenditure.
TABLE III.—Savings and Depreciation: See Table VI. Distribution between sources is in same proportions as distribution of gross saving at current prices as shown in N.I. and E., Table 6.
    Fixed Capital Consumption: N.I. and E., 1957, Table 56.
TABLE IV.—Gross Fixed Capital Formation: Totals by type of asset at 1948 prices for 1938 and 1948 to 1956, N.I. and E., 1957, Table 49; Distribution between sectors in same proportions as at current prices in Table 53.   Totals for 1946 and 1947, Table 11.
TABLE V.—Net Fixed Capital Formation: N.I. and E., 1957, Tables 54 and 56.
TABLE VI.—Gross Domestic Capital Formation: As in Table IV.
    Physical Increase in Stocks: N.I. and E., Tables 6 and 11.
    Net Foreign Investment: Balances of Payments surpluses at market prices (N.I. and E., 1957, Table 6) converted to 1948 prices at average of the Board of Trade's import and export price indexes. (The justification for the use of this index is that a balance-of-payments surplus may involve forgoing either imports or resources used for exports.   It is assumed here that it involves half of each.)
    Total Investible Funds: Total of above.
    Gross Saving, Capital Grants, and Transfers and Errors and Omissions: form same proportions of total investible funds at 1948 prices as they do at current prices in N.I. and E., 1957, Table 6.

[1] Statistical tables constructed on the same principles but revised to 1961 appear in Chapter 8.

CHAPTER 6

PROGRESS, PRICES, AND THE POUND[1]

EVER since the war, discussion of British economic policies
has been confused by the fact that governments have pursued
a number of different objectives, sometimes consistent, often
conflicting, sometimes at different periods, often simultaneously. Some of these, such as a progressive increase in the
equality of incomes, are for the moment in abeyance; but
there remain at least five which are in vogue to-day. These
include 'full employment' in one or more of the possible
meanings of the phrase; a maximum rate of current output;
a maximum rate of increase in output; the ending of inflation;
and the stability of sterling in terms of foreign currencies and
particularly in terms of the United States dollar. It is the
purpose of this article to examine how far and in what circumstances these objectives are likely to be consistent with each
other and, where they are inconsistent, which should be given
priority.

Let us begin by looking at the first three, which are sometimes assumed to be identical. 'Full employment' is rarely,
if ever, used to mean the employment of every individual
registered as available for work; 100 per cent employment is
probably unobtainable except by compulsion, and even then
would contain some concealed unemployment. Even at the
height of the war, with labour desperately scarce and in the
presence of a considerable element of compulsion, the proportion of the civilian labour force actually employed never exceeded 99½ per cent. We therefore need some other criterion
of an optimum level of employment. Two possible ones suggest themselves: one is the level of employment which is
consistent with the maximum amount of production in the
current year; the other is the level of employment which is
consistent with the maximum long-run rate of growth of output.
If demand for goods and services, and thereby the demand

---

[1] Published in the *District Bank Review*, March 1958.

for labour, is such as to force employment above a certain (in this country, very high) level, there is a danger that more projects will be started than there exist resources to complete, and that, as the result of so-called 'bottle-necks', some of the resources used will either be wasted altogether or will be locked up for long periods in uncompleted and useless forms. Grossly excessive demand may also lead to losses of care and efficiency in carrying out work, increased absenteeism, a high rate of economically purposeless labour turnover and other difficulties. In such conditions, a reduction in the pressure of excess demand, while probably causing some slight increase in transitional unemployment, will also bring such an increase in efficiency in the use of resources that total production rises. It is doubtful whether even the most enthusiastic advocate of full employment would wish to push it to beyond the point of maximum current output.

The alternative definition, for which the case is at least equally strong, is the level of employment which is consistent with securing, not the maximum rate of current output, but the maximum long-run rate of growth of output. This level is, for a number of possible reasons, likely to be below that at which current output is at its maximum. One possible cause for divergence is a development such as occurred in 1952, when a sharp and unexpected rise in personal saving brought a check to demand for some types of durable consumption goods, especially textiles, a fall in current output of manufactures, and an appreciable rise in unemployment. The rise in saving, however, permitted in course of time a considerable rise in fixed investment, first in house-building and later in industry and commerce. Since the rate of growth of output depends, among other things, on the volume of new investment, it can be hoped that in such circumstances the drop in current output will be followed in due course by a rise in the rate of growth of output.

Another and perhaps even more fundamental reason why a reduction in excess demand, leading to a reduction in current output, may be followed by an increase in the rate of growth of output is its effect on the average level of business efficiency. Under conditions of excess demand it is relatively easy for firms to stay in existence even if their costs of production are above the average, so that there may be a wide margin between the most and the least efficient. As excess demand is reduced, high-cost firms have either to increase their efficiency or go out of business, the margin between the most and the least efficient narrows and average efficiency rises. For a time, while the process of adjustment is going on, current production may well be reduced; but as it proceeds and resources come increasingly into the hands of the most efficient concerns, the way becomes open for an accelerated rate of increase. It remains true, however, that if this accelerated rate of long-term growth is to be maintained, production and employment must always be kept below the level which could be secured in the current year by the creation of additional demand. If conditions of excessive demand are permitted to reappear, a year or two of exceptionally large increases in output will be paid for by a subsequently lower rate of growth, as the effects of decreased competition begin to make themselves felt.

Both the temporary check to production caused by the removal of excess demand and the temporary increase caused by its reappearance are likely to be exaggerated in the published statistics, since these inevitably fail to make adequate allowance for changes in quality. In any case, the statistics tend to underestimate the effects of improvements in the design and performance of manufactured goods, so that, in the long run, the rise in production is probably greater than is shown. This tendency to underestimate may, however, be more than offset in periods of increasingly excessive demand, because the rise in prices may take place partly in the form of reductions in quality, and especially in durability and reliability. It is probable, however, that more important than the fall in the quality of the goods is the fall in the quality of the services which accompany them. Long and unkept delivery dates, inadequate information, dilatory correspondence, difficulties about spares and repairs, and even economies in politeness, are only some of the many forms which reductions in quality of service may take during periods of excess demand, but which do not offset in the official estimates the rise in the number of physical units produced. Similarly, when excess demand is reduced, the statistics reflect inadequately, or not at all, the improvements in the quality of goods, and still more

D2

of services, which accompany the check to the volume of production.

GROWTH OF OUTPUT AND STABILITY OF PRICES

If we are prepared to accept as an optimum the level of employment which is consistent with a maximum rate of growth of output, we are able to reduce the number of our possible objectives from five to three : the maximum rate of growth of output, the ending of inflation, and equilibrium in the supply and demand for foreign currencies. Let us first consider how far the first two are compatible in a closed economy, without foreign trade, where changes in production are identical with changes in real national income, and no balance-of-payments problems can arise.

There are two possible definitions of a situation which is neither inflationary nor deflationary. One is stability of the general level of prices and the other stability of average money incomes. With rising output, stability of incomes implies a gradual fall in the prices of final products, while stability of prices implies a gradual rise in money incomes. In defining stability of prices we should exclude the effects of indirect taxes or subsidies, which are irrelevant for the present purpose, and the best definition seems to be that price stability is a condition in which the national money income at factor cost is rising at the same rate as the national real income — which, in a closed system, is the same thing as saying that money income is rising at the same rate as output.

As objectives there is something to be said both for stable incomes and for stable prices. On grounds of equity there is much to be said for the first, which would spread the benefits of increasing productivity over the whole community in the form of lower prices. There is little substance in the contention that the whole benefit should go to those actually employed, for the long-term rise in output is in the main due to the skill, energy, saving, and risk-bearing of a relatively small number of scientists, business executives, and investors : and in so far as it is due to the savings or enterprise of the Government, all citizens should share in the benefits. On the other hand, stability of average incomes implies that, to attract labour from less to more needed uses, earnings would have to fall in some occupations if they were to rise in others. This would not necessarily involve corresponding rises and falls in wage rates, for changes in the relative opportunities for over-time earnings might conceivably supply the necessary incentives. Nevertheless, it would probably be a good deal easier in practice to obtain an appropriate distribution of labour if the incentives could be applied in the form of rises in wages in some sectors coupled with stability, or smaller rises, in others. The differential rises in wage rates would, of course, have no necessary relationship to the increases in output per head in particular occupations. In general, one would expect that earnings in industries, probably mainly manufacturing, with the highest increases in output per head would rise less than output, while those in industries in which the increase in output was low, probably service industries, would rise more than output. Thus stability in prices of ultimate products would involve progressive falls in some prices, probably mainly of manufactures, and progressive rises in others, probably mainly services.

If, on balance, we decide to choose, as the second objective, stability of average prices rather than stability of average incomes, how far is this choice likely to be consistent with the first objective, a long-run maximum rate of increase in output ? The answer seems to depend on the answer to two other questions, one about the effects on business enterprise of a reduction in excess demand sufficient to secure stability of average prices, and the other about the attitude of trade unions to the prospect of annual increases in average wages no greater than in proportion to the rise in aggregate output per person employed. To enable us to examine these questions separately, let us first assume a society where neither trade unions nor employers have monopoly powers, so that wages are determined by the supply and demand for labour in a freely competitive market. In these circumstances, for wages to rise proportionately with output per head would imply a permanent slight excess demand for labour at existing wage rates, the amount of the excess depending on the average time-lag between the achievement by employers of the economies of more efficient production and the time when they were obliged by competition

to pass a large part of these on to labour in higher wages. The
longer the time-lag, the greater would be the excess demand
for labour and the lower the level of unemployment. For
this excess demand for labour to exist, there would also have
to be a slight potential excess of demand for ultimate goods
and services, which could be satisfied only because of the rise
in output. It seems likely that this level of demand would
provide an adequate incentive to efficient producers to expand
output to meet it. Indeed, it is possible that it would be
slightly too high to provide the conditions for the maximum
increase in efficiency, so that the long-run increase in output
might be slightly lower than it would have been in conditions of stable incomes, falling prices, and slightly higher
unemployment.

The level of unemployment which is in practice consistent
with stability of prices will vary greatly according to circumstances. A small amount of transitional unemployment, widely
spread throughout all districts and industries, is much more
likely to prevent excess demand for labour from forcing up
wages faster than aggregate output than a larger amount of
structural unemployment, concentrated in a few districts or
industries. It is because unemployment in the United Kingdom
is much more evenly distributed now than a year ago that the
marked reduction in excess demand has brought with it only a
very small increase in total unemployment. In this country,
with its short distances and relative lack of concentration of
industry, it can be hoped that structural unemployment can be
kept small and that the minimum level of total unemployment
consistent with stability of prices may not be more than about
2 per cent or not far above the present level. In other countries,
however, where distances are greater or industry more concentrated, the minimum level may be a good deal higher than
this.

THE EFFECTS OF COLLECTIVE BARGAINING

Let us now remove the assumption of a free and competitive
market for labour and recognise that in fact, in this country,
wage rates are largely fixed by a process of collective bargaining
between large trade unions on the one side and large employers
or employers' organisations on the other. Strictly speaking,

the result of bargaining between two opposed monopolies is unpredictable; it depends partly on the relative strengths of the two sides and partly on what each side expects the other to do. One thing, however, can be said with some confidence, and that is that a system of collective bargaining, as it exists in this country, imposes a long delay between the presentation of a claim and the final determination of the result. Thus, in conditions of excess demand for labour, the existence of collective bargaining is likely to add to the delay before the excess demand at existing wage rates is reflected in a rise in wage rates. Thus rises in wage rates tend to lag further behind rises in productivity or prices, actual wage rates are further below their equilibrium levels, and unemployment is lower.

There is a school of thought which holds that the effect of collective bargaining in delaying rises in wage rates is more than offset by the effects of the monopoly power of the trade unions in forcing up wage rates faster than they would have risen on a free market; and that it has been these monopoly-enforced rises in wage rates which have provided the initial impetus for the rises in prices and costs which have occurred during the past few years. Two difficulties in accepting this interpretation of events may be mentioned here. If the general level of wage rates had been forced up by trade union pressure, it is difficult to see why actual weekly earnings, which are largely within the control of employers, should have risen faster than wage rates; whereas if they have been forced up by the competition of employers for scarce labour this development is quite intelligible. Secondly, it is difficult to see why, if the resumption of the rise in prices in 1954 was due to trade union pressure for higher wages, it was accompanied by a proportionately larger rise in the trading profits of companies than in wage payments. This evidence, again, fits the interpretation that wage rates rose as the result of the increased demand for labour, which in turn was the result of increased demand for ultimate products and of higher profits.

The belief that it is the monopoly power of the trade unions which provides the initial impetus towards inflation leads naturally to the conclusion that, if they could be persuaded not to use their powers in this way, the tendency towards inflation could be checked. It is true, of course, that

if not only wage rates but actual wage payments could some-
how be prevented from rising faster than average output, the
demand for labour could be kept permanently in excess of
supply, and unemployment permanently below the equilibrium
level, without rises in prices; though such a policy would, of
course, involve difficult problems of labour rationing, and
would be unlikely to promote the maximum rate of growth
of output. It is, however, unnecessary to examine in detail
the effects of such a policy, since it would not be enforcible
for long, at least in a democracy. In conditions of excess
demand, mere restraint on the part of trade union leaders
would not be nearly enough.

Even if they were able to prevent agreed wage rates from
rising faster than output, the competition between employers
for workers would cause them to try to attract them by offering
additional amenities, guaranteed overtime or actual wage payments above the standard level. It is for this reason that,
during the period of wage restraint, while wage rates rose by
only 24 per cent between 1946 and 1951, weekly earnings rose
by 43 per cent and national money income by 44 per cent.
After wage restraint was largely abandoned, from 1951 to 1956,
wage rates rose by 36 per cent or half as much again; but
during the same period earnings rose by only 44 per cent, or
hardly more than in the previous quinquennium, while the
rise in national money income, at 43 per cent, actually showed
a decrease. In addition, the attempt to maintain a policy of
wage restraint for long periods in the presence of excess demand
leads to a growing breach between the trade union leaders and
their members, with growing unofficial strikes and the formation of breakaway unions. To make a policy of wage control
effective would almost certainly require legal action, enforced
by severe penalties for infringement both upon employers and
employed; and even then it is doubtful if collusive evasion
could be prevented without methods of enforcement which
would not be tolerated in this country.

While, however, it is not believed that the excessive demands
of trade unions are responsible for inflation in the past, an
immense responsibility rests on trade union leaders now that
excess demand has been largely eliminated. The elimination of
most of the excess demand both for final goods and services

and for labour means that in future employers will be able to raise average wages only in proportion to the rise in total output. If average wage rates are forced up faster than this, it will be at the cost of increased unemployment. If only some trade unions have great monopoly power and are prepared to use it ruthlessly, they may be able to obtain exceptional rises in the real incomes of their members, but only at the cost of a worsening of the position of other wage-earners, either in the form of lower wages or, more probably, of increased unemployment. If all trade unions have great monopoly power, they may be able to improve the position of those of their members who remain employed, but only at the cost of a rise in unemployment.

Whether the trade unions really have the monopoly power to act in this way is by no means certain ; but even if they have, there is reason to hope that trade union leaders will prove to be no less responsible and far-sighted than they have been in the recent past, and that it will prove possible to keep the rise in average wage rates down to a level which would not be inconsistent either with stable prices or the maintenance of a high level of employment. Between last June, by when the 1957 round of wage claims had been settled, and last December, the general index of weekly wage rates rose by just over 1 per cent. If by next June the index has risen by not more than an additional 2 per cent, making a total of 3 per cent over the whole twelve months, it will be possible to say with some confidence that, in spite of the existence of trade unions, price stability in this country is not inconsistent with either a high level of employment or a high rate of growth of output.

PRICE STABILITY AND THE BALANCE OF PAYMENTS

There still remains our final question, whether price stability and a high rate of growth, even if mutually compatible in a closed system, are also consistent with equilibrium between the supply of and demand for foreign currencies in a country situated as is the United Kingdom to-day. To begin with, the introduction of foreign trade complicates the internal picture by making changes in real and money national incomes depend, not only on internal production, but also on changes in the prices of imports and exports, as well as, usually to a smaller extent, on changes in net investment income from abroad. If the terms of trade improve (that is to say, if a given quantity of exports will pay for more imports), real national income is increased and money incomes can rise more than in proportion to production without causing a rise in prices. The anti-inflationary effects of an improvement in the terms of trade are greatest if it takes the form of a fall in import prices, for this increases real income without also increasing money incomes; while a rise in export prices increases real and money incomes together. Similarly, a worsening of the terms of trade cancels out part of the benefit of the rise in production, and increases the inflationary effect of a given rise in money incomes. The effect of worsening terms of trade is most inflationary if import prices rise, for this reduces real incomes without reducing money incomes, while if export prices fall both are reduced. A simultaneous rise in import and export prices is certainly inflationary, for money incomes are increased without any corresponding rise in real incomes.

How large can be the effect of changes in the terms of trade may be seen from the recent experience of the United Kingdom. Between 1951 and 1956 the gross real domestic product is estimated to have risen by about 14 per cent, or slightly less than between 1946 and 1951. As the result, however, of changes in external factors, mainly the terms of trade, real national income rose by nearly 18 per cent between 1951 and 1956, as against only 11 per cent between 1946 and 1951. It would therefore have been possible to allow wages and other incomes to increase by more than half as much again in 1951–56 as in 1946–51 without causing inflation. Thus, in deciding how large a rise in money incomes is consistent with stability of prices, the Government must take account, not only of the increase in production, but also of the external changes which affect the real national income.

If a country, which is attempting to prevent either a rise or a fall in its internal price level, is faced with either a persistent rise or a persistent fall in prices in the rest of the world, it may be forced to choose between maintaining a stable price level and stable exchange rates. If, when prices are rising abroad, it attempts to prevent internal prices from rising by restricting money incomes, it is likely to find itself developing an un-necessarily large favourable balance of payments; and though for a time it may be able to offset this tendency by removing restrictions on imports or reducing tariffs, it is likely sooner or later to be forced to choose between sharing in the world inflation and raising the exchange value of its currency. Similarly, if prices in the rest of the world are falling, the attempt to maintain internal prices and incomes will rapidly lead to a large adverse balance of payments, which can be prevented only temporarily, if at all, by increased tariffs and import restrictions; and sooner or later the choice will have to be made between a fall in the internal price level and de-valuation. So long as the rate of fall in prices does not exceed the rate of rise in the real national income per head, so that average money incomes do not decline, a falling price level may not involve too much difficulty. But if, to secure a fall in prices greater than this, wages and other money incomes have to be substantially reduced, many governments would prefer devaluation. There can therefore be no guarantee that stable exchange rates are consistent with a maximum rate of growth and stable prices.

To say, however, that stable exchange rates might, in certain circumstances, be inconsistent with maximum growth and stability of prices does not mean that they will in fact prove to be so. Nor does the possibility that fluctuating exchange rates might, in certain circumstances, permit the maintenance of growth and price stability mean they can always be relied upon to do so. A major world depression would certainly mean heavy losses of output and a large rise in unemployment among those now engaged in producing for export. The rise in unemployment might well be larger than the rise in 1929–32, partly because the numbers employed on exports are now much larger and partly because a larger pro-portion of exports now consists of goods for which the demand would fall particularly heavily in a major depression. Even if all considerations of exchange stability were abandoned and every effort made to expand internal demand, there would certainly be a long time-lag before the resources released from exports could be reabsorbed. Indeed, the quickest way of checking the rise in unemployment would probably be to try to re-expand export demand by liberal foreign loans and credits. For devaluation to be an effective remedy, we must postulate, not a sudden fall in world demand, but merely a slow downward drift of prices.

Whether, in fact, world prices can, in the long run, be expected to decline, to remain stable, or to rise further must be a matter of opinion. On the whole, with the knowledge and powers that governments now command, prolonged falls in price levels seem less likely than before the war, and it seems more probable that they will remain stable or even tend to rise, though probably a good deal more slowly than in recent years. In view of the fact that, to meet its obligations and ensure the stability of sterling, the United Kingdom will need to maintain an average favourable balance of payments on income account of something like £400 millions a year, restriction of internal demand may have to be somewhat stricter than in some other countries. Nevertheless, provided home demand is kept at a level which enables and obliges producers to seek out export markets with efficiency and enthusiasm, there seems to be a very good chance that policies sufficient to maintain stability of prices at home will also be sufficient to ensure an adequate balance-of-payments surplus. We should not assume the contrary at least until the experiment has been tried.

CHAPTER 7

INFLATION IN THE UNITED KINDGOM
1948-57 [1]

PRODUCTION, REAL INCOME, AND MONEY INCOME,

INFLATION may be defined as a condition in which the national money income is rising faster than the national real income. The most general cause of a rise in national real income is an increase in the output of goods and services; but over limited periods the national real income may also be considerably affected by changes in the investment income received from (or paid to) overseas countries and by changes in the terms of trade. During the years 1950 and 1951 the greater part of the rise in production was offset by a worsening of the terms of trade, so that real national income rose little, while since 1951 the recovery in the terms of trade has substantially augmented the effect on real income of rising production. Thus while production rose by an average of about $3\frac{1}{2}$ per cent a year between 1948 and 1951, real national income rose by only about 2 per cent a year, while from 1951 to 1956,

TABLE I

PRODUCTION, REAL INCOME, MONEY INCOME, AND PRICES
(1948 = 100)

Year	Production	Gross National Income		Ratio of Money Income to Real Income	Consumption Price Index
		Real	Money		
1951	110·5	106·5	123·1	115·8	115
1955	124·0	122·4	162·5	132·6	130
1956	125·7	125·4	175·0	139·2	136
1957 (est.)	128	128·5	182	143	140

[1] *Memorandum presented to the Council on Prices, Productivity, and Incomes*, November 1957. Published in *Economica*, May 1958.

while production rose by about 3 per cent a year, real national income rose by an average of about $3\frac{1}{2}$ per cent.[1]

Meanwhile, money national income rose by an average of rather over 7 per cent a year from 1948 to 1951 and by $7\frac{1}{2}$ per cent a year from 1951 to 1956; but since real income rose by $3\frac{1}{2}$ per cent a year in the later period and only 2 per cent in the first, the rise in the ratio of money income to real income (which is a general price index for the total of goods and services produced in the economy) fell from 5 per cent a year in the period 1948–51 to under 4 per cent a year in 1951–56. In 1956–57 production has probably risen by about 2 per cent, real national income by about $2\frac{1}{2}$ per cent (thanks to the further improvement in the terms of trade), national money income by about $5\frac{1}{2}$ per cent, and the ratio of money income to real income by about 3 per cent. The rise in the ratio of money to real income is slightly larger than the rise in the price index for consumers' expenditure, mainly because prices of goods and services bought by public authorities have risen rather more steeply than other prices.

COST AND DEMAND THEORIES OF INFLATION

Two theories are current to account for the recent excessive rise of money incomes. One is that it is primarily due to the success of the trade unions in forcing up wages, and the other that it is due to a general excess of demand, which pulls up the price paid for labour in the same way that it pulls up other prices. My own view is that it is difficult to sustain the first theory in any circumstances without making assumptions which in effect amount to the existence of a demand inflation; but whether or no a cost inflation can exist in any conditions, it is even more difficult to advance it as the reason for the renewed rise in prices which has developed in this country since the temporary check in 1953.

If the original reason for the recent rise in prices had been the forcing up of wages by the trade unions against the opposition of the employers, one would have expected that in the

---

[1] 1961 estimates put the average annual increase in output between 1948 and 1951 at $3\frac{1}{4}$ per cent and in real national income at $2\frac{1}{4}$ per cent; while between 1951 and 1956 the average annual increase in output becomes $2\frac{1}{2}$ per cent and in real national income $3\frac{1}{4}$ per cent.

initial stages of the renewed inflation the wage rises would
have been, to some extent at least, at the expense of profits.
In fact we find that, between 1953 and 1955, income from
wages rose by 17 per cent and gross trading profits of companies by over 24 per cent. There is no evidence here that
wage increases were at the expense of profits. It is rather that
business was so profitable that it was able to pay the increased
wages and salaries while at the same time substantially increasing its profit margin. This would seem to support the view
that wages went up, not so much because trade unions asked
for higher wages as because employers could afford to pay
them.

A second reason for doubting whether the actions of the
trade unions in pressing for higher wages provide an adequate
explanation of the rise in national money income is that wage
rates, which are fixed by collective bargaining between employers' organisations and trade unions, have in most years
risen considerably less than have the actual earnings of wage-
earners. Part of the difference can be accounted for by piece-
rate earnings and part by more overtime ; [1] but a large, perhaps
the greater part, can be accounted for only on the assumption
that many employers were in fact paying wages at rates increasingly above the trade union scale. This is again much more
in conformity with a picture of wages pulled up by competition
between employers for scarce labour than of wages pushed up
by trade union pressure against the opposition of reluctant
employers.

Only in three years since 1948 have earnings failed to rise
more than wage rates : in 1952, in 1956, and probably in
1957. In 1952 and 1956 the percentage rise in earnings was
almost the same as in wage rates, while in 1957 it was probably
appreciably less. In all three years the Government, largely
by the use of monetary policy, was trying to check the growth
of demand, in all three there seems to have been a fall in
profit margins, and in all three the average ratio of unemployment to vacancies was significantly higher than in years when

[1] The average length of the working week as fixed by wage agreements
fell by 0·2 per cent between 1948 and 1951 and a further 0·2 per cent between
1951 and 1956, while the average number of hours worked by all classes of
wage-earners rose by 2·2 per cent between 1948 and 1951, and by a further
0·6 per cent between 1951 and 1956.

earnings were rising faster than wage rates. While rises in the average level of wage rates remained large in the actual years 1952 and 1956, both were followed by years of much smaller wage increases. A rise of 8½ per cent from 1951 to 1952 was followed by a rise of only 4½ per cent from 1952 to 1953, while a rise of 8 per cent from 1955 to 1956 has been followed by a rise of (probably) 5½ per cent from 1956 to 1957. If these precedents are any guide, the rise from 1957 to 1958 should be appreciably less than 5½ per cent. The delay of a year before the effects of reduced demand are seen in a check to the rise in the yearly average of wage rates is explicable by the fact that most wage increases usually take place in the first quarter of the year. The greater rise in earnings than in wage rates in all years except those in which demand is to some degree checked, seems to indicate that excess demand is at least a very important cause of the over-rapid rise of money incomes.

TABLE II

WAGE RATES AND EARNINGS

(1948 = 100)

	Average Index of Trade Union Wage Rates	Average Index of Earnings (men)	Earnings as a Percentage of Wage Rates
1951	113	119	105
1952	123	129	105
1953	129	138	107
1954	134	147	110
1955	144	160	111
1956	155	172	111
1957 (est.)	163	177	109

There is, of course, a sense in which it can be said that trade unions, by demanding higher wage rates, could generate the additional demand which would enable employers to pay them and at the same time maintain or increase their profit margins. Even though the Government, by limiting demand, could force employers either to refuse demands for wage increases or to cut down the number of their employees as the result of granting them, it might nevertheless regard the resulting strikes or temporary loss of output as politically unacceptable. The trade unions would then be in a position to oblige the Government to maintain conditions of excess demand in order to avoid strikes and maintain full employment. Strictly speaking, a politically secure government can always take steps to remove excess demand and check an inflation, but it is conceivable that trade unions could make the process so expensive in terms of strikes, unemployment, and loss of output that all but the most courageous of governments might shrink from the attempt. In fact, however, it seems unlikely that the unions will press their demands for higher wages to the point either of prolonged strikes or of serious unemployment. History seems to indicate that the great majority of long and bitter strikes have occurred when the unions are defending either their real or money wages, or their own negotiating rights ; and there is no reason now why money wages should fall or why wage-earners should not receive their full share of the rise in real national income. If wage rates ceased to rise altogether, this rise in real income would appear in the form of a fall in the average level of prices, probably in the form of an appreciable fall in the prices of manufactured goods combined with stability in the price of services. Alternatively, average wages could rise proportionately with the national real income without bringing a rise in average prices. In this case a (smaller) fall in prices of manufactured goods would just offset a rise in prices of services. There is a good deal to be said for the second course, in the interests both of industrial peace and of the mobility of labour : it is easier to raise wages in one sector while keeping them stable in another than to raise them in one and lower them in another. In neither case should the rise in real wages be appreciably smaller than under a system of creeping inflation, where most of each rise in money wages is absorbed by the rise in prices.

CAUSES OF EXCESS DEMAND

Strictly speaking, the question of what causes an excess demand has no meaning ; excess demand is produced by the demand for all uses jointly, and it is open to anyone to hold the view that, in some absolute sense, any particular use is too large. Nevertheless, if we find that some particular use of resources has shown a marked increase proportionately to others during a period when excess demand has developed or been intensified, it does not seem wholly unreasonable to attribute the rise in excess demand to the increase in that particular use of resources. If this is so, it would seem that we can attribute the excess demand which has developed since 1953 to the rapid rise in investment, and especially in fixed investment, which has occurred since that year. We can distinguish five main uses of the national real income: (1) personal consumption; (2) public authorities' expenditure on goods and services; (3) fixed investment; (4) investment in increasing the volume of stocks; and (5) foreign investment, which, if we regard increases in the gold reserve as foreign investment, is identical with the favourable balance of payments on current account. Since 1953 these various uses of the national income are estimated to have been as follows:

TABLE III

USES OF GROSS REAL NATIONAL INCOME

(at 1948 prices)

	Personal Consumption		Public Authorities' Expenditure on Goods and Services		Gross Fixed Investment		Stocks		Balance of Payments		Errors and Omissions	To
1953	9099	68·1	2306	17·3	1849	13·8	95	0·7	141	1·1	−133	13,:
1954	9503	68·4	2287	16·4	1995	14·3	35	0·3	175	1·2	−92	13,9
1955	9796	67·9	2255	15·6	2124	14·7	230	1·6	−59	−0·4	59	14,4
1956	9847	66·7	2285	15·5	2234	15·1	165	1·1	170	1·1	58	14,7
1957 (est.)	10,100	66·7	2250	14·9	2300	15·2	260	1·7	170	1·1	50	15,:

If these figures can be regarded as giving even an approximate indication of the real position, it would seem that the use of resources on income account both by persons and by public authorities has absorbed a substantially declining share of real national income. The decline in the proportion absorbed by personal consumption is due to the very remarkable rise which has taken place in personal saving, while the fall in the share taken by public authorities is due to the success of the Government in stabilising its expenditure, in real terms, at the level reached in 1952. On the other hand, investment, both in fixed assets and in stocks, has absorbed a considerably larger share. Gross fixed investment, at 1948 prices, rose by over 20 per cent between 1953 and 1956, while net investment, after deducting the amount estimated to be needed to make good wear and obsolescence, rose by nearly 40 per cent. Of the rise in gross investment, nearly 90 per cent was in private industrial and commercial investment. It is this rise, superimposed on the earlier rise in (mainly private) house-building, which seems to have over-strained the resources of the economy and led to the development of excess demand. The causes of the uprush by nearly 50 per cent in gross private industrial and commercial investment are no doubt complex. They probably include the introduction of the investment allowance, the effects of official urging, and perhaps a change in business sentiment following the earlier change of government; but almost certainly the lifting of restrictions on commercial building played a part, as the lifting of restrictions on private house-building had done earlier in stimulating the rise in the number of new houses built. It is one of the great disadvantages of physical controls that the amount of frustrated demand concealed behind them cannot be estimated, and that their removal may release a flood of demand which is unusually insensitive to other types of control.

In view of the heavy additional demand for resources occasioned by the great rise in investment, action designed to slow down this rise is not unreasonable; though it is, of course, open to anyone to maintain that the level of investment is still too low and that steps should have been taken to restrict consumption and promote still more saving rather than to control the rise in investment.

FISCAL AND MONETARY POLICIES

The distinction often made between fiscal and monetary policies for checking an excessive rise in money incomes is not a clear one; for fiscal measures may well have an effect on the quantity of money, as when an increased budget surplus is used to repay Government debts to the banks. A more convenient comparison is between those measures which check the rise in incomes directly by withdrawing money from, or

reducing its flow into, the income circulation, and those
which seek to check it indirectly by withdrawing money from,
or checking its flow into, the capital circulation, thus raising
interest rates and discouraging investment. The most usual
form which fiscal policy takes is to raise taxation without a corresponding rise in Government expenditure, thus withdrawing
money directly from the income circulation and either cancelling it by paying off Government debt to the banks or transferring it to the capital circulation by paying off Government
debt to the banks' customers. The effect of this policy is to
increase aggregate saving, reduce interest rates, and stimulate
investment. The return of the money to the income circulation, via increased investment, is, however, never complete,
for the lower interest rates also reduce the (opportunity) cost
of holding money idle and so increase the volume of idle
money; further, what does return via increased investment
returns to the income circulation only after a time-lag, the
length of which depends largely on business expectations.
Thus a continuing policy of using an increased budget surplus
to pay off Government debt will tend to bring a continuing
check to the rise in the income circulation and in money incomes. Similar results are obtained by reducing Government
expenditure without a corresponding reduction in taxation,
and by preventing money from being created, or transferred
from the capital circulation, for the purpose of financing increased consumption (as, for instance, by restrictions on hire-
purchase finance).

The alternative policy of withdrawing money from the
capital circulation, as, for instance, by paying off Government
debt to the banks with money borrowed from the banks'
customers, reduces the supply of loanable funds in the market
and causes interest rates to rise. A similar result follows from
preventing new money from being created to replace the
money withdrawn from the capital circulation to the income
circulation to finance a rise in income. (This might roughly
correspond to a fall in bank deposits, the money in which
practically all capital transactions are carried out, equal to the
rise in the issue of notes, the money used almost entirely in
the income circulation.) The rise in interest rates has two
effects: on the one hand it discourages investment, and so

slows down the flow of money from the capital to the income circulation, and on the other it raises the opportunity cost of holding idle balances and so stimulates an increase in the velocity of circulation. The fall in the quantity of money in the capital circulation can, however, never be more than partially made good by releases from idle balances, since these releases take place only as the result of a rise in interest rates and are reversed if interest rates fall again.

If the rise in money incomes continues while the total quantity of money remains stable, more and more money will be withdrawn from the capital circulation, and since this loss can be offset only partly by the release of idle balances, rates of interest will continue to rise until the rise in aggregate money incomes is brought to an end. How long this will take, and how high interest rates will have to rise, depend largely on the expectations, in the early stages of inflation, of business men, but in the later stages also among consumers. If consumers are expecting prices to double each week, it may take a rate of interest of 100 per cent a week to prevent them anticipating their next week's purchases ; though even in this extremity the knowledge that the Government was taking drastic action to stop the inflation might so affect expectations that a much lower rate of interest might be sufficient. In the early stages of an inflation, however, it is the expected profitability of investments rather than the expected rise in the price of consumption goods which is the incentive for the transfer of money into the income account ; and at this stage a comparatively moderate rise in interest rates may be enough to reduce the profitability of investment sufficiently to end the net transfer of money to the income circulation. Generally speaking, it is the construction of the most durable assets which will be rendered relatively least attractive by the rise in interest rates, for the more durable the asset the higher is the proportion of interest cost and the lower the proportion of depreciation allowance in the total annual cost of ownership. High interest rates are therefore more likely to discourage the creation of long-lived, safe assets, such as houses and commercial buildings, where the rate of depreciation is very low, than that of machinery or vehicles, where it is relatively high. If, however, the rise in interest rates is expected to be temporary, investment even in durable assets will not be much discouraged if it can be financed temporarily on short term at rates not far above the long-term rate; for borrowers will hope to be able to obtain long-term re-finance at lower rates in the fairly near future. For high long-term rates to be effective they must be accompanied either by very much higher short-term rates or by quantitative restriction of short-term loans.

Both fiscal and non-fiscal methods of checking a rise in incomes face considerable difficulties. To be effective, increased taxes must be imposed on those who cannot maintain their expenditure on consumption either by reducing their saving or by spending capital: that is to say, on the general mass of taxpayers. And to increase taxation of this sort beyond a certain point may be both politically difficult and likely to have undesirable effects on the incentive to work. It was presumably considerations of this sort which prevented the then Government from increasing taxes in 1950–51 to keep pace with the rise in defence expenditure, and so preventing a sharp fall in the budget surplus, the rise in which had played so important a part in slowing down the rise in incomes in 1948–49.

The great difficulty in carrying out the alternative policy, of making money scarce in the capital circulation, is that the Government itself is now by far the greatest short-term debtor in the country, with not only some £3000 millions of Treasury bills in non-official hands but also many hundreds of millions of short-term bonds maturing every year. Any holder of these whom Government policy makes short of money has only to decline to renew them on maturity to be sure of having his shortage relieved; and the only way in which the Government can meet these maturing obligations without creating new money is to borrow sufficient from the public (the banks' customers, not the banks) at whatever rate it is necessary to offer. Further, any other holder of maturing Government short-term obligations, even if he does not need money himself, will refuse to subscribe to new short-term securities in their place unless he is offered as high a short-term rate as he can get elsewhere — and that, when the shortage of money is severe and long-term rates are higher than they are expected to be in the future, may be very high indeed. Thus the

Government has to choose between paying high rates for long periods, by issuing long-term securities at high rates, offering extremely high rates for short periods, and attempting, by means of quantitative restrictions, to prevent borrowers from competing with the Government for the scarce funds. Until recently the Government was relying mainly on the first and third of these methods ; since September it has been obliged to have recourse to the second as well.

The two methods, of reducing the supply of money to the income circulation directly through budgetary policy and limiting it indirectly through restricting the supply of money to the capital circulation, are complementary rather than competitive. Budgetary policy has a considerable effect on the aggregate level of national saving ; monetary policy seeks to keep investment within the quantity of saving so determined. The need for monetary policy is always present, but the higher the level of saving in relation to the demand for investment the less drastic its enforcement needs to be. Thus the bigger the budget surplus the less drastic will be the monetary policy needed to prevent inflation and (in the absence of a spontaneous increase in the expected profitability of investment) the lower the rate of interest consistent with the absence of inflation. The decision about the size of the budget surplus and the level of interest rates depends partly on considerations about what is technically or politically possible and partly on expectations about the effect of different measures on the incentive to work, but very largely on opinions about how much the standard of living of the present generation should be sacrificed in order to accelerate the rise in real national income and in the standard of living of the next generation.

COSTS, PROFIT MARGINS, AND PRICES

If the earlier argument is accepted, it follows that rises in profit margins, wages, and salaries are, just as much as the higher prices themselves, merely the symptoms of excess demand and links in the transmission of its effects. Higher profit margins transmit the excess demand only when they lead to the payment of higher wages, salaries, and (to a very minor extent) dividends, or when they give rise to increased investment. If higher profits are ploughed back to reserve and used to finance an unchanged investment programme, the effect is to increase the level of aggregate saving without increasing attempted investment and is therefore disinflationary. Thus, for instance, a rise in electricity prices not accompanied by a rise in wages of electricity employees would enable the electricity industry to provide more of the finance needed for its investment programme and relieve the Treasury of part of its responsibility for providing finance for new power stations. The Treasury would then be able to devote part of the budget surplus to repaying Government debt, with the effects outlined on p. 112. The effects of a rise in electricity prices and profit margins would thus be identical with those of the imposition of an excise duty on electricity, the proceeds of which were used to increase the budget surplus and repay Government debt.

A rise in import prices is not in itself inflationary, in the sense used here, since it does nothing in itself to raise money incomes. If export prices do not rise, the rise in internal prices will be due, not to a rise in money income but to a fall in real income caused by the worsening terms of trade. If, however, import and export prices rise together, money incomes will rise as the result of the rise in export prices (or more strictly of the rise in the domestic component in export prices), while, since the terms of trade are unchanged, real incomes have not improved. The result will therefore be inflationary.

Of the renewed rise of prices since 1953 very little can be attributed to the rise in import prices. From 1953 to 1956 the import price index rose by less than 4 per cent. This by itself would cause a rise in the internal price level of less than 1 per cent, or less than a twelfth of the rise in the price index for consumer expenditure.

WAGES, SALARIES, AND COLLECTIVE BARGAINING

Reasons have been given above [1] for believing that the causal factor in the rise in wages and salaries has been, not the demands of trade unions, but the ability of employers to grant them without reducing their demand for labour. Excess

demand has kept business so profitable that employers have
been in competition with each other for scarce labour, and it
is this competition which has forced up labour earnings, with
wages following with, in most years, a lengthening time-lag.
It is probably true that the very existence of collective bargaining, with its administrative delays, has caused wage rates to
rise more slowly than they would have done under similar
conditions of excess demand in a free labour market, where
there were neither trade unions nor employers' associations.

This does not mean, however, that trade union leaders are
powerless to influence the rate of rise of wage rates and perhaps
also of earnings, for while they cannot increase them they
can, in collaboration with employers' associations, bring about
a still larger gap between the actual rise and the rise that would
have taken place, as the result of excess demand, in a free
market.   The effect of a 'wage freeze', loyally applied by both
employers and employed, could in theory prevent an excess
demand for labour from bringing with it an excessive rise in
incomes, though it would still involve difficult problems of
labour distribution.   It could, therefore, perpetuate a condition
of over-full employment without inflation — indeed, inflation
would be checked by price control of wages and salaries.   In
fact, however, it is most unlikely that, without powers of
enforcement more severe than would be tolerated in a free
country, this solution of the problem could be more than
temporary.   The continued pressure of excess demand for
labour would inevitably cause some employers to find ways
of evading the prohibition on paying higher wages, while trade
union leaders would find it increasingly difficult to retain the
support of their rank and file members.   While, therefore, a
'wage-freeze' might provide a temporary relief in a period of
emergency, it is unlikely to provide a permanent solution of
the problem of maintaining full employment without inflation.

The time when it is really essential to get the support of
the trade union leaders for a policy of moderation in pressing
wage demands is when the excess demand has been removed
from the system.   In any case, the removal of excess demand
will bring with it some rise in transitional unemployment.   In
this country, with its short distances, good communications,
and well distributed industries, it is believed that the minimum

level of unemployment consistent with the absence of excess demand may be much lower than in many other countries — perhaps not more than of the order of 2 per cent of the working population, or, say, 500,000 persons, most of whom would be unemployed for relatively short periods while moving from one job to another. But if the trade unions used their monopoly power to drive up wages in industries and districts where the labour force would otherwise be expanding, the labour released in industries and districts where it was contracting would remain unemployed. It is not too much to say that while the trade unions, when faced with a determined government, cannot cause inflation, they can determine within wide limits how much unemployment is consistent with its absence.

OTHER RESTRICTIVE PRACTICES

What is true of trade unions is also probably true of other monopolists. During a period of excess demand it is doubtful if they appreciably accelerate the rise in prices, though from the time of Elizabeth I popular opinion has always thought they do. Indeed, it is possible that price agreements, which, like wage agreements, take time to revise, if anything slow down the rise in prices at the cost of causing delays in delivery. In periods of excess demand there is little incentive to limit output, while the function of cartels in keeping high-cost firms in existence side by side with low-cost firms is adequately performed by the excess demand itself. Here also the time when monopoly has the power of doing serious harm is after the excess demand has been removed. With its disappearance, the restriction of output to increase or maintain prices becomes once more attractive, while the sharing of markets again becomes necessary for the survival of high-cost firms. The restriction of output to maintain prices causes unemployment to be higher than would otherwise be necessary, while the maintenance in existence of high-cost firms slows down the rise in real national income.

DISINFLATION AND OUTPUT

The elimination of excess demand will inevitably cause a temporary check to the rise in output, or even a temporary fall. How long this check will last will depend partly on how soon employers, the demand for whose products has fallen, release labour and other resources for alternative uses; but with the disappearance of excess demand there will also almost certainly be a permanent fall in the aggregate number of hours worked throughout the country, as the result partly of the withdrawal from the working population of marginal workers, whom it only just pays to employ even under conditions of excess demand; partly of some increase in unemployment; and partly of the reduction in the hours of overtime worked. In general, the hours no longer worked will be those for which the payments were highest in relation to output; incomes will therefore fall more than output, at least as soon as redundant labour has been discharged, and in spite of the fall in output the net effect of the operation will be disinflationary.

How large and prolonged the check to output will be will depend on how long employers retain redundant labour and how soon the resources so released can find new employment; but given all possible Government assistance in facilitating transfer and the co-operation of the trade unions, it is believed that the initial loss does not need to be very large, at least so long as trade in the rest of the world remains active and workers can be absorbed in export occupations. In the longer run, it is believed that the effect may be to accelerate rather than to slow down the rise in production, for the loss of a small number of high-cost working hours is likely to be more than made up by the increased incentive to labour economy and other forms of efficiency induced by more competitive conditions. The recent experience of the motor car industry, which after last year's check to home demand is now producing more cars with less labour, and exporting a higher proportion of them, is a hopeful augury.

E

CHAPTER 8

MONETARY POLICY AND THE CONTROL OF THE POST-WAR BRITISH INFLATION [1]

THE NATURE OF INFLATION

INFLATION may be defined as a condition in which money incomes are rising faster than the flow of goods and services on which to spend them — that is to say, faster than the real national income. The real national income, in turn, depends mainly on the volume of current domestic output, and though at times it may also be affected by changes in the relative prices at which part of the output is exchanged for imports, and in the amount of investment income received from, or paid to, foreign countries, these last two factors are usually of secondary importance. Broadly, therefore, it may be said that inflation is a condition in which incomes are rising faster than output.

To check inflation it is necessary either to accelerate the rise in output without a corresponding acceleration of the rise in incomes, or to slow down the rise in incomes without a corresponding slowing-down of the rise in output. Unfortunately, in conditions where inflation already exists, attempts to accelerate the rise in output tend to involve more than proportionate rises in incomes, while although the checking of a rise in incomes usually involves some check to the rise in output, the slowing-down of the rise in output is usually less than the slowing-down of the rise in incomes. Thus to check inflation it is usually necessary to slow down the rise in incomes, even though this will probably involve at least a temporary check to the rise in output.

In order to check a rise in incomes, it is necessary to check the rise in those forms of expenditure which create incomes. Not all expenditure is income-creating. If more money is spent on buying existing durable goods, or on titles to assets

[1] Paper prepared for the American Assembly, September 1958. Statistical tables prepared on principles described in Chapter 5 and revised to September, 1961.

or to money, the rise in their prices does nothing directly to raise the level of incomes. If A buys an existing house from B, the sale in itself does nothing to raise incomes (except, perhaps, the income of the house-agent). Only if B then proceeds to spend the money by having a new house built, or in other ways which involve the creation of incomes by payments for the services of persons or of their assets, does the higher price paid by A lead to higher incomes. If it is possible to ensure that money paid for existing assets is not used except to pay for more existing assets, its expenditure is not inflationary, however far it raises asset prices ; all that it does is to bring down the rate of interest. There is, however, a strong probability that the higher prices of existing assets and the lower rates of interest will make it more profitable to construct new physical assets, and that sooner or later income-creating expenditures will also rise unless they are in some way prevented from doing so.

In an isolated country, the effects of income rising faster than output will show themselves entirely in a rise in prices. If, however, there are a number of countries of which only one is inflating, the excessive rise in incomes and in demand there will not only force up internal prices, but will attract additional imports from abroad and will divert resources away from producing exports to satisfying the home demand. Internal inflation, at a rate faster than in other countries, thus tends to bring a rise in imports, a fall in exports, and an adverse balance of payments. The larger amount of goods thus made available on the home market will slow down the internal rise in prices. Indeed, in an extremely open economy, with negligible transport costs, almost the whole of the effects of the inflation would be seen in the balance of payments, while internal prices would rise hardly at all until the currency was devalued. In a country, such as the United Kingdom, which exports a large fraction of what it produces and imports a large fraction of what it consumes, the effects of inflation on the balances of payments often give rise more rapidly to anxiety than do those on the internal price level.

The task of checking inflation is rendered more difficult by the fact that it is frequently inconsistent with other objectives of policy, such as a maximum rate of output and a very low level of unemployment. An excess demand for goods and services leads directly to an excess demand for labour. When there are many more jobs vacant in a country than there are people genuinely looking for them, it is likely that anyone who leaves one job for any reason will quickly find another in his own line of business and his own district. If, however, the demand for labour is no greater than the supply, so that the number of vacancies is not greater than that of men seeking work, there is a much greater probability that to find work a man will have to change his job or leave his district, or both. This will inevitably take longer, and the number of unemployed will rise. If, therefore, political considerations require a government to try to maintain a lower level of unemployment than is consistent with the absence of inflation, the problem of stopping inflation may be insoluble.

TYPES OF ANTI-INFLATIONARY POLICY

If a government genuinely desires to check an inflation, it has three types of technique which it may use. In the first place, it may attempt to restrict income-creating expenditure, either on consumption or on the production of new assets, by means of direct controls on the spending of money. Secondly, it may attempt to reduce expenditure on consumption by a faster rise in tax payments by the public than in Government expenditure. A third method is to try to discourage income-creating expenditure indirectly, by reducing the quantity of money (or preventing it from rising as rapidly as money incomes), and so forcing up the rate of interest.

Sometimes it is only the last of these which is classified as 'monetary policy', as distinguished from direct controls and budgetary policy. All three of them, however, affect either the quantity of money or its velocity of circulation, and all three, therefore, have their monetary aspects. Further, all three have been in use in the United Kingdom in greater or less degree, throughout the post-war period, and it is not possible to discuss the practice of any one of them without reference to the others. We shall therefore regard all three of them as coming under the heading of 'monetary policy' in its wider sense, and shall proceed to consider them in turn.

DIRECT CONTROLS

The first method, that of restricting the rise in income-creating expenditure by means of direct controls, was developed during the war, and has been in use, though to a steadily diminishing extent, ever since. Direct controls can be classified under four main headings : those which prevent businesses from maintaining the (money) value of their inventories; those which limit the amounts which can be spent on consumption and so enforce a rise in saving ; those which restrict fixed investment directly ; and those which attempt to restrict investment indirectly by restricting financial investment.

1. *Price Controls.*—The first-mentioned type of direct control is also the form which usually appears first in time. When a massive increase in Government expenditure, usually for war purposes, simultaneously raises incomes and diverts resources away from the production of consumption goods, the first attempt to prevent the rise in consumer demand and the fall in consumer goods output from causing a rapid rise in prices is to impose direct *price control* on many types of consumption goods. This prevents retailers and wholesalers from raising prices rapidly enough to keep their sales down to the reduced level of replacement supplies. Hence, stocks of consumer goods are progressively depleted. Holders of stocks therefore find themselves in possession of growing amounts of money which they cannot spend on replacements, and which they are obliged to use for debt repayments, or to invest in Government or other securities, or to hold idle.

2. *Rationing.*—This stage can continue, however, only so long as stocks last. When they approach exhaustion, consumers can no longer find as much in the shops as they would like to buy at the prices fixed, and are therefore obliged to save part of their incomes. Under such conditions the distribution of the available supplies among consumers becomes extremely arbitrary. In order to obtain a fairer distribution, systems of *rationing* are introduced for supplies of most new goods, except for those regarded as luxuries, to the extent that these are still allowed to be produced.

3. *Fixed Capital.*—The third type of direct control consists of *restrictions on the creation of new fixed capital*. This control

is likely to be most effective over new building, where it is possible to enforce a strict system of licensing. Output of other forms of fixed capital is more difficult to control directly, and recourse is often had to indirect methods, such as the control of supplies of iron and steel and of other materials, as well as of labour, necessary to their production. Control over the distribution and use of other types of new fixed capital is also more difficult to enforce than over new building.

The combined effect of the preceding three types of control is to limit the amount of money people can spend in ways which create additional incomes. If the restrictions are fully effective, the level of incomes can be rendered independent of the quantity of money in the economic system as a whole, and the quantity of money can be expanded indefinitely without causing inflation. If people hold money idle, the Government can safely create more to take its place ; while if they use it to buy existing assets, they force down the rate of interest and enable the Government to borrow cheaply.

4. *Securities Issues.*—The purpose of the fourth type of direct control, that over new capital issues and the borrowing of money, seems to be twofold. On the one hand, this control attempts to prevent other borrowers from competing with the Government for funds and so to concentrate the excess money on the market for Government securities. On the other hand, it provides a second line of defence against unauthorised private investment. So long as there is a general excess of money in the system, so that very few persons or firms are short of cash, it is doubtful whether this type of control goes far toward the achievement of either of its objectives. Only when money begins to become scarce, so that many investors would have to obtain capital from someone else in order to finance investment they are not otherwise prevented from carrying out, is this type of control likely to have any appreciable effect.

5. *Limitations of Direct Controls.*—Once the necessary machinery for enforcement has been created, the policy of checking a rise in money incomes by means of direct controls can be very effective — under certain conditions and for a limited time. As a permanent policy, effective for the control of inflation under all conditions, it is likely to break down. In

the first place, its success depends on the willingness of the population to work and sell in exchange for money, part of which they cannot spend, at least on the things they want. So long as they continue to expect that they will be allowed to spend their involuntary savings in the not too distant future, they may be willing to continue to accept payment in money. But as the prospect of being able to spend freely their accumulated money savings becomes increasingly remote, they will become increasingly unwilling to add further to them, and ultimately it may become possible to obtain the use of services or to buy useful goods only if payment is made in kind. A controlled inflation pushed to extremes reaches the same ultimate result as an open inflation — money ceases to be used as a medium of exchange, and the economy resorts to barter.

A second difficulty is that the efficient enforcement of direct controls depends largely on the effective restriction of supplies. In time of war, when resources are extensively and often compulsorily employed for military purposes, it is relatively easy to prevent the substantial diversion of resources to the production of goods and services of low priority. But when, at the end of a war, large quantities of resources are released from military use, it becomes increasingly difficult to prevent their diversion to what the Government regards as low-priority uses, and to prevent their products from being sold to the public. While the rationing system may continue to be effective for a limited number of essential commodities, it is likely to be much less effective for a wide range of non-essentials of which there was little production during the war. The result is that many of the resources released from the war, instead of going into high-priority uses such as capital goods and exports, or into expanding the output of essential consumption goods, tend to be absorbed into the production of consumption goods which, though officially regarded as of low priority, are in keen demand from an over-liquid and luxury-starved public. The final effects of trying to maintain a system of direct controls, when it can no longer be enforced effectively, are not only an inflationary rise in incomes but a serious distortion of the structure of production.

Another disadvantage of the use of direct controls is that they keep down the amount of actual inflation only at the cost of building up behind them a very large potential inflation in the form of an excessive stock of money. This excessive stock of money is one of the main reasons why it has been so difficult to control inflation in the United Kingdom since the war. In 1938 clearing bank deposits averaged £2213 millions, or 46 per cent of national income; by 1945 they had risen to £4541 millions, or 54 per cent; and by 1947 to £5454 millions, or 64 per cent. This 50 per cent rise in the ratio of bank deposits to national income is an indication of the potential inflationary pressure built up behind the controls.

SAVING THROUGH BUDGET SURPLUSES

The second principal method of keeping down incomes is the use of surpluses in the governmental budget. In principle, the operation of this method is simple: money is subtracted from incomes by increased taxation or reduced Government expenditure, and is used for the repayment of Government debt. The method is most effectively disinflationary when the budget surplus is used to repay debts to the banks, through Treasury redemption or purchase of Government securities from them.

In this situation the money subtracted from incomes is cancelled, at least until it is re-created by the expansion of other bank assets. If the surplus is used to repay Government debt due to the central bank (the Bank of England), thus reducing the commercial banks' cash reserves, or if it is used to retire Treasury bills held by the discount market and the banks, thus reducing the banks' liquid assets ratios, the repayment may have not only the primary effect of reducing the quantity of bank deposits directly but also the secondary effect of obliging the banks themselves to reduce their deposits further by cutting down their non-liquid assets. The effects of debt repayment to the banks come, however, under the heading of operations on the quantity of money, which are dealt with in the next section. Here we shall deal only with the effects of budget surpluses which affect the use of money rather than its quantity.

Even if a budget surplus is used to pay off debt to (or reduce the need for borrowing from) the general public, its effects will still be disinflationary, though less so than if it had been used to cancel money. Most investors whose Government securities are paid off will treat the proceeds as capital. They will therefore not spend them on consumption, but will either hold them idle or will re-invest them, usually in existing assets. Not until they come into the hands of someone who uses them to pay for the construction of new physical assets will they again become income, and this will happen only after a longer or shorter time-lag. The effect of an increase in the budget surplus and its use to pay off securities held by the public will therefore be to reduce consumption and check the rise in incomes, while at the same time tending to bring down the rate of interest and usually, after a time-lag, to permit an increase in investment. It is, however, possible for the higher taxes or reduced Government expenditure to make business prospects so much worse that, even with lower interest rates, there is no incentive to increase the production of new assets. If this is so, the disinflationary effects of the policy will be greatly increased.

So far, the effects of an increased budget surplus seem to be identical with those of an increase in the level of voluntary saving. The truth, however, is less simple. In the first place, an increased budget surplus checks the rise in incomes only if it involves an immediate reduction in income-creating expenditure. It is unlikely that this fall in expenditure will ever be equal to the whole of the rise in the budget surplus, and in some cases it may be very much smaller. There are, for instance, some taxes, such as death duties and stamp duties on the transfer of securities and property, which are normally paid almost wholly out of capital. An increase in these, yielding a budget surplus used to repay Government debt to the public, merely pays back as capital money originally paid out of capital, and has little or no net effect.

Again, if very high taxes are imposed on rich men, especially those with property, they are likely to be paid in part, and often to a considerable extent, either out of capital or at the expense of a reduction in current saving. Only if the increased taxes are imposed on the relatively poor is it at all certain that they will involve an almost equal reduction in current consumption. Thus the more progressive the system of taxation, the more likely it is that taxes will be paid out of capital or at the expense

E 2

of new savings, and the less effective they are likely to be in checking an excessive rise in incomes.

The United Kingdom is fortunate to have found two forms of tax which, though probably highly regressive in incidence, have aroused relatively little political controversy. One of these consists of the extraordinarily high excise and customs duties imposed on tobacco, beer, and most other alcoholic drinks, which together provide well over a fifth of the total tax revenue. The other is the flat-rate national insurance contribution, paid by every employed person, which at present provides more than half the total amounts paid out by the National Insurance Funds, in retirement, sickness, unemployment and other benefits, and to which the political objection is very much less than if it had been called by its true name of a poll tax on employed persons. If these taxes were replaced by still higher levels of progressive income taxation, there can be little doubt that, with an unchanged budget surplus, the amount of money withdrawn from the income circulation would be substantially reduced.

In addition to the difficulty that direct taxes on high incomes are likely to be paid either out of capital or at the expense of savings, there is the additional difficulty that very high marginal rates of income taxation are likely to have undesirable effects in distorting the use of resources. This is because they diminish the incentive to earn additional taxable income. The choice is probably less between work and leisure, in the sense of idleness, than between work which produces taxable income and work which produces non-taxable benefits, sometimes in the form of unpaid services within the household. In addition, very high rates of income taxation provide a great incentive both for the legal avoidance and the illegal evasion of tax liability, and large amounts of valuable resources may be devoted to these activities, and to their prevention, instead of to increasing the real national income. When, therefore, taxation is already very high, governments may well hesitate before seeking to check inflation by raising it further. Indeed, in most western countries a reduction rather than an increase in the proportion of national income taken in taxation would probably be desirable as a means of increasing the rate of growth of the real national product.

The economic disadvantages of seeking to check an inflation by obtaining a larger budget surplus through a reduction in Government expenditure are much less marked. Reductions in expenditure through mere administrative economies, though no doubt always possible, are, however, likely to be limited. Really substantial reductions of expenditures are usually possible only by major changes in the activities or policies of the Government, many of which would be almost, if not quite, as unpopular as an increase in taxation. The most popularly acceptable are likely to consist of reductions in defence expenditure, so long as these do not obviously increase the danger of war or of defeat in war. Even here, however, large and rapid reductions are likely to release highly localised and specific resources for which it is difficult quickly to find alternative uses. Hence the fall in money incomes is likely to be accompanied by some corresponding fall in national product. On the whole, the most that can reasonably be hoped for in most countries, in the absence of a major change in the international political situation, is that Government expenditure should be stabilised in real terms while real national income continues to rise ; or at any rate that Government expenditures should rise more slowly than national income. If even this modest hope could be realised, a gradual rise in the budget surplus could be made consistent with a gradual fall in the proportion of the national income taken in taxation.

CONTROLLING THE QUANTITY OF MONEY

1. *Through Budget Surpluses.*—So far, we have considered methods of checking an inflation by methods which involve changes in the uses of a fixed quantity of money, as between consumption on the one hand and investment and idle balances on the other. Such methods, while tending to check a rise in money incomes, also tend to reduce interest rates and so to offset part of the initial effect. We now turn to methods which affect not only the distribution of money between the different purposes for which it is used, but also its aggregate quantity. We may distinguish between three methods : first, those which withdraw money from incomes while permitting a rise in capital expenditures ; second, those which withdraw money from

both income and capital expenditures together; and finally, those which withdraw it initially from capital expenditures only. The first of these methods brings some reduction in the rate of interest, and so to some extent offsets the effect of the initial withdrawal of money from incomes. The last method exercises its effects entirely through a rise in interest rates and a consequent check to investment. The second method, while exercising a doubly disinflationary effect on incomes, has an indeterminate effect on interest rates, depending on how far the fall in the demand for money to finance investment, brought about by the reduction in the expected yield of new physical assets, offsets or outweighs the fall in the supply of money available for investment.

An example of a withdrawal of money from incomes, accompanied by a smaller rise in money available for investment, is a budget surplus used to pay off Government securities held by the banks, or to repay a bank advance to a nationalised industry. The immediate effect is a fall in bank deposits, a fall in the banks' non-liquid assets, and a rise in both their cash and liquid assets ratios.[1] The banks will therefore be in a position to lend more or to buy more securities, thus tending to bring down

---

[1] Banks in the United Kingdom keep their surplus funds in the form, not of cash reserves, but of liquid assets other than cash. These non-cash liquid assets consist partly of very short loans to the discount market (call money) and partly of bills maturing in not more than three months. The loans to the discount houses are now used mainly to finance holdings of Treasury bills, while some 90 per cent of the banks' bill holdings also consist of Treasury bills. Since 1935 the banks themselves have not purchased Treasury bills directly from the Treasury, but have bought them from the market, usually when they have not more than two months to run. The clearing banks keep their cash reserves as nearly as possible at the agreed minimum of 8 per cent of deposits, but try to keep their combined holdings of cash, call money, and bills at appreciably above the conventional minimum of 30 per cent. The size of the desired excess varies with the season, being at its highest in December, before the seasonal flow of tax payments begins, and at its lowest in March, when issues of Treasury bills are normally at their lowest. Thus a minimum level of 30 per cent in March corresponds to perhaps 33 per cent in December.

The discount houses have the privilege of borrowing money in virtually unlimited amounts from the Bank of England at Bank Rate against the security of Treasury bills, though the Bank usually employs open market operations to prevent them from having to do so as the result of merely accidental fluctuations: that is to say, it supplies additional cash to the market by buying bills or lending money through its agents at the ordinary market rate. If the banks are short of cash but have surplus liquid assets, they call in loans from the discount market, thus obliging the market to borrow from the Bank. If the Bank wishes to force up short-term rates, it

long-term interest rates, a tendency which will be reinforced
by the fall in the expected yield of capital brought about
by the increase in tax receipts or the fall in Government
expenditure.

An example of a case where the withdrawal of money from
incomes leaves the quantity available for investment unchanged is more difficult to find in a system where money
consists of a mixture of notes and deposits. In a system where
money is created by Government decree, it might be secured
by merely cancelling notes to the extent of the surplus. In a
cheque-using system, it would be necessary, in repaying Government debt to the banks, to do so in a way which would leave
unchanged the proportions between the different classes of
bank assets. It would therefore be necessary to use an amount
equal to about 8 per cent of the budget surplus to repay debt
to the Bank of England, thus reducing the commercial banks'
cash reserves: about 25 per cent to repay Treasury bills held
by the commercial banks and discount houses; about one-
third to repay Government securities held by the commercial
banks; and about one-third to repay the bank advances of
local authorities or nationalised industries.

Examples of the case where money is withdrawn from both
consumption and investment uses are the use of an overall
budget surplus to repay Government debt to the Bank of
England and its use to repay Treasury bills held by the discount houses or the clearing banks. If debt is repaid to the
Bank of England, the fall in the Bank's assets will be accompanied by an equal fall in the cash reserves of the commercial
banks. These will have to replenish their cash reserves by
calling in loans from the market, which will be forced to borrow
from the Bank at Bank Rate. Thus the effect will be a rise in
short-term interest rates and, with the depletion of the banks'
holdings of call money, a fall in their liquid assets ratio. In

allows the discount houses to come to the Bank and borrow at Bank Rate;
if not, it supplies the necessary cash through open market operations.

The non-liquid assets of the clearing banks, which normally constitute
nearly two-thirds of their total assets, consist partly of advances and partly
of Government securities, usually redeemable in not more than ten years.
In recent years the banks' holdings of securities and advances have been
about equal, though it is believed that the banks would like to return to the
proportions of the 1920s, when the total of advances was twice as large as
that of securities.

fact, the Treasury does not operate by varying its debt to the Bank of England (leaving that to the open market operations of the Bank itself). In practice, if the Treasury wishes to use an overall budget surplus in a way which will exercise the maximum disinflationary effect, by reducing the quantity of money not only in the income circulation but also in the capital circulation, it employs it in paying off Treasury bills as they mature. This has a double effect on interest rates. By making Treasury bills scarce, it tends to bring down short-term interest rates. At the same time, unless the banks and discount houses can obtain a larger share of the smaller issue, it reduces the banks' liquid assets ratio.

Since their proportion of loans to securities has for many years been smaller than they would like, the banks' first reaction to an inadequate liquid assets ratio will probably be to sell securities, thereby tending to bring about a rise in interest rates, especially on short-dated securities, at the same time that their bidding for Treasury bills is forcing down bill rates. Later, however, as their supply of shorter-dated securities becomes exhausted, the banks will become increasingly reluctant to force the sale of their longer-dated securities on a falling market, and can be expected to begin instead to restrict loans.

In point of fact, there has been no recent year when the Government has had a budget surplus, on account of current operations, large enough to cover the whole of its extra-budgetary expenditure, let alone leaving a margin for debt redemption. Though there was a time, in 1948–50, when it was able to do so, in recent years it has been able to repay short-term debt to the banks, if at all, only out of money borrowed elsewhere.

2. *Debt Management Policy.*—Even though the Government is unable to achieve an overall budget surplus, it is still possible for the monetary authorities (that is to say, the Treasury and Central Bank acting in conjunction) to control the quantity of money by changes in the amounts and forms of their debts to banks and others. In a purely note-using economy, a reduction in the quantity of money could be achieved by the Treasury's borrowing money from the public and hoarding or destroying it. Alternatively if the notes were the liability of the Central Bank, the same result could be achieved by the

Central Bank's selling its assets and cancelling the notes received in exchange. In a modern cheque-using economy, however, the process is more complicated.

In the United Kingdom to-day, the vast majority of bills in existence are the obligations of the Treasury. Hence a large rise in Bank Rate is widely regarded as a method which, though likely to be effective if carried far enough, is an expensive one which should be reserved for moments of great emergency. The cost of high short-term money rates to the Treasury is greatly increased by the fact that very large amounts of short-term Treasury liabilities are held by overseas owners of sterling balances, who do not pay income tax and increased interest payments to whom constitute an additional burden on the balance of payments.

In view of the high cost to the Treasury of large rises in short-term rates of interest, and of the belief that for checking an inflation it is a rise in the long-term rate of interest which is mainly relevant, attention has in recent years been directed to the possibility, not of making cash scarce in relation to other liquid assets, but of reducing the supply to the banks of *all* types of liquid assets taken together. This is possible because some 90 per cent of all bills in existence now consist of Treasury bills. By restricting the volume of Treasury bills on the market it is possible to restrict the amount of liquid assets available for the banks.

There are three possible ways of cutting down the supply of Treasury bills available to the discount market and the banks :

(*a*) to sell more of an unchanged volume of Treasury bills to non-bank buyers ;
(*b*) to sell more securities to the banks themselves, using the proceeds to pay off Treasury bills ;
(*c*) to pay off Treasury bills out of the proceeds of sales of securities to non-bank buyers.

In the early stages of credit restriction, when financial and other institutions are still very liquid, a moderate rise in bill rates may be sufficient to induce non-banking investors to take up substantial quantities of Treasury bills. But as money becomes increasingly tight, it takes increasingly high bill rates to induce non-bank holders even to retain their existing holdings, and other methods become correspondingly more attractive. Similarly, the sale of securities to the banks is possible only while they have a substantial surplus of liquid assets ; so that, while this method may be useful in the initial stages of reducing their surplus liquid assets ratios, it ceases to be practicable as soon as their liquidity position becomes less comfortable. While therefore these measures may be useful in the early stages of credit restriction, to push the reduction of the banks' liquid assets ratios to the point where they will be obliged to restrict their holdings of non-liquid assets necessitates recourse to the sale of securities to the public.

The main way in which the Treasury sells additional securities to the public is to make periodical large issues on the capital market. In so far as these are not subscribed for by the public, they are taken up by 'Government departments' (mainly, it is believed, by the Bank of England), and subsequently sold off gradually on the stock exchange as opportunity offers. Thus, in fact, Government securities are kept continuously on offer to the public at market rates. The chief difficulty which this policy has encountered is that the Treasury, before it can obtain funds with which to pay off its short-term bills, has to provide not only for all governmental expenditure (plus the cost of any acquisitions of gold by the Exchange Equalisation Account not covered by sales of additional bills to holders of increased sterling balances), but also for the repayment or conversion of several hundred millions of medium-term securities maturing each year. Banking and other holders of these can always replenish their stock of liquid assets by allowing them to mature without replacement ; and the Treasury is always under the necessity of finding new holders to take their place. Once, therefore, the restriction of the quantity of money held for investment has been carried a certain distance, it becomes increasingly difficult for the Treasury to carry it further by means of the so-called 'funding policy', or even to prevent the liquid assets and deposits of the banks from rising again.

3. *Banking and Credit Controls.*—It is largely because of the difficulty which the Treasury and Bank of England have found in keeping the banks' liquid assets down to a level which would compel them to restrict their holdings of non-liquid assets, that governments have from time to time 're-

quested' the banks to restrict their loans, even when the banks' own liquidity positions would have allowed them to expand them substantially. These requests have in the main taken two forms : (*a*) to restrict certain classes of loans, for uses which the Government regarded as of low priority ; (*b*) more recently, to restrict total loans, regardless of their purpose. Such direct restrictions are unlikely to be practicable or effective, except in times of obvious emergency and over short periods. It has therefore been proposed that the 'funding policy' should be reinforced by giving the authorities the power to fix and vary the minimum liquid assets ratio which the banks would be required to maintain. With this power, analogous to the power of the Federal Reserve to alter legal reserves of member banks in the United States, the authorities would be able to raise the minimum liquid assets ratio sufficiently to absorb any surplus liquid assets. An alternative suggestion has been made to revive the system of Treasury Deposit Receipts, instituted during the war and suspended at the end of 1951. Under this system the banks were required to subscribe each week for varying quantities of non-liquid and non-marketable short-term Government securities, thus being compelled to sterilise a varying proportion of their liquid assets. One advantage claimed for this device is that the banks' liquid assets ratios could be adjusted continuously by small amounts, whereas liquid assets ratios themselves could be adjusted only from time to time and by relatively large amounts.

Recently the Government has introduced, simultaneously with the removal of direct limitations on the level of bank advances, a variant of the Treasury Deposit Receipt system. It is now proposed that the Bank of England should have power to require the banks to hold, in addition to their normal cash reserves, 'special accounts' at the Bank of England equal to a proportion of their deposits which could be varied from time to time. These special accounts, which would bear interest at approximately the Treasury bill rate, would not be regarded as constituting part of the banks' liquid assets, and their institution would therefore reduce the banks' liquid assets ratios. It is believed that the new powers are intended for use only in emergency, and to supplement rather than replace the policy of keeping down the banks' liquid assets by budgetary and funding policies. While the new system, which closely resembles that in force in Australia, is much preferable to the direct limitation of advances which it replaces, it is to be hoped that more orthodox measures will in future be sufficiently effective to prevent the development of any new emergency serious enough to require it to be put into operation.

OPERATION OF ANTI-INFLATIONARY POLICIES IN POST-WAR BRITAIN

1945-47 — DIRECT CONTROLS

While some of the policies discussed above, and especially the financial controls over the lending and borrowing of money and the raising of new capital, have been in force in the United Kingdom with varying degrees of rigour throughout the whole post-war period, we can divide the past thirteen years (1945–1958) into three distinct phases, each clearly characterised by the emphasis given in Government policy to one or other of the three main classes of counter-inflationary policy just described.

In the first phase, which lasted from the end of the war until nearly the end of 1947, the main emphasis was on direct economic controls. During the war, and especially in the years after 1942, there had been built up an elaborate series of controls on consumption and investment. These were very effective in slowing down the rise in prices and incomes during the later years of the war. The rise in the volume of bank deposits, however, which in the early years of the war had lagged behind the rise in incomes, was accelerated in the later years; and by the end of the war the ratio of bank deposits to national money income was considerably higher than in 1938 (see Table I and Chart I). Since, however, the controls were largely successful in keeping this new money out of consumption expenditures, it was possible to confine its effects almost entirely to investment in existing assets and securities, where it kept prices of assets high and interest rates low.

It was, no doubt, the remarkable effectiveness of the physical controls in the later years of the war which induced the Government in the immediate post-war years to embark

upon a policy of expanding the money supply substantially
further, while relying on direct controls to prevent it escaping

CHART I

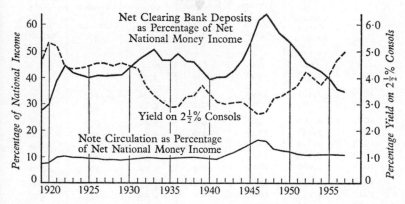

into consumption expenditures and raising incomes and prices
there. The motives behind this policy seem to have been
mainly four :

(1) to bring down the interest burden of the national debt,
especially on the securities which it was proposed to issue
as compensation to the former owners of nationalised
industries ;
(2) to promote the rapid re-employment of men released from
the armed forces ;
(3) to provide capital on easy terms for those forms of investment of which the Government approved ;
(4) to carry further the curtailment of investment incomes.

The budget deficit of over £850 millions [1] for 1946 was
therefore financed mainly by borrowing from the banks ; so
that between January 1946 and January 1947 clearing bank
deposits rose by £900 millions, or nearly 20 per cent. But at
levels of under 3 per cent, long-term interest rates proved very
resistant to even so massive an injection of money as this.
Although during 1946 the ratio of deposits to national income

[1] These and subsequent budget figures are those given in the National
Income estimates for the Revenue Account of the Central Government.
They cover calendar years and include the cash surpluses of the National
Insurance Funds.

TABLE I
NATIONAL MONEY INCOME, CLEARING BANK DEPOSITS, NOTE CIRCULATION, AND YIELD ON CONSOLS

	Estimated Net National Money Income	Average Clearing Bank Deposits	Ratio of Deposits to National Income	Yield on Consols	Average Note Circulation	Ratio of Note Circulation to National Income
	£m.	£m.	%			
1913	2,368	740	31·2	3·39	155	6·5
1919	5,461	1500	27·5	4·62	413	7·5
1920	5,664	1710	30·2	5·32	449	7·9
1921	4,460	1764	39·6	5·21	437	9·8
1922	3,856	1730	44·9	4·42	400	10·4
1923	3,844	1629	42·3	4·31	388	10·1
1924	3,919	1622	41·4	4·39	391	10·0
1925	3,980	1610	40·4	4·44	383	9·6
1926	3,914	1615	41·2	4·55	375	9·6
1927	4,145	1661	40·1	4·56	373	9·0
1928	4,154	1709	41·1	4·47	372	9·0
1929	4,178	1743	41·7	4·60	362	8·7
1930	3,957	1747	44·1	4·48	359	9·1
1931	3,666	1711	46·7	4·39	355	9·7
1932	3,568	1745	48·9	3·74	360	10·1
1933	3,728	1906	51·1	3·39	371	9·9
1934	3,881	1830	47·2	3·10	379	9·8
1935	4,109	1947	47·4	2·89	395	9·6
1936	4,388	2156	49·1	2·93	431	9·8
1937	4,750	2220	46·7	3·28	480	10·1
1938	4,816	2213	46·0	3·38	486	10·1
1939	5,160	2175	42·2	3·72	507	9·8
1940	6,120	2408	39·4	3·40	575	9·4
1941	7,080	2849	40·3	3·13	651	9·2
1942	7,800	3145	40·3	3·03	807	10·3
1943	8,300	3544	42·7	3·10	966	11·6
1944	8,500	4012	47·2	3·14	1136	13·4
1945	8,480	4541	53·6	2·92	1284	15·1
1946	8,087	4922	60·4	2·60	1358	16·8
1947	8,587	5454	63·6	2·76	1384	16·1
1948	9,556	5703	59·7	3·21	1254	13·1
1949	10,208	5761	56·5	3·30	1269	12·4
1950	10,762	5800	54·0	3·54	1287	12·0
1951	11,757	5918	50·3	3·78	1342	11·4
1952	12,707	5844	46·0	4·23	1435	11·3
1953	13,604	6012	44·2	4·08	1532	11·3
1954	14,535	6225	42·8	3·75	1630	11·2
1955	15,361	6171	40·2	4·17	1760	11·4
1956	16,746	5998	35·8	4·73	1875	11·2
1957	17,675	6122	34·7	5·01	1967	11·1

rose from about 55 per cent to about 65 per cent (as compared with 46 per cent in 1938), the market yield on $2\frac{1}{2}$ per cent Consols fell only from $2\frac{3}{4}$ per cent to just over $2\frac{1}{2}$ per cent.[1]

By the end of 1946 it was becoming clear that, in peace-time conditions, the physical controls could no longer be relied upon to keep the excess money out of consumption expenditures. The effects of excessive purchasing power, combined with those of price controls, showed themselves in a series of physical shortages, of which the most serious was of coal. In spite of the controls, the rise in consumer expenditures and in labour earnings and prices began to quicken (see Tables II and III). Perhaps most serious of all, the diversion of resources to meet the rising home demand checked the rise in the volume of exports, which had shown an encouraging start in the second half of 1945 and the first half of 1946.

Early in 1947, therefore, the attempt to hold down long-term interest rates by the creation of large amounts of new money was abandoned; the ratio of bank deposits to national income began to fall; and long-term interest rates started on their long climb which, apart from a temporary check in 1953–1954, did not reach its peak until 1957. The effects of the 1946 expansion, however, continued to be felt throughout 1947, culminating, in spite of heavy drawings on the North American Loan, in the balance-of-payments crisis of the autumn; and in November an emergency budget inaugurated a new policy.

1948–51 — BUDGET SURPLUSES

The autumn budget of 1947, supplemented by the spring budget of 1948, imposed additional taxation at a time of falling Government expenditure. They inaugurated the period of massive saving through Central Government budget surpluses which is associated with the name of Sir Stafford Cripps. During the four years 1948–51, the Central Government budget surpluses on income account aggregated over £2300 millions (see also Table IV), while aggregate cash surpluses, including receipts and payments on Central Government capital account, totalled over £2600 millions. During the same period the

---

[1] See Table I. For a fuller discussion of this period see the author's 'Cheap Money Policy' (*Economica*, August 1947).

TABLE II

PRODUCTION PRICES AND INCOMES IN THE UNITED KINGDOM

(Yearly Percentage Changes)

	Production and Real Income			Money Incomes				Prices	
	Index of Industrial Production	Gross Domestic Product	Gross Real National Income	Trade Union Weekly Wage Rates	Weekly Earnings	Gross National Money Income	Ratio of Money Income to Real Income	Prices of Consumption Goods and Services	Index of Retail Prices
1947	+6·1	+1·1	+0·1	+4·3	+8·8	+6·8	+6·7	+6·9	+5·7
1948	+7·6	+4·6	+4·2	+4·7	+10·1	+11·1	+6·6	+7·5	+7·3
1949	+6·2	+4·2	+3·7	+2·8	+3·6	+6·5	+2·7	+2·0	+2·9
1950	+5·9	+4·0	+3·0	+1·7	+4·2	+5·6	+2·5	+2·7	+2·7
1951	+3·1	+2·1	+0·7	+8·6	+10·6	+9·7	+8·9	+9·4	+9·8
Total 1947-51	+32·6	+16·6	+12·0	+23·9	+43·4	+46·4	+30·6	+31·6	+31·8
1952	−2·3	−0·8	+1·6	+8·5	+7·8	+8·5	+6·8	+6·0	+8·8
1953	+5·5	+4·0	+4·7	+4·6	+6·8	+6·8	+2·0	+1·5	+3·1
1954	+6·0	+4·4	+4·0	+4·4	+6·8	+6·5	+2·4	+2·0	+1·8
1955	+5·7	+3·6	+3·5	+6·6	+8·8	+5·9	+2·3	+3·4	+4·4
1956	± 0	+0·9	+2·4	+7·9	+7·7	+8·9	+6·3	+4·4	+4·9
Total 1952-56	+15·4	+12·6	+17·2	+36·2	+44·2	+42·4	+21·5	+18·4	+25·1
1957	+2·0	+1·8	+1·7	+5·0	+4·6	+5·7	+3·9	+2·7	+3·9

TABLE III
USES OF REAL NATIONAL INCOME
(£m. at 1954 Prices)

	Consumers' Expenditure				Public Authorities' Expenditure on Goods and Services			Saving and Depreciation			Gross National Income	
		Percentage of				Percentage of			Percentage of			
	£m.	National Income	1948	1948 per Head of Population	£m.	National Income	1948	£m.	National Income	1948	£m.	Percentage of 1948
1938	10,730	72·4	100·2	105·0	2350	15·8	99·2	1752	11·8	91·3	14,832	98·9
1946	10,330	71·8	96·5	97·7	3480	24·2	147·0	572	4·0	29·8	14,382	95·9
1947	10,680	74·2	99·8	100·3	2380	16·5	100·5	1340	9·3	69·8	14,400	96·0
1948	10,706	71·4	100·0	100·0	2368	15·8	100·0	1919	12·8	100·0	14,993	100·0
1949	10,940	70·3	102·3	102·0	2521	16·3	106·6	2087	13·4	108·8	15,554	103·7
1950	11,317	70·7	105·6	104·8	2546	15·9	107·5	2148	13·4	112·0	16,011	106·8
1951	11,167	69·2	104·3	103·5	2752	17·0	116·2	2222	13·8	115·8	16,141	107·6
1952	11,116	67·8	103·7	102·2	3048	18·6	128·8	2228	13·6	116·1	16,392	109·3
1953	11,581	67·5	108·1	106·1	3141	18·3	132·6	2428	14·2	126·4	17,150	114·4
1954	12,119	67·8	113·2	110·7	3135	17·6	132·4	2600	14·6	135·4	17,854	119·0
1955	12,558	67·9	117·2	114·4	3063	16·6	129·4	2857	15·5	148·8	18,478	123·2
1956	12,691	67·1	118·4	115·0	3077	16·3	129·9	3138	16·6	163·4	18,906	126·2
1957	12,994	67·5	121·3	117·2	2981	15·5	125·8	3260	17·0	169·8	19,235	128·3

local governments made capital expenditures (mainly on building small houses to rent at subsidised rates) to the extent of
£1200 millions; and nationalised industries made capital expenditures to the extent of over £700 millions, in excess of their
own savings. Thus the aggregate net savings of all the public
authorities combined were some £700 millions in excess of
their combined net capital expenditures. More than half this
surplus was used to reduce Central Government debt to the
banks, which fell by some £400 millions between the end of
1947 and the end of 1951. This repayment of Government
debt was sufficient to offset the greater part of the rise of over
£700 millions in bank loans, and net deposits rose by less than
£350 millions, or about 6 per cent. This rise was substantially
less than that in real national income, which, in spite of the
worsening of the terms of trade, was over 10 per cent for the
period (see Table II). If, therefore, velocities of circulation of
money had remained constant, it could have been expected
that the inflation would have been checked and prices stabilised.

In fact, however, the effects of the preceding monetary
expansion continued to work themselves out; the rise in
prices, though slowed down for a time, was never wholly
checked. The rise in national money income, which was over
11 per cent from 1947 to 1948, slowed down to only 6½ per cent
from 1948 to 1949; as the rise in real national income was
nearly 4 per cent in each year, the rise in the price level slowed
down [1] from about 7 per cent in 1947–48 to only 2½ per cent
in 1948–49. The devaluation of the pound during 1949 however (which was necessitated by the difficulties of the rest of
the sterling area rather than by those of the United Kingdom
itself), together with the worsening of the terms of trade due
to the (partly consequential) rise in import prices, brought some
intensification of inflationary pressure in 1950 and still more
in 1951, when prices rose by something like 9 per cent.

Over the whole four years, prices rose by some 22 per cent
and national money income by about 38 per cent. This rise
in national money income, accompanied by a rise of only 6 per

[1] Except where otherwise stated, the phrase 'the price level' refers to a
price index obtained by dividing the index of money national income by the
index of real national income. It is, therefore, an index of prices at factor
cost of all goods and services (including imports) used in the country, both
for consumption and for investment. See Table II.

cent in bank deposits, reduced the ratio of deposits to national income from 65 per cent at the end of 1946 and 63 per cent at the end of 1947 to about 50 per cent at the end of 1951. This fall in the ratio, reflecting an increase in velocity of circulation of money, was accompanied by a considerable rise in long-term interest rates. The yield on 2½ per cent Consols came up from 2½ per cent at the end of 1946 and 3 per cent at the end of 1947 to 3¾ per cent in September 1951. This rise in interest rates, however, would still have been quite inadequate to equate with saving an otherwise unrestricted level of investment. Hence, even at the higher level of saving established in 1948, severe controls on domestic investment were maintained throughout the period. These were less effective for the control of investment in inventories than in fixed assets; and in 1951 the rise in import prices caused by the Korean War induced a major inventory boom. It was largely this additional source of internal demand which, together with drawings on London balances by sterling area countries, brought on the balance-of-payments crisis which developed in the second half of 1951 (see Table VI).

While the policy of budget surpluses ultimately proved inadequate to cope with the inflationary pressures induced by the pound sterling devaluation of 1949 [1] and by the Korean War, it had considerable success for a time. Personal consumption per head, which had risen sharply in 1947, remained almost unchanged thereafter in spite of the progressive relaxation of rationing. It did not rise much above the 1947 level until 1953. The proportion of real national income devoted to personal consumption thus fell from 74 per cent in 1947 to 71 per cent in 1948 and 69 per cent in 1951. In 1948 the whole of the rise in real national income was saved, and the

---

[1] Many observers at the time thought that the extent of the devaluation, from $4·04 to $2·80 to the pound, was excessive. It is believed that the lower rate was decided on in the expectation that the moderate United States business recession of 1949 would develop into a major depression. In fact, at the moment of devaluation the United States down-turn had already come to an end, and even before the outbreak of the Korean War in mid-1950 there had been a considerable recovery. It is arguable that if the devaluation had been to a rate of, say, $3·20 to the pound, this would have been sufficient to bring sterling area costs and prices into line with those in the United States and other countries, and that the subsequent inflations in the United Kingdom and other countries of the sterling area would have been correspondingly less marked.

proportion of the (gross) national income available for (gross) investment rose from 9 per cent to 13 per cent (see Table III). This permitted not only a much-needed increase in the pace of industrial re-equipment, but also a marked improvement in the balance of payments. With the help of generous aid from the United States, this enabled the most urgent capital needs of other sterling area countries to be met without a further depletion of the gold reserves.

After 1948, however, a large part of the resources withheld from private consumers was devoted to financing increased Government expenditure on goods and services, first on the health service and later on defence. For the rest of the period, therefore, saving rose hardly faster than national income, and the proportion of national income available for investment increased only from 12·8 per cent in 1948 to 13·8 per cent in 1951. Not until 1951, however, when to the rise in rearmament expenditure was added a very large investment in inventories, did the level of saving again prove seriously inadequate to meet the demands on it, and the policy break down in a new wave of inflation and a balance-of-payments crisis.

1952–58 MONETARY POLICY

(A) 1951–52 — *the First Period of Tight Money.*—On taking office in October 1951, the new Conservative Government were faced with a difficult situation. The combined effects of the United Kingdom's own adverse balance of payments, and of heavy withdrawals of sterling balances by other countries of the sterling area, were causing the gold reserves to fall at an alarming pace; while, in spite of the down-turn in import prices, both wage rates and retail prices were rising rapidly. Some action to check the loss of gold and the internal inflation was urgent. Possible measures available were the intensification of physical controls, a further increase in saving through budget surpluses, and a return to the traditional methods — in abeyance for twenty years or more — of checking an outflow of gold through a restriction of the quantity of money and a rise in short-term interest rates.

Any attempt to secure a larger budget surplus was rendered difficult by the very high existing level of taxation and rising expenditure on defence. In fact, apart from the largely political and much criticised excess profits levy, no very serious attempt to do so was made. Direct controls were certainly intensified, especially over the volume of imports (to the great hardship of foreign exporters) and over some types of investment. But the main innovations were the raising of the Central Bank discount rate, first to $2\frac{1}{2}$ per cent and then to 4 per cent; and the 'persuasion' of the banks to convert some £500 millions of liquid assets into short-dated Government securities, thus reducing their liquid assets ratio from 39 per cent in October 1951 to 33 per cent in December and 32 per cent in January. The results of these policies were seen in rises in Treasury bill rates from $\frac{1}{2}$ per cent in September 1951, to nearly 3 per cent in June 1952, and in the yield of $2\frac{1}{2}$ per cent Consols from $3\frac{3}{4}$ per cent to nearly $4\frac{1}{2}$ per cent. Further, by June 1952, bank advances were falling rapidly and bank deposits were £100 millions lower than they had been twelve months before, bringing their ratio to national income down from 51 per cent to 46 per cent, the same figure as in 1938. At the same time, a marked check to internal demand was shown by a fall in the volume of personal consumption and by a perceptible rise in unemployment, especially in the textile industries. Most important of all, the balance of payments improved sharply and, in spite of continued withdrawals of sterling balances, the fall in the gold reserves, which was still large in the first quarter of 1952, almost ceased in the second quarter.

This dramatic change in the situation within a period of a few months was widely acclaimed as a great success for the new monetary policy. Subsequent information, however, seems to show that, while the introduction of a restrictive monetary policy was no doubt of great importance in influencing international financial opinion and checking speculative sales of sterling, its internal effects were no more than to reinforce and perhaps accelerate the operation of two other factors. The first of these was the continued fall of import prices, which improved the balance of payments not only directly through its effect on the terms of trade, but also indirectly by helping to bring to an end the accumulation of inventories. The second was a quite unforeseen and probably largely autonomous rise in personal saving (see Table IV). Ever since its decline

Table IV
SOURCES OF SAVING
(£m. at 1954 Prices)

	Persons and Unincorporated Businesses	Companies and Public Corporations	Tax, Dividend, and Interest Reserves	Public Authorities	Total Savings and Depreciation	Depreciation of Fixed Assets	Total Net Saving
1938	829	1102	66	−245	1752	1073	679
1946	469	698	−55	−540	572	(1090)	(−518)
1947	213	553	343	231	1340	(1115)	(−225)
1948	35	942	188	754	1919	1145	774
1949	(100)	(1179)	−22	830	2087	1171	916
1950	50	1244	96	758	2148	1217	931
1951	24	1060	511	627	2222	1256	966
1952	415	1386	−22	449	2228	1286	942
1953	493	1552	41	342	2428	1331	1097
1954	406	1700	172	322	2600	1388	1212
1955	596	1717	30	514	2857	1435	1422
1956	871	1675	139	453	3138	1469	1669
1957	855	1785	21	599	3260	1508	1752

at the end of the war personal saving had been very small. Its virtual disappearance had been widely ascribed to permanent causes, and especially to the great redistribution of personal incomes brought about by inflation and high income taxes. The causes for its sudden rise from £24 millions in 1951 to £415 millions in 1952 are still by no means clear. The most generally accepted explanation is that it marked the exhaustion of many of the involuntary war-time savings, the spending of which as supplies became available had hitherto been offsetting most of the positive saving, which had been carried on largely through such institutions as life insurance offices and building societies. In retrospect, it seems likely that the fall in import prices and the rise in personal saving would have brought a considerable check to the demand both for inventories and for consumption goods, even without the change in monetary policy.

(B) 1952–54 — *the Expansion of Investment.*—After the middle of 1952, the check to the internal inflation and the much improved balance-of-payments position encouraged the authorities to permit a relaxation of their restrictive monetary policies. Bank holdings of Government debt rose steadily, and, in spite of the fact that loans continued to fall for some time, bank deposits began to expand again, rising by some £200 millions, or 3 per cent, during each of the next two years. Although Bank Rate was not reduced until October 1953, the yield on Consols fell from 4½ per cent in June 1952 to just over 4 per cent in June 1953, and 3¾ per cent in June 1954. At the same time the Government relaxed their administrative restrictions on investment.

The combined effects of easier money and the relaxation of restrictions appeared first in house-building, where the Government were under an election promise to increase the number of houses built from 200,000 to 300,000 a year. The number of houses completed by public authorities, mainly for letting at subsidised rents, rose from about 175,000 a year to about 260,000 in 1953 and 1954, while privately-built houses, which had previously been kept down by licensing restrictions to under 30,000 a year, increased to 65,000 in 1953 and over 90,000 in 1954, thus enabling the Government more than to fulfil its promises (see also Table V).

TABLE V

GROSS DOMESTIC FIXED CAPITAL FORMATION

(£m. at 1954 Prices)

	Vehicles, Ships, and Aircraft			Plant and Machinery			New Dwellings			Other Buildings, etc.			Total		
	Private Sector	Public Sector	Total	Private Sector	Public Sector	Total	Private Sector	Public Sector	Total	Private Sector	Public Sector	Total	Private Sector	Public Sector	Total
1938	..	..	282	..	..	522	..	..	600	..	..	596	1403	597	2000
1946	..	..	..	..	..	..	..	..	..	..	..	..	..	..	1360
1947	..	..	400	..	..	515	..	..	449	..	..	320	..	..	1674
1948	289	75	364	492	171	663	56	369	425	187	230	417	1024	845	1869
1949	290	100	390	492	232	724	68	348	416	236	273	509	1086	953	2039
1950	236	96	332	524	270	794	63	345	408	265	300	565	1088	1011	2099
1951	218	80	298	504	355	859	62	337	399	230	317	547	1014	1089	2103
1952	199	66	265	440	377	817	97	380	477	212	344	556	948	1167	2115
1953	233	78	311	424	404	828	169	454	623	216	368	584	1042	1304	2346
1954	260	73	333	489	431	920	226	419	645	270	374	644	1245	1297	2542
1955	289	89	378	558	435	993	251	333	584	336	374	710	1434	1231	2665
1956	304	112	416	599	421	1020	267	301	568	400	408	808	1570	1242	2812
1957	320	136	456	673	415	1088	266	280	546	401	453	854	1660	1284	2944

The housing boom of 1953–54 brought with it a period both of prosperity and of relative stability. After the check to demand in 1952, the rate of rise in national money income declined from 8½ per cent between 1951 and 1952 to under 7 per cent from 1952 to 1953. At the same time, the recovery in production and the improving terms of trade brought the rate of rise of *real* national income up to 5 per cent so that the rise of prices slowed down from 9 per cent in 1951 and 7 per cent in 1952 to barely 2 per cent in 1953. In fact, from March 1953 to June 1954, the level of retail prices was almost stationary. In spite of the fall in the average annual budget surplus from £600 millions in 1948–51 to £300 millions in 1952–54, and of the rise in house-building, the much higher level of personal saving and the low rate of inventory accumulation kept total domestic investment well within the limits of total saving, and the balance-of-payments surplus remained reasonably adequate (see Table VI).

About the middle of 1954, just after Bank Rate had been reduced to 3 per cent, signs began to appear that the period of stability was coming to a close. Early in 1953 the Government had become concerned that the rise in fixed investment was confined to house-building, and that little increase was occurring in industrial and commercial investment. Steps were therefore taken, by tax concessions and the removal of restrictions, to encourage investment in assets other than houses. For many months these measures seemed ineffective. But from the middle of 1954 industrial and commercial investment began to expand rapidly; and by the end of 1954 it was clear that total investment was again beginning to outrun the level of saving and that inflationary pressure, which had been dormant for over a year, was beginning to appear again. In the second half of 1954 retail prices, which had been stationary since April 1953, rose by over 2 per cent, while the stock exchange recovery quickened toward a boom. After the beginning of 1955 a marked rise in inventory accumulation, which had been very small during the past three years, reinforced the rapidly rising level of domestic fixed investment (see Table V and VI). Imports increased sharply; the balance of payments on income account became unfavourable; and the gold reserve began to fall.

TABLE VI
SOURCES AND USES OF INVESTIBLE FUNDS
(£m. at 1954 Prices)

	Investible Funds				Gross Domestic Fixed Capital Formation	Surplus Available for Stock Accumulation and Foreign Investment	Use of Surplus	
	Gross Saving	Capital Grants and Transfers from Abroad	Errors and Omissions	Total Investible Funds			Physical Increase in Stocks	Net Foreign Investment
1938	1752	—	—	1752	2000	− 248	—	− 248
1946	572	228	—	800	1360	− 560	− 79	− 481
1947	1340	221	—	1561	1674	− 113	+ 480	− 593
1948	1919	303	+ 75	2297	1869	+ 428	+ 235	+ 193
1949	2087	235	+ 1	2323	2039	+ 284	+ 35	+ 249
1950	2148	205	+ 60	2413	2099	+ 314	− 240	+ 554
1951	2222	87	+ 20	2329	2103	+ 226	+ 565	− 339
1952	2228	35	+ 25	2288	2115	+ 173	+ 40	+ 133
1953	2428	27	+ 149	2604	2346	+ 258	+ 130	+ 128
1954	2600	11	+ 127	2738	2542	+ 196	+ 56	+ 140
1955	2857	13	− 79	2791	2665	+ 126	+ 288	− 162
1956	3138	13	+ 101	3252	2812	+ 440	+ 261	+ 179
1957	3260	4	+ 99	3363	2944	+ 419	+ 231	+ 188

(C) 1955–58 — *the Second Period of Tight Money.*—Encouraged by its apparent success in 1952, the Government placed the whole responsibility of checking the renewed inflation on a purely monetary policy. At the end of January 1955, Bank Rate was raised from 3 per cent to 3½ per cent, and at the end of February to 4½ per cent. At the same time, successful efforts were made to keep down issues of Treasury bills by sales of securities. Security sales, both by the Treasury and by the banks, brought a sharp rise in long-term rates, and the yield on 2½ per cent Consols rose from rather over 3½ per cent in October 1954 to nearly 4¼ per cent in June 1955. No doubt remembering 1952, the Government was so confident of its power to check inflation by purely monetary means that it made substantial reductions in taxation in its April budget, taking 6d. off the income-tax rate.

The conditions of 1955, however, were very different from those in 1952. Import prices, instead of falling, were rising; the country was feeling the reaction from several years of under-stocking; and plans for increased industrial and commercial investment were still only beginning to take effect. In spite, therefore, of the Government's technical success in squeezing the liquidity of the banks, and in checking, in July, the rise in prices of equity securities, internal demand, wage rates and retail prices continued to rise rapidly. Meanwhile, the level of imports remained high and gold reserves fell at an increasing rate. In October the Government introduced an emergency budget, increasing the purchase (sales) tax, and announcing drastic restrictions on instalment sales finance, the discontinuation of further housing subsidies, and reductions in investment by public authorities. In February 1956, Bank Rate was raised to 5½ per cent.

The year 1956 saw a new development almost as surprising as that of 1952. Personal saving, which in 1955 had already shown an appreciable rise above the 1952–54 level, took a new upward leap to over twice its 1954 total (see Table IV). A minor part of the rise can be attributed to the restrictions on instalment selling. Whether the remainder can be attributed to the direct effect of higher interest rates, or to the slight rise in unemployment and uncertainty about the stability of future incomes, remains a matter of conjecture. Whatever the cause,

F

the higher level of personal saving, together with an increase in the budget surplus from an average of £300 millions in 1952–54 to one of over £450 millions in 1955 and 1956, brought a major improvement in the economic situation. Although, in spite of higher interest rates, industrial and commercial fixed investment continued to rise rapidly, while house-building fell only slightly, the rise in total saving was large enough to provide a much larger margin for other forms of investment, such as inventory accumulation and foreign investment (see Table VI). In spite, therefore, of a continued high level of inventory accumulation, an adverse balance of payments of £166 millions in 1955 was converted into a favourable one of £187 millions in 1956. This balance, while still smaller than that which the weakness on international capital account would have made desirable, would probably have been large enough to insure the stability of sterling but for the Suez crisis. This gave rise to heavy speculative sales of sterling and was prevented from having a disastrous effect on an already weak capital position only by a loan of £200 millions from the International Monetary Fund. In spite, therefore, of the rise in saving and the improvement in the underlying economic position, no relaxation of monetary restriction was possible. By the end of 1956 the yield on 2½ per cent Consols had almost reached 5 per cent.

In the early months of 1957 the Government took advantage of an improvement in market sentiment to undertake a vigorous funding policy, which in February enabled Bank Rate to be reduced to 5 per cent without causing much change in long-term money rates. Personal and total saving continued to rise about as fast as fixed investment; but a continued rise in inventories prevented any appreciable rise in the balance-of-payments surplus.

In the late summer, fresh speculative sales of sterling, perhaps partly due to expectations of a revaluation of the German mark, together with heavy withdrawals of sterling balances by India, caused further heavy outflows of gold and a new sterling crisis. This time the Government overcame its dislike of high short-term interest rates sufficiently to allow Bank Rate to be raised to the crisis level of 7 per cent. At the same time the banks were asked not to allow their total advances to rise further for any purpose.

The drastic rise in Bank Rate marked the turning of the tide. Since then, the decline in speculative pressure has allowed the great improvement in the internal economic position to show its effects. After September 1957, the tightness of money and the rise in long-term rates, with the yield on $2\frac{1}{2}$ per cent Consols momentarily reaching almost $5\frac{1}{2}$ per cent, at last checked the upward surge of domestic fixed investment. At the same time the rise in inventories seems to have slowed down and the margin of savings available for overseas investment has almost certainly increased further. Even without the sharp fall in prices of imports during 1958, there would probably have been a favourable balance of payments in 1958 of the order of £300 millions, which is about the level thought necessary to ensure the long-term stability of sterling.

The fall in import prices is both a help and a source of difficulty. On the one hand it has raised the real national income, has facilitated the task of checking the internal inflation and has perhaps tended to make the balance of payments more favourable. On the other hand, it makes it more difficult to sell exports and creates the danger that productive capacity, so painfully diverted from serving the internal demand, may run to waste. So far, however, overseas countries have been able to maintain their imports fairly well, partly by drawing down their sterling balances, and the favourable balance of payments for the first half of 1958 has certainly shown a very large increase.

Meanwhile, the internal inflationary pressure has markedly declined. In spite of trade union pressure, the index of wage rates has risen by barely 2 per cent over the past twelve months, as compared with nearly 5 per cent during the previous year. The rise in retail prices has slowed down in recent months and is now believed to have come to an end. Unemployment, though still low by any absolute standard, is nearly twice as high as in most post-war years. Above all, it would seem that the last vestiges of concealed inflation have now been squeezed out of the British economy. The last of the physical controls have been abandoned; and it is doubtful if such financial controls as remain are now having any important effect. Bank deposits are scarcely larger than they were four years ago, while national money income has risen by over 20 per cent.

Hence the ratio of deposits to national income has fallen to only 35 per cent, by far the lowest figure recorded since 1920.

In view of the improved balance of payments and the reduction in inflationary pressure, the Government have felt justified in taking cautious steps to permit some re-expansion of home demand. Since March 1958, Bank Rate has been reduced in three steps from 7 per cent to 5 per cent (though funding policy seems still to be carried out with some vigour, and the yield on 2½ per cent Consols is still about 5 per cent) and the direct restriction on bank advances has been withdrawn. With bank deposits at their present low level in relation to national income, it will probably be safe — and indeed necessary, if a fall in output is to be avoided — to allow them to rise henceforward at least in proportion to productive capacity, that is to say, by something like 3 per cent or £200 millions a year. If their rise over the coming year is no greater than this, there is good reason to hope that prices can be stabilised at about their present level.

The post-war British inflation is over. In the absence of a new inflation in the world as a whole, it will need deliberate action by the British Government to restart it.

CHAPTER 9

BRITAIN'S FOREIGN INVESTMENTS:
THE POST-WAR RECORD [1]

THE term 'foreign investments' has two possible meanings. In one sense it means the amount of capital exported during the period, in the other the changes in the value of the foreign assets owned by U.K. residents. The two senses are, of course, connected, for the greater the exports of capital have been in the past, the larger the stock of investments is likely to be to-day. But the present stock of foreign investments is very far from being a mere cumulative total of past capital exports. Not only may foreign investments be acquired with capital borrowed abroad, but earlier capital exports may have been lost as the result of defaults, expropriations, or disappointed hopes of profit. Alternatively, they may have been augmented as the result of good fortune, wise management or the ploughing back abroad of profits earned abroad (in so far as they are not included in the balance-of-payments figures). In addition, the market values of foreign investments may change, not as the result of any change in yield, but merely in consequence of changes in rates of interest ruling in home markets. Thus the current value of a country's foreign investments may well fall, at least for a time, even though it continues to export capital; while conversely it may rise substantially even though current exports of capital are small or even negative. This article will examine the position of the United Kingdom both as an exporter of capital and as an owner of foreign investments.

I

THE UNITED KINGDOM AS AN EXPORTER OF CAPITAL

Since the war, the United Kingdom's record as an exporter of capital has been perhaps the most disappointing part of its history. In spite of the fact that real national income is to-day

---

[1] Published in *Lloyds Bank Review*, July 1956.

probably more than 25 per cent above the pre-war level and probably 70 per cent higher than in 1913, British capital exports, which in 1913 were the equivalent of about £800 millions at to-day's prices, have in the last three years averaged only some £60 millions a year, while over the whole of the post-war period they have been substantially negative. The failure of Britain to maintain since the war a margin of saving over domestic investment sufficient to supply out of her own resources more than a fraction of the capital needs even of those countries in the Commonwealth which are accustomed to look

TABLE I

SOURCES OF FUNDS INVESTED BY THE UNITED KINGDOM OUTSIDE THE DOLLAR AREA

	1946–1949	1950	1951	1952	1950–1952	1953	1954	1955	1953–1955	T 1
United Kingdom Balance of Payments on Current Account :	£m.	£m.	£m.	£m.	£m.	£m.	£m.	£m.	£m.	
Balance of Payments on Income Account	−709	300	−407	126	19	75	155	−147	83	−
Defence Aid	—	—	4	121	125	102	50	44	196	
Total	−709	300	−403	247	144	177	205	−103	279	−
Imports of Capital from Dollar Area :										
Grants	388	239	54	—	293	—	—	—	—	
Increases in Sterling Balances	−3	48	−41	−4	3	28	35	−39	24	
Other Capital Imports	1278	118	−34	40	124	3	38	58	99	1
Total	1663	405	−21	36	420	31	73	19	123	2
*Withdrawals from Gold and Dollar Reserves : * (addition −)*	156	−575	344	175	−56	−240	−87	229	−98	
Total Invested Outside Dollar Area	1110	130	−80	458	508	−32	191	145	304	1

* In terms of *dollars*, the changes in our gold and dollar reserves have been as follows :

$m.	$m.
1946–49, fell by 788	1953–55, rose by 274
1950–52, rose by 158	1946–55, fell by 356

Sources : *U.K. Balance of Payments White Papers* (Cmd. 8976, 9430, and 9731).

to her for finance is perhaps the most important cause of her decline as a world power.

While, however, the United Kingdom has been able to spare little of its own resources for investment abroad, it has hitherto been able partially to fill the gap left by its own inadequacy by a substantial re-export trade in imported capital. The most important source of this imported capital has been the dollar area, mainly the United States and, to a smaller extent, Canada. The extent of these imports of capital is shown in Table I. In this the ten post-war years are divided into three periods : the first is the period of reconstruction, from 1946 to 1949, ending with the devaluation of sterling ; the second, from 1950 to 1952, covers the period of the Korean war ; while the third, from 1953 to 1955, covers a period of 'normality' which offers no particular excuses for inadequacy. In the first of these three periods the United Kingdom was a heavy net importer of capital, in spite of substantial withdrawals from its exiguous gold reserves, as the result of the very large adverse balances of payments in 1946 and 1947. In the second period this adverse balance was converted into a favourable balance of payments of £144 millions, of which £56 millions were used to replenish the gold reserve, leaving an average of less than £30 millions a year for foreign investment. In the third period the aggregate favourable balance of £279 millions left, after adding £98 millions to the gold reserves, only £60 millions a year to finance the export of capital.

IMPORTS OF CAPITAL FROM THE DOLLAR AREA

Table I also makes clear how it was that the United Kingdom, in spite of the small size of its own favourable balance, has been able to make quite large amounts of capital available to the non-dollar world. In the first period, from 1946 to 1949, no less than £1663 millions were imported from the dollar area, £388 millions as gifts and £1275 millions by way of loans. This enabled the United Kingdom not only to meet its own adverse balance but to provide over £1100 millions of capital for the rest of the non-dollar world. After 1949, with the exhaustion of the dollar loans raised in 1946 and the tapering off of Marshall Aid, imports of capital from the dollar area rapidly declined, to £420 millions in 1950–52 and £123 millions, presumably from non-governmental sources, in 1953–1955. This rapid fall in capital imports from the dollar area much more than offset the slow improvement in the United Kingdom's own balance of payments, and our exports of capital to the non-dollar world fell rapidly from £1110 millions in 1946–49 to £508 millions in 1950–52 and £304 millions in 1953–55.

While the grants and loans made by the United States to Britain between 1946 and 1951 were not intended to provide the United Kingdom with resources to invest abroad, there can be little doubt that the fact that Britain was thus enabled to export substantial quantities of capital to the rest of the world was an important factor in promoting world economic recovery. It is probably a pity that means could not have been found to continue the process, for the United Kingdom has all the qualifications for a successful exporter of capital — specialised institutions, financial connections, long experience : all the qualifications, that is, except one, the availability of adequate resources to invest. If it had been possible for the United States to have continued to supply this sole deficiency, the results might in the long run have proved beneficial both for the ultimate suppliers of the capital and for its ultimate users.

DISTRIBUTION OF UNITED KINGDOM CAPITAL EXPORTS

The way in which the shrinking outflow of capital from the United Kingdom has been distributed to the non-dollar world is shown in Tables II to IV. In the official statistics the figures are classified primarily according to the form of investment and only secondarily by area. The three main classifications are grants on capital account (to be distinguished from grants on income account, such as Defence Aid and the grants made by the United Kingdom to various colonies) ; net repayments of the very large sterling balances held by foreign banks, governments and others in London ; and 'other capital exports', a residual item which represents the net balance of an enormous number of individual capital transactions in both directions, and incidentally contains all the errors and omissions from the other accounts, current as well as capital. In the tables given

TABLE II

U.K. CAPITAL EXPORTS TO NON-DOLLAR, NON-STERLING COUNTRIES

	1946–1949	1950	1951	1952	1950–1952	1953	1954	1955	1953–1955	Total 1946–1955
	£m.	£m.	£m.	£m.	£m.	£m.	£m.	£m.	£m.	£m.
Other Western Hemisphere Countries:										
Grants	15	2	11	—	13	—	—	—	—	28
Increases in Sterling Balances	83	35	−12	51	74	−34	32	−1	−3	154
Other Capital Exports	−179	−34	−30	5	−59	−19	−47	3	−63	−301
Total	−81	3	−31	56	28	−53	−15	2	−66	−119
E.E.C. Countries:										
Grants	86	96	—	—	96	—	—	—	—	182
Increases in Sterling Balances [1]—										
E.P.U.	—	80	−246	−53	−219	21	78	−1	98	−121
Other	−11	72	−51	112	133	−13	−18	33	2	124
Other Capital Exports	168	15	79	25	119	47	7	25	79	366
Total	243	263	−218	84	129	55	67	57	179	551
Other Non-Sterling Countries:										
Grants	11	1	—	—	1	—	—	—	—	12
Increases in Sterling Balances [1]	108	22	−22	123	123	27	−60	15	−18	213
Other Capital Exports	88	41	71	−4	108	19	51	−8	62	258
Total	207	64	49	119	232	46	−9	7	44	483
Total Non-Dollar, Non-Sterling Area:										
Grants	112	99	11	—	110	—	—	—	—	222
Increases in Sterling Balances [1]—										
E.P.U.	—	80	−246	−53	−219	21	78	−1	98	−121
Other	180	129	−85	286	330	−20	−46	47	−19	491
Other Capital Exports	77	22	120	26	168	47	11	20	78	323
Total	369	330	−200	259	389	48	43	66	157	915

[1] Increase −

Sources: As for Table I.

here the order of classification is reversed, the main classification being by area and the sub-classification by form of investment. This change brings to light certain features which are not immediately obvious in the official presentation. The situation revealed and presented in Tables II to IV is briefly as follows. During the first four post-war years, of the £1110 millions of capital exported to the non-dollar world, £757 millions, or more than two-thirds, went to the sterling area. After 1949, however, there was a striking change. Of the £812 millions of capital exported during the next six years, no less than £546 millions, or just about two-thirds, went to

TABLE III

U.K. CAPITAL EXPORTS THROUGH NON-TERRITORIAL ORGANIZATIONS

	1946–1949	1950	1951	1952	1950–1952	1953	1954	1955	1953–1955	T...
	£m.	£m.	£m.	£m.	£m.	£m.	£m.	£m.	£m.	£
Decreases in Sterling Balances [1]—	− 576	− 1	11	− 1	9	56	35	7	98	−
Other Capital Exports	560	1	4	3	8	− 2	5	− 6	− 3	
Total	− 16	—	15	2	17	54	40	1	95	

[1] Increase −

Sources: As for Table I.

non-sterling countries, while a further £112 millions was exported through the agencies of the International Bank and the International Monetary Fund, no doubt also largely to non-sterling countries, leaving only £154 millions, or less than 20 per cent, for the sterling area.

The proportion of capital exports going to the non-sterling area in 1946–49 would almost certainly have been a good deal higher if it had not been for the large import of capital from Argentina in 1948 as the result of the sale of the Argentine railways. For the rest, it seems probable that, apart from the grants, made partly to U.N.R.R.A. and partly as a concomitant of Marshall Aid, exports of capital to non-sterling countries have been largely involuntary, occurring as the result of realisations by foreigners of sterling assets rather than of positive

British investment. This was certainly true of the withdrawals from foreign-owned sterling balances, where repayments of £491 millions over the ten years greatly exceeded the sterling debt of £121 millions incurred to the European Payments Union, and was probably also true of much of the £323 millions of 'other capital exports'.

UNITED KINGDOM CAPITAL EXPORTS TO THE STERLING AREA

While the share of total capital exports which has gone to the sterling area since 1949 has been very small, its share of 'other capital exports', which include all exports of long-term capital, has been quite large, with £775 millions out of a total of £1026 millions. This has been possible only because the sterling area as a whole, so far from running down its sterling balances, has increased them over the six years by no less than £621 millions, thus collectively providing on short-term the great bulk of the capital it has borrowed on long-term.

It is further possible to ascertain from the United Kingdom Balance of Payments White Papers that more than the whole of this increase in sterling balances came from the colonies, whose balances rose by about £650 millions (the transfer of Northern Rhodesia and Nyasaland out of the category of colonies during the period makes the exact figure uncertain), while the combined sterling balances of the non-colonial sterling area probably fell slightly. In addition, the colonies seem to have bought some £90 millions of dominion and colonial sterling securities on the London market, which are included in their own totals of their sterling balances, though not in those of the United Kingdom.

THE COLONIAL STERLING BALANCES

The two main causes of the remarkable increases in the colonial sterling balances during the past six years seem to have been, on the one hand, the large rises in the real, and still more in the money, incomes of those colonies which have enjoyed increased prices for their main exports ; and, on the other, the absence of local capital markets in which the swelling official

162   *Studies in an Inflationary Economy*

TABLE IV
U.K. CAPITAL EXPORTS TO STERLING AREA

	1946–1949	1950	1951	1952	1950–1952	1953	1954	1955	1953–1955
	£m.	£m.	£m.	£m.	£m.	£m.	£m.	£m.	£m.
Colonial Territories:[1]									
Decreases in Sterling Balances *	(−110)	(−141)	−173	−100	(−414)	−55	−121	−61	−237
Decreases in Colonial Holdings of Non-U.K. Sterling Obligations *	n.a.	(−10)	(−26)	−22	(−58)	−18	−14	1	−31
Other Capital Exports	n.a.	(34)	(37)	92	(163)	111	113	65	289
Total	n.a.	(−117)	(−162)	−30	(−309)	38	−22	5	21
Non-Colonial Sterling Area:									
Grants	−46	—	—	—	—	—	—	—	—
Decreases in Sterling Balances *	(219)	(−240)	(114)	212	(86)	−197	6	135	−56
Other Capital Exports	n.a.	(157)	(153)	15	(325)	25	124	−62	87
Total	n.a.	(−83)	(267)	227	(411)	−172	130	73	31
Total Sterling Area:									
Grants	−46	—	—	—	—	—	—	—	—
Decreases in Sterling Balances *	109	−381	−59	112	−328	−252	−115	74	−293
Decreases in Colonial Holdings of Non-U.K. Sterling Obligations * } 694 {		(−10)	(−26)	−22	(−58)	−18	−14	1	−31
Other Capital Exports		(191)	(190)	107	(488)	136	237	3	376
Total	757	−200	105	197	102	−134	108	78	52

Figures in brackets are partly estimated.   * Increase − ; n.a.—not available.
[1] Excluding Hong Kong, Northern Rhodesia, and Nyasaland throughout.
Sources: *U.K. Balance of Payments White Papers* (Cmd. 8976, 9430, and 9731), *I randum on the Sterling Assets of the British Colonies* (Colonial No. 298, 1953), *Colonial Annual Reports on the Colonial Territories* (Cmd. 9169, 9489, and 9769).

and other reserve funds could be invested with safety and liquidity. These funds have therefore been invested very largely in London. Colonial Office estimates of the composition of these funds at the end of each of the past four years are shown in Table V.

TABLE V

OWNERSHIP OF COLONIAL STERLING BALANCES [1]

End of	1952	1953	1954	1955	Increase 1952–55
	£m.	£m.	£m.	£m.	£m.
Currency Board Holdings and Currency Funds with Crown Agents	363	372	395	439	76
Other Funds with Crown Agents—					
Special [2]	189	201	232	238	49
General [3]	235	266	322	347	112
Miscellaneous Known Official Funds [4]	144	144	139	143	− 1
Funds with U.K. Banks	240	268	301	279	39
Total	1171	1251	1389	1446	275

[1] *Including* Hong Kong, *excluding* Northern Rhodesia and Nyasaland.
[2] Funds of Colonial Governments and other public bodies held under statute or earmarked for special purposes (*e.g.* sinking, savings banks, renewals, and pension funds).
[3] Other Funds of Colonial Governments and other public bodies (*e.g.* general revenue balances, invested surpluses and general purpose reserve funds).
[4] Uganda Price Assistance Funds, sterling securities of West African Marketing Boards, etc.

Sources : *Colonial Office Annual Reports on the Colonial Territories* (Cmd. 9489 and 9769).

EXPORTS OF CAPITAL TO THE COLONIES

The fact that the colonies have greatly increased their sterling balances in London since 1949 does not in itself prove that they have been net exporters of capital to the United Kingdom, for their exports of capital in the form of increasing sterling balances could have been more than offset by their imports of capital in other forms. No information is available in the United Kingdom balance-of-payments statistics which would enable us to separate 'other capital exports' to the colonies from those to the rest of the sterling area. In the various reports issued by the Colonial Office, however, information is provided on the basis of which, by making some reasonably probable assumptions, it is possible to arrive at estimates of 'other capital exports' to the colonies for the years since 1949. These estimates must, however, exclude Hong Kong, whose balance of payments still seems to defy the official statisticians; Hong Kong is therefore included with the non-colonial sterling area. Further, as mentioned earlier, the Colonial Office figures of colonial sterling balances include holdings of colonial and dominion sterling obligations, while the United Kingdom figures cover only United Kingdom obligations. By comparing the two sets of figures it is possible to obtain estimates of colonial holdings of dominion and colonial sterling obligations. Since these were presumably purchased on the London market, they have been included in Table IV as a separate item. Some difficulty has been caused by the omission of Northern Rhodesia and Nyasaland from the colonial totals after 1951, and this has necessitated a small degree of estimation in the figures for 1950 and 1951. It should also be noted that the estimates of capital exports to the colonies exclude a substantial amount of grants made to various colonies by the United Kingdom Government on income account. These totalled about £140 millions in the six years from 1950 to 1955.

The start of our calculations is the Colonial Office's estimate of the collective balance of payments on income account of the colonies as a whole. Since a favourable balance of payments on income account is the same as an export of capital, and an unfavourable balance as an import of capital, we have estimates of the aggregate import or export of capital to or from the colonies. If we make the further assumption, which may not be very far from the truth, that (with the exception of the £7 millions loan made by the International Bank in 1955 to the East Africa High Commission) all colonial capital transactions are with the United Kingdom, it is possible to obtain, by subtraction, estimates of 'other capital exports' from the United Kingdom to the colonies. By then subtracting these totals from those of the whole sterling area, we obtain estimates of total and 'other' capital exports to the non-colonial sterling area.

These estimates are naturally subject to a very wide margin of error; it can only be hoped that they are sufficiently near the truth for their general implications not to be seriously mis-leading. In so far as they can be relied on, they indicate that, whereas in 1950–52, when prices of many colonial exports were very high, the colonies were large net exporters of capital to, and the rest of the sterling area large net importers of capital from, the United Kingdom, during the last three years 'other capital exports' to the colonies have been at least as large as the increase in their sterling balances. Indeed the figures (though they cannot be relied upon within such fine limits) indicate that the colonies were small importers of capital on balance. It is probably very largely as the result of this change that exports of capital to the rest of the sterling area fell sharply to a negligible figure, and that an acute shortage of capital has developed in several countries in spite of efforts to import capital from elsewhere.

COLONIAL CAPITAL TRANSFERS BY AREAS

In addition to its estimates for the colonies as a whole, the Colonial Office gives similar figures for five separate areas — West Africa, East Africa (including Aden), the West Indies, the Malayan Area, and Other Territories (excluding Hong Kong) — from which are derived the estimates shown in Table VI. Of these five areas, only two — West Africa and Malaya — seem at any time to have been substantial exporters of capital. The largest importer of capital during the past three years has been East Africa, where the rise in 'other capital exports' is attributed mainly to the cost of constructing the new oil refinery at Aden, which is included for statistical pur-poses in East Africa. The exports of capital from Malaya, which occurred mainly in the Korean war period, have clearly been greatly influenced by the price of rubber, while in West Africa a similarly dominant rôle is played by the price of cocoa.

The position of the United Kingdom as an exporter of capital to the non-dollar world has thus passed through three phases during the past ten years. In the first, up to 1949, it was able to act as an intermediary for passing on a large pro-portion of the grants and loans received from the United States, mainly to the sterling area and, it may be surmised, particularly

to the non-colonial sterling area.   In the second, up to the end
of 1952, it was still able to act as an intermediary, though on a
smaller scale, by passing the imports of capital received from

TABLE VI

U.K. CAPITAL EXPORTS TO COLONIAL TERRITORIES [1]
BY AREAS

	1950	1951	1952	1950–1952	1953	1954	1955	19 1ç
	£m.	£m.	£m.	£m.	£m.	£m.	£m.	£
West Africa:								
Decrease in Sterling Balances [2] *	− 56	− 77	− 29	− 162	− 38	− 88	− 19	− »
Other Capital Exports	14	27	− 3	38	10	20	10	
Total	− 42	− 50	− 32	− 124	− 28	− 68	− 9	− »
East Africa (including Aden):								
Decrease in Sterling Balances [2] *	(− 29)	(− 28)	(− 37)	(− 94)	− 11	3	20	
Other Capital Exports	(35)	(23)	(47)	(105)	64	44	20	»
Total	(6)	(− 5)	10	(11)	53	47	40	»
West Indies:								
Decrease in Sterling Balances [2] *	− 11	− 3	− 9	− 23	− 17	− 16	4	−
Other Capital Exports	14	16	25	55	16	19	18	
Total	3	13	16	32	− 1	3	22	−
Malayan Area:								
Decrease in Sterling Balances [2] *	− 57	− 88	− 31	− 176	1	− 23	− 59	−
Other Capital Exports	− 30	− 34	12	− 52	16	24	16	
Total	− 87	− 122	− 19	− 228	17	1	− 43	−
Other Territories:								
Decrease in Sterling Balances [2] *	2	− 3	− 16	− 17	− 8	− 11	− 6	−
Other Capital Exports	1	5	11	17	5	6	1	
Total	3	2	− 5	—	− 3	− 5	− 5	−

Figures in brackets are partly estimated.   * Increase −
[1] Excluding Hong Kong, Northern Rhodesia, and Nyasaland.
[2] Including holdings of non-U.K. sterling obligations.
Sources : As for Table IV.

the colonies in the form of rapidly rising sterling balances,
partly back to the colonies in the form of long-term investments, but mainly to the non-colonial sterling area.   In the

third period, now ending, the rise in colonial sterling balances has been barely sufficient to cover long-term investment in the colonies, including Aden.   It seems probable that we are now entering upon a fourth period, in which the rise in colonial sterling balances may slow down or cease altogether, and may provide little or nothing towards the export of long-term capital even to the colonies.

There seem to be two main reasons why we should expect the rise in colonial sterling balances to slow down, or even be reversed, in the near future.   One is the fall in prices which has recently occurred in the main export products of the two areas whose sterling balances have risen most in the past — Malaya and West Africa.   The other is that it is especially in these areas that the movement towards self-government is proceeding most rapidly.   As colonies achieve self-government, it is reasonable to expect that resources which formerly went to swell the London balances will be increasingly diverted to local uses, either because they no longer reach the various funds at all or because the funds will be encouraged to invest at home, even though in a less liquid form, rather than in London. Indeed, it may well be that there will be a tendency to draw upon the London balances to finance local investment rather than to increase them further.   The United Kingdom will therefore be unable to rely on this source for finance for other countries, including both the colonies which are not yet self-governing and the rest of the sterling area.

With the disappearance of its two major sources of imported capital, the United Kingdom will henceforward be obliged to rely much more completely on its own resources to provide capital for export.   If it is to continue to replenish its inadequate gold reserves, to supply finance for the remaining colonies and for the rest of the sterling area, and to meet the continued realisation of sterling assets by the non-sterling world, it will need a very much larger surplus in its balance of payments on income account than it has managed to achieve at any time since the war — or indeed since 1913.   The Government has put the necessary annual surplus at from £300 to £350 millions, or say £1000 millions over the next three years.   To quadruple the surplus achieved between 1953 and 1955 will be no easy task.

II
THE UNITED KINGDOM AS AN OWNER OF FOREIGN INVESTMENTS

A partial light is thrown on changes in the United Kingdom's foreign investments in the estimates, published by the Bank of England, of *United Kingdom Overseas Investments*. These estimates, first published in 1950 for the years 1938 to 1948, and subsequently annually, provide a continuation of those published by Lord Kindersley in the *Economic Journal* before the war. They cover that part of the country's overseas investments which consists of the overseas investments of U.K. residents through the medium of securities quoted on, unofficially dealt in, or otherwise known to the London Stock Exchange, and provide estimates not only of the nominal values of the securities held at the end of each year, but also of the interest and dividends received from them during the year, the nominal values of the securities bought, sold, or redeemed, and the cash paid or received for them by British residents. The securities are classified by type of security, by type of industry, and by countries. These elaborate and detailed estimates obviously take a long time to make, for the latest figures available, published in 1955, refer only to 1953.

It is difficult to say how large a proportion of total British foreign investments is covered by these figures. The coverage is obviously less wide than that covered by the item 'interest, profits and dividends' received from overseas given in the balance-of-payments White Papers, which totalled £285 millions in 1953, as compared with the £160 millions in the Bank of England estimates. The balance-of-payments figures, however, probably include amounts not ultimately due to British residents, which are passed on to overseas owners and appear also in the payments figures, while the Bank of England estimates are net. It is probable, therefore, that these estimates cover the greater part — perhaps two-thirds or more — of the country's total overseas assets. If so, they make it clear that British residents have done a good deal better since the war as owners of overseas assets than they have as suppliers of foreign capital.

SALES AND PURCHASES OF OVERSEAS SECURITIES

During the war, the United Kingdom had to realise roughly a third of its total holdings of overseas securities, the cash proceeds of which amounted to about £950 millions. The process of selling out continued for several years after the war, and during the period 1946–49 net sales and redemptions realised a further £290 millions, largely from the sale and re-payment of securities in Argentina and other countries in South America, but also in Canada, Australia, and New Zealand. It was not until the period 1950–52 that the net realisations ceased, and not until 1953 that there was any appreciable net new investment in overseas securities.

The classification by countries and areas in the Bank of England's estimates is different from that in the balance-of-payments statistics, but in Table VII an attempt has been made to regroup them in a form which would make them comparable

TABLE VII

UNITED KINGDOM OVERSEAS INVESTMENTS
NET CASH RECEIPTS OR PAYMENTS FROM THE SALE,
REDEMPTION, OR PURCHASE OF OVERSEAS SECURITIES
(U.K. Receipts −, U.K. Payments +)

	1939–1945	1946–1949	1950–1952	1953	Total 1946–1953
	£m.	£m.	£m.	£m.	£m.
Dollar Area	− 398	− 66	− 4	+ 18	− 52
Other Non - Sterling Area :					
Other Western Hemisphere	− 59	− 188	− 43	− 8	− 239
O.E.E.C. Countries	− 6	− 8	—	− 1	− 9
Other	− 20	− 14	− 3	− 3	− 20
Total	− 85	− 210	− 46	− 12	− 268
Sterling Area :					
Colonies	− 4	+ 7	+ 30	+ 9	+ 46
Other	− 470	− 50	+ 18	+ 37	+ 5
Total	− 474	− 43	+ 48	+ 46	+ 51
Unclassifiable	+ 3	+ 29	+ 10	+ 19	+ 58
Grand Total	− 954	− 290	+ 8	+ 71	− 211

with the estimates of imports and exports of capital given in Tables I to IV. This comparison makes it clear that, with the exception of 'Other Western Hemisphere' countries, especially in 1946–49, and sterling area countries other than the colonies in 1953, the cash received or paid as the result of the purchase, sale, or redemption of the securities of overseas public authorities and of companies operating overseas represented only a very minor part of the collection of transactions called in Tables I to IV 'Other Capital Imports' and 'Other Capital Exports'.

INCOME FROM FOREIGN INVESTMENTS

The effect on annual income of the heavy sales of overseas securities during the war is shown in Table VIII. Income from fixed interest securities fell between 1938 and 1945 by £28 millions, from £77 millions to £49 millions, while dividends on shares fell by £19 millions, from £78 millions to £59 millions. The fall in fixed interest receipts continued in the following

TABLE VIII

UNITED KINGDOM INCOME FROM OVERSEAS INVESTMENTS

	1938	1945	1949	1952	1953
	£m.	£m.	£m.	£m.	£m.
Interest on Government and Municipal Loans:					
Commonwealth	44	27	18	17	17
Other	11	5	3	4	11
	55	32	21	21	28
Interest on Company Loans:					
Commonwealth	12	7	5	4	4
Other	10	10	2	3	5
	22	17	7	7	9
Total Loan Interest	77	49	28	28	37
Dividends on Shares:					
Commonwealth	46	33	52	71	69
Other	32	26	36	55	54
Total Dividends	78	59	88	126	123
Total Income from Overseas Investments	155	108	116	154	160

years, the income from them falling to £28 millions in 1949, remaining at that level in 1952, and recovering to £37 millions only in 1953 as the result of the resumption of interest payments by Germany and Japan. Share dividends, on the other hand, rose continuously, reaching £88 millions in 1949 and £126 millions in 1952, and though they fell back slightly in 1953, it seems probable that the rise has since been resumed. Thus in spite of net sales and redemptions realising nearly £1200 millions between 1939 and 1953, total income from overseas securities had by 1953 more than recovered its 1938 level. It was, however, very differently constituted, for whereas in 1938 almost exactly half consisted of interest on loans, either to public authorities or to companies, by 1952 the proportion derived from loans was under 20 per cent of the total, rising again to 23 per cent in 1953 but probably falling again since. The country's much greater dependence for its foreign investment income on dividends on shares provides it with a considerable hedge against further losses of real income in case of a further rise in world prices, but renders its balance of payments even more vulnerable to the effects of a world depression, especially since more than half its total dividends comes from oil, mines (other than gold), and plantation companies.

CAPITAL VALUES OF OVERSEAS SECURITIES

The Bank of England does not attempt to make any estimates of the market values of overseas securities owned by United Kingdom residents, but contents itself with giving figures for nominal values, which, of course, have little practical significance, especially for ordinary shares. The Bank estimates that aggregate nominal capital fell from £3545 millions in 1938 to £2417 millions in 1945, fell further to a minimum of £1967 millions in 1948, and thereafter recovered only very slightly to £1982 millions in 1952 and £2013 millions in 1953. But clearly a rise in aggregate income of nearly 50 per cent since 1945 cannot have been without its effect on capital values, and in Table IX an attempt is made to give some idea of capital values by capitalising the income from the different classes of securities at what seem to be appropriate rates. In Table IX (B) constant rates are used, varying from 4 per cent for the loans of Commonwealth governments and municipalities to 6 per cent for most company shares; while in Table IX (c) the rates used for capitalising the income fluctuate roughly in accordance with changes on the London market, varying for Commonwealth governments and municipalities between 3 per cent

TABLE IX

ESTIMATED AGGREGATE VALUES OF U.K. OVERSEAS INVESTMENTS

	1938	1945	1949	1952	1953
	£m.	£m.	£m.	£m.	£m.
(A) *Nominal Values:*					
Government and Municipal Loans	1521	904	795	790	798
Company Loans	734	445	281	245	260
Total, Fixed Interest Securities	2255	1349	1076	1035	1058
Shares	1290	1068	963	947	955
Total, Overseas Securities	3545	2417	2039	1982	2013
(B) *Income Capitalised at Constant Interest Rates:*					
Government and Municipal Loans	1325	780	560	500	640
Company Loans	415	310	135	140	165
Total, Fixed Interest Securities	1740	1090	695	640	805
Shares	1275	970	1445	2060	2035
Total, Overseas Securities	3015	2060	2140	2700	2840
(C) *Income Capitalised at Fluctuating Interest Rates:*					
Government and Municipal Loans	1490	1030	585	430	570
Company Loans	460	375	150	120	150
Total, Fixed Interest Securities	1950	1405	735	550	720
Shares	1275	1230	1445	1750	1860
Total, Overseas Securities	3225	2635	2180	2300	2580

in 1945 and 4¾ per cent in 1952, and for most shares between 5 per cent in 1945 and 7 per cent in 1952. (The constant rates used in Table IX (B) are approximately the averages of the fluctuating rates used in IX (C).) The purpose of publishing the two separate tables is to make it possible for readers to distinguish changes due to changes in income yields from changes due to fluctuations in interest rates on the London market.

The Bank of England's estimates of nominal values are given, for purposes of comparison, in Table IX (A).

The results of these calculations obviously give only the very roughest idea of the changes in the true market values, to ascertain which would clearly take more labour than the Bank of England has yet felt justified in devoting to the purpose. A particularly likely source of error is that these calculations are applied to the actual current yields, while market prices are determined by many factors besides current income yields. For instance, where fixed interest securities are redeemable in the fairly near future, the yield to maturity, upon which market prices are based, is at present often far above (and in other periods may sometimes be below) the flat yield, which necessarily forms the basis of calculation here. This would tend to cause an undervaluation of fixed interest securities in times of high interest rates and an overvaluation in times of low interest rates. Again, where there are expectations of a future default on, or resumption of interest payments on, fixed interest securities, or of a future increase or decrease in dividends on shares, market prices may change well before interest or dividend payments alter. Nevertheless, it is hoped that the capitalised values calculated here may be sufficiently relevant to give some idea of the changes in capital values of British overseas investments since the war.

Although by 1953 the total income from overseas investments had risen above its pre-war level, it seems clear that, even in the absence of changes in interest rates, the aggregate capital value of the investments would still have been below the pre-war level, since a much higher proportion of the income was derived from relatively high-yielding shares and a much lower proportion from relatively low-yielding loans. Even so, in the absence of a rise in interest rates, it seems likely that by 1953 aggregate capital values would have recovered by far the greater part of the fall due to earlier sales and redemptions. The rise in interest rates has, however, probably deprived owners of something like half of the capital appreciation which they would otherwise have enjoyed. As Table VII shows, the net cash proceeds of overseas securities sold or redeemed between 1939 and 1953 is put at £1165 millions. If there had been no capital appreciation or depreciation on the remaining securities, this is also the amount by which aggregate capital values would have declined. In fact, Table IX (c) puts the decline in value, after allowing for changes in interest rates, at only £645 millions. This would make the capital appreciation on the remaining securities something like £500 millions, as against the £1000 millions which would have been enjoyed if interest rates had remained unchanged throughout. Since 1953 interest rates have again risen, but it may be hoped that part or all of the loss of market value due to this cause has been offset by a further rise in overseas investment income.

CONCLUSIONS

The general impression left by this examination of the United Kingdom's record since the war, both as an exporter of capital and as an owner of foreign investments, is that, in ten years, it has made little progress either towards being able to supply the urgent capital needs of the rest of the Commonwealth or towards restoring its own international financial position. In spite of an unprecedentedly rapid rise in production, in no single year, still less in any series of years, has it had a surplus of saving over fixed investment at home sufficiently large to provide both for an increase in stocks commensurate with the rise in output and a favourable balance of payments commensurate with the capital needs of those developing countries which traditionally look to it for finance; such temporary improvements as have occurred in its balance of payments have been achieved only at the expense of decreases or inadequate increases in stocks, and have disappeared as soon as stocks have had to be replenished.

Until recently, the United Kingdom's meagre exports of long-term capital out of its own resources have been supplemented by the re-export of capital supplied from overseas, until 1950 mainly in the form of gifts and loans from the United States and Canada, and more recently in the form of the rising sterling balances of the colonies. Now that the second of these forms of capital imports is also disappearing, the United Kingdom will in future be dependent on its own balance-of-payments surplus for supplying even the long-term capital which it is morally bound to provide for the colonies.

Such improvement as has taken place in recent years in the United Kingdom's own international financial position has been due mainly to the capital appreciation in its shares in overseas companies, which now constitute some three-quarters of its foreign investments. Between 1945 and 1953 these are estimated to have risen in value by perhaps £600 millions, thus making good perhaps nearly half the fall in the value of its overseas fixed interest securities, caused partly by war-time and post-war sales and partly by higher interest rates. If, however, we look, not merely at foreign assets but at the net margin between foreign assets and foreign liabilities, we find that the capital appreciation on overseas shares offsets only a very small fraction of the net worsening in the whole international financial position. In addition to the net loss of perhaps £1200 millions in the value of overseas fixed interest securities, the excess of short-term sterling liabilities to overseas creditors over the value of the gold and dollar reserves has risen from nothing in 1938 to some £3000 millions in 1945 and hardly less to-day, while in addition the long-term dollar debt, incurred mainly after the war, stands at over £2000 millions. As the result of these changes, a pre-war surplus of foreign assets over foreign liabilities of perhaps £4000 millions has been converted into a deficit of perhaps £1000 millions or more. In the ten years which have elapsed since the war the country has made little progress even towards emerging from its unaccustomed position as a net international debtor, still less towards starting the task of rebuilding the great net surplus of foreign assets which earlier generations accumulated in the century before the First World War. It is urgently necessary that the United Kingdom should henceforward restrain its home demand sufficiently both to supply its share of the resources so urgently needed by the developing countries of the Commonwealth and at the same time to begin to restore the international financial position which has been lost, partly as the result of two world wars, but partly also as the result of policies pursued in the years of peace succeeding them.

CHAPTER 10

THE NEW GOLD STANDARD[1]

As a prelude to my paper this evening, I should like to draw your attention to two charts and their accompanying Table I, both covering the same three series over two different periods of three years each. The three series are the gold reserves in the hands of the Bank of England and the Exchange Equalisation Account, the rate of discount on three months' fine bank bills, and the yield on 2½ per cent Consols; the two periods are from January 1906 to December 1908 and from July 1953 to June 1956. The two charts present both similarities and contrasts. The most striking similarity is that in both charts the bill rate rises as the gold stock falls and falls as the gold stock rises. If we define a gold standard, very broadly, as a system under which the value of the currency is fixed in terms of gold, or in terms of another currency which in turn is fixed in terms of gold, where the foreign exchange reserves are held wholly or mainly in the form of gold, and where fluctuations in the size of the gold reserve are accompanied by inverse fluctuations in interest rates, there can be little doubt that our present system falls within the definition. It is, however, a system which differs widely both in objectives and in techniques of operation from the classical gold standard as it existed, for instance, in the years between 1900 and 1914. It is the purpose of this paper to examine these differences.

One great difference between the two charts which leaps to the eye is the disparity between the absolute sizes of the gold reserves. Even if we make the fullest allowance for changes in the level of the national money income, the average ratio of the gold reserve to national income was something like four times as large in 1953–56 as it had been in 1906–8. It is true that the value of the gold in circulation in the earlier period is estimated at nearly four times the reserve, but by the beginning of the twentieth century gold in circulation had become almost

[1] Paper read to the Manchester Statistical Society, 13th March 1957.

entirely unavailable for meeting an outflow from the country, and must be omitted from any effective reserve.

That it was possible to maintain the position of sterling as the leading world currency, in which were made not only the international payments to and by the United Kingdom but also many of those between overseas countries, upon the basis of so microscopic a gold reserve can be attributed mainly to two circumstances. In the first place, the rest of the world looked to London not only for the finance of many goods in transit overseas but also as a convenient place for the investment of temporarily surplus short-term funds. A rise in short-term rates there made it a less attractive place to borrow in but more attractive to lend in, so that a sufficient rise in rates in London relatively to those in other centres could attract a net balance of short-term funds; and, what is equally important, the universal confidence in the exchange stability of sterling permitted overseas owners to move their funds to London without hedging them by sales of sterling on the forward markets. The second circumstance was that continental central banks maintained much larger gold reserves than did the Bank of England and were in a position to release gold whenever the net inflow of short-term funds to London caused the exchange rates to reach gold point.[1] A close analogy to the position of London, and of the Bank of England, in the years before 1914 is with a commercial bank which is able to conduct a large business on a very small cash reserve because it is owed large amounts on call by highly liquid customers, who, in effect, carry its cash reserves for it.

In consequence of this situation, the primary function of a rise in short-term interest rates in the years before 1914 was to call in short-term funds and gold from the rest of the world whenever the gold reserve (and with it the note reserve of the Banking Department of the Bank of England) showed a fall that threatened to reduce it to a dangerously low level. The reserve, in effect, acted not so much as a reserve as a sensitive thermostat, designed as the result of a small change to set in motion powerful forces to reverse the movement. Provided that the fall in the reserve was not thought to be due to purely temporary causes, its cause was irrelevant. Whether

<hr>

[1] See R. S. Sayers, *Central Banking after Bagehot*, pp. 14-15.

GOLD RESERVES AND INTEREST RATES IN THE U.K.
A.   1906–08

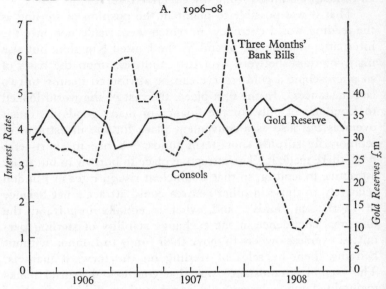

GOLD RESERVES AND INTEREST RATES IN THE U.K.
B.   1953–56

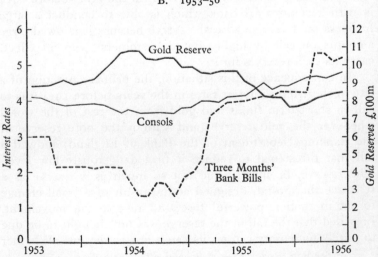

TABLE I
GOLD RESERVE AND INTEREST RATES

	1906–08				1953–56		
End of Month	Gold Reserve £m.	3 months' Bank Bills	Consols	End of Month	Gold Reserve £m.	3 months' Bank Bills	Consols
1906				**1953**			
Jan.	29·6	$3\frac{3}{4}$	2·78	July	877	3·00	4·13
Feb.	32·4	$3\frac{7}{8}$	2·76	Aug.	882	3·00	4·12
Mar.	36·3	$3\frac{9}{16}$	2·77	Sept.	888	3·00	4·00
Apr.	33·4	$3\frac{7}{16}$	2·78	Oct.	900	2·19	3·43
May	30·2	$3\frac{1}{2}$	2·79	Nov.	915	2·19	3·88
June	33·4	$3\frac{3}{8}$	2·82	Dec.	899	2·19	3·89
July	35·9	$3\frac{1}{8}$	2·87	**1954**			
Aug.	35·6	$3\frac{1}{16}$	2·84	Jan.	908	2·19	3·90
Sept.	33·3	$4\frac{1}{4}$	2·89	Feb.	923	2·13	3·91
Oct.	27·7	$5\frac{3}{4}$	2·91	Mar.	959	2·19	3·89
Nov.	28·4	$5\frac{15}{16}$	2·88	Apr.	1007	2·16	3·80
Dec.	28·8	6	2·90	May	1066	2·13	3·72
1907				June	1078	1·66	3·78
Jan.	31·1	$4\frac{3}{4}$	2·87	July	1076	1·31	3·69
Feb.	34·1	$4\frac{3}{4}$	2·88	Aug.	1042	1·31	3·66
Mar.	34·6	$5\frac{1}{8}$	2·93	Sept.	1036	1·66	3·66
Apr.	34·6	$3\frac{3}{8}$	2·91	Oct.	1048	1·63	3·66
May	33·7	$3\frac{3}{16}$	2·94	Nov.	1045	1·31	3·64
June	33·8	$3\frac{3}{4}$	2·97	Dec.	986	1·78	3·76
July	34·6	$3\frac{5}{8}$	2·97	**1955**			
Aug.	34·6	$4\frac{1}{2}$	3·07	Jan.	987	1·97	3·83
Sept.	37·7	$3\frac{3}{4}$	3·04	Feb.	958	2·34	3·98
Oct.	33·4	$4\frac{3}{8}$	3·02	Mar.	953	3·51	3·99
Nov.	30·6	$6\frac{7}{8}$	3·07	Apr.	959	3·75	3·98
Dec.	32·0	$5\frac{5}{8}$	3·02	May	959	3·94	4·11
1908				June	957	4·00	4·15
Jan.	34·7	$4\frac{1}{4}$	2·99	July	909	4·00	4·18
Feb.	36·8	$3\frac{3}{4}$	2·87	Aug.	878	4·06	4·34
Mar.	38·6	$2\frac{7}{8}$	2·87	Sept.	838	4·16	4·48
Apr.	35·3	$2\frac{5}{8}$	2·87	Oct.	820	4·16	4·30
May	35·6	$2\frac{1}{16}$	2·89	Nov.	815	4·22	4·38
June	37·3	$1\frac{1}{4}$	2·86	Dec.	757	4·22	4·39
July	36·2	$1\frac{3}{16}$	2·86	**1956**			
Aug.	34·9	$1\frac{1}{2}$	2·89	Jan.	768	4·22	4·53
Sept.	36·8	$1\frac{3}{8}$	2·92	Feb.	789	4·25	4·61
Oct.	35·0	$1\frac{7}{8}$	2·95	Mar.	813	5·36	4·65
Nov.	34·2	$2\frac{1}{4}$	2·95	Apr.	832	5·33	4·61
Dec.	31·4	$2\frac{1}{4}$	2·99	May	846	5·14	4·66
				June	852	5·20	4·74

it was due to a worsening of the balance of payments on current account, to excessive long-term overseas investment or to withdrawals of foreign-owed short-term balances, the immediate reaction was to raise Bank Rate, make it effective upon market rates, and call in short-term funds from abroad. If the rise in rates needed for this purpose happened to have other effects, such as checking the outflow of long-term capital, reducing investment in inventories or in domestic fixed capital, or otherwise checking demand, these were incidental. On some occasions, no doubt, these secondary effects happened to fit in with the economic needs of the country and helped to keep the economy in equilibrium; on others, as during the United States financial panic in the autumn of 1907, they merely transmitted an irrelevant disturbance to the system. It is to the fact that the main function of a rise in short-term rates was to call money from abroad that we can attribute both the violence and the brevity of the rises in bill rates shown in our chart.

In the new gold standard the order of the objectives is reversed. No longer can a rise in short-term rates attract short-term funds unhedged to London : that power was largely exhausted in the effort to establish and maintain the pound at an unduly high parity in the years between 1922 and 1931, and its last vestiges have been dissipated in the devaluation of 1949 and the balance-of-payments crises of 1947, 1951, and 1955. To-day the primary function of monetary policy is to check an inflationary rise in expenditure and incomes, with the secondary effects of improving the balance of payments, checking the export of long-term capital, and raising the gold reserve. A larger gold reserve is needed to-day — a reserve indeed much larger than in fact we hold — not only because it is no longer possible by raising interest rates to attract short money from abroad, but also because there may well be circumstances in which we should not wish to do so if we could, as for instance, if a loss of gold is caused by a financial panic abroad at a time when there is no excessive rise in domestic incomes. It may be doubted whether interest rates would now be used even to correct a persistent adverse balance of payments if this was not accompanied by any tendency for money incomes to rise faster than real income. In a country running either a persis-

tently over-adverse or over-favourable balance of payments as
the result of its attempting to maintain internal stability in an
unstable world, it is likely that alterations in the rate of exchange would now be preferred to measures designed to keep
in step with the rest of the world at the cost of unnecessarily
promoting either deflation or inflation at home. It is probably
true to say that, whereas under the old gold standard interest
rate policy was designed to stabilise the stock of gold, but might
incidentally serve to stabilise the economy, under the new gold
standard it is designed to stabilise the economy, but may incidentally also serve to stabilise the stock of gold. The reason
why, since the re-introduction of interest rate policy at the end
of 1951, rises in interest rates have been associated with losses
of gold, and falls in interest rates with gains, is that during
this period gold losses have been associated with adverse
balances of payments, which in turn have been largely attributable to excessive demand at home, while gold gains have been
associated with more favourable balances of payments and
relaxations of internal inflationary pressure. Thus policies
designed to reduce excess demand have incidentally served also
to restore a falling gold reserve. It is, however, fair to say
that the gold losses have imported an urgency into the efforts
to check excess demand which might otherwise have been
absent; for this reason, the fact that inflationary pressure in
most of the rest of the world has recently been markedly less
than in this country has been a factor making for stability here.

With the view that under the new gold standard the objectives of policy differ widely from those of the old there will
probably be general agreement. What is less generally recognised is that differences of objective involve equally wide
differences of method. In the years before 1914 the main
emphasis was necessarily on changes in short-term rates of
interest; the accompanying changes in long-term rates were in
general extremely small. For instance, while between January
1906 and December 1908 the bill rate fluctuated from under
$1\frac{1}{4}$ per cent to nearly 7 per cent, the yield on Consols varied
only between $2\frac{3}{4}$ per cent and just over 3 per cent. This
absence of any substantial fluctuations in long-term rates is
entirely appropriate to a situation where the primary function
of changes in rates is to attract short-term capital from abroad

and the duration of fluctuations in short-term rates is measured
in months or even weeks. If, however, the main objective of
interest rate policy is to control the rate of change in the
national money income, it is the changes in the long-term rate
which become of primary importance, and the fact that between
mid-1953 and mid-1956 the yield on Consols fluctuated between
under $3\frac{3}{4}$ per cent and over $4\frac{3}{4}$ per cent need occasion no sur-
prise; in fact, it will be the contention of this paper that the
fluctuations could well have been even wider.

Higher interest rates are, of course, by no means the only
instruments now at the disposal of the Government for the
restriction of excess demand. Other possible instruments
include controls on expenditure, controls on borrowing and
other capital transfers, and changes in fiscal policy. All these
measures fall into one of two groups—those designed to restrict
consumption and increase aggregate saving, and those designed
to restrict investment. The two groups should be regarded
as complementary. The restrictions on consumption help to
determine the level of saving which the country is able to
achieve without inflation, while the restrictions on investment
help to keep the total of investment within the limits thus
determined. Criticism of measures to restrict investment,
based on the ground that more investment is desirable in the
national interest, is thus misdirected. The real responsibility
for any inadequacy in the total of investment lies with the inadequate level of non-inflationary saving, not with the measures
designed to prevent investment from exceeding that level.

Another criticism which is sometimes levelled against interest-
rate policy as a means of keeping total investment within the
limits of saving is that, whereas controls on the expenditure or
transfer of money can discriminate against whatever may at
the moment be officially regarded as the less essential forms
of investment, restriction through limitation of the quantity
of money and higher interest rates is random and non-discriminatory. It is, however, quite untrue to say that a rise in
interest rates is non-discriminatory in its effects, though of
course the forms of investment which it tends to discourage
most may not be the same as those which any particular
government would regard as least desirable. Broadly speaking,
the effectiveness of higher interest rates in discouraging the

creation of durable assets varies directly with the durability
of the asset. The reason for this is that interest charges form
a much higher proportion of the annual cost of ownership
of a long-lived asset, where the annual charge for depreciation
is small, than of a short-lived asset, where it is large. The
effect of differences in durability is reinforced if the long-lived
investment is also safer than the short-lived. Thus for a highly
durable, safe investment, such as a block of flats, a rise from
4 to 6 per cent in the rate of interest paid on the capital borrowed to finance its construction may involve a rise, say, from
6 to 8 per cent, or a third, in the annual cost of ownership.
We may contrast this with a piece of machinery carrying a
high risk of early obsolescence, on which the annual depreciation might well be 20 per cent or more, so that the rise in the
total annual cost of ownership would be only from 24 to 26 per
cent, or by one-twelfth. The effect of a rise of 2 per cent in the
rate of interest is thus likely to be much more significant in the
first case than in the second, and is much likelier to discourage
the construction of such assets as houses, flats, and perhaps
commercial buildings than less durable, riskier investments
such as industrial plant and machinery, and perhaps industrial
buildings.

For a rise in interest rates to exercise its full effect in discouraging the construction of highly durable assets, it must
fulfil one of two further conditions. Either an equal rise in all
rates of interest must be expected to be permanent, or a rise in
long-term rates must be accompanied either by a much larger
rise in short-term rates or by the impossibility of obtaining
additional short-term loans on any terms. If the rise in long-
term rates is expected to be only temporary, and if it is possible
to obtain additional short-term loans at less than extremely
high rates, it will pay to finance the construction of even highly
durable assets by means of short-term loans, in the expectation
of subsequently refinancing them on long-term when long-
term rates have fallen. How large the rise in short-term rates
might have to be before it became worth while to borrow on
long-term immediately is indicated in the following example.
Let us suppose that the long-term rate is now 6 per cent, and
is confidently expected to fall to 5 per cent within a year. If a
man who wishes to borrow for twenty years can wait a year

G

before borrowing on long-term, he will save £1 per cent a year for nineteen years, equivalent to a capitalised value of over £12. It will thus pay him to borrow for one year at anything up to 12 per cent above the long-term rate of 6 per cent, that is, at anything up to 18 per cent, rather than borrow immediately on long-term. If he can borrow freely for a year at anything appreciably less than 18 per cent, the effectiveness of the 6 per cent long-term rate in checking investment will be diminished ; while if the short-term rate is no higher than the long-term rate, a plentiful supply of short-term finance will reduce the effect of the higher long-term rate to insignificance. If the fall in the long-term rate is expected in less than a year, the equilibrium short-term rate will be even higher — 30 per cent if the fall is expected within six months, 54 per cent if within three. In view of the short duration of the high interest rate periods in 1906–8, the disparity between the ¼ per cent fluctuations in the yield on Consols and the 5 per cent fluctuations in the yield on bills does not look unreasonable.

Even in the years before 1914 not all short-term interest rates fluctuated as freely as those on bills. In the United Kingdom, bankers have never relied merely on changes in interest rates to control the volume of their advances ; in times of stringency they have always limited them quantitatively, refusing them outright rather than quoting a rate high enough to discourage them. To-day, with the almost complete disappearance of the inland bill and the greatly reduced significance of the international trade bill, bank advances constitute almost the only regular source of short-term finance to industry. It thus appears that, within the limits of their permitted fluctuations, changes in short-term rates affect investment decisions only to a small extent, the main control over the volume of advances and over their use to finance investment being exercised by quantitative limitation. Most of such influence as a rise in short-term rates still has seems to be exercised either psychologically, as giving evidence of the authorities' intentions, or via its effects on long-term rates. The two main ways in which restriction of credit now operates on investment decisions are therefore through the quantitative restriction of short-term credit and a rise in rates on long-term loans.

To bring about a restriction of short-term credit by the

banks one of two things is necessary : either the banks must be
made unwilling to increase, or even to maintain, the total of
their advances, or they must be forbidden to do so. The first
method is likely to be the more efficient, for under it the banks
become the willing collaborators of the Government instead
of its resentful servants. It is sometimes said that if the banks
are put in a position where they themselves wish to reduce
advances, the criteria used in deciding which loans to refuse
will be those that accord with the policy of the banks and not
with that of the Government. But this is not necessarily so ;
for if, at the same time as the banks are made to want to
reduce advances, they are given a list of official priorities, or
rather of non-priorities, they will often welcome the opportunity
of putting the blame for the refusal of an advance on the official
directive, even if for their own purposes they would have preferred to refuse someone else. If, on the other hand, the banks
are merely given a directive at a time when they themselves
are in a position to expand advances, there will inevitably be a
tendency for them to try to find means of bringing an application within the limits of the official policy. The wish of the
Government to concentrate the restriction of advances on particular classes of borrowers is therefore no reason for leaving
the banks in a position where they are prevented from expanding advances only by the official directive.

To place the banks in a position where they themselves wish
to restrict advances two things are necessary. The first of
these is that their ratio of liquid to non-liquid assets is below
the level they would wish ; and the second that, of their non-
liquid assets, they wish to reduce advances rather than, or as
well as, investments. The traditional form of the first of these
conditions is that the central bank should take steps, by
reducing its own assets, to reduce the clearing banks' cash
reserves below the customary minimum and so force them to
reduce their non-cash assets. More recently, however, it has
been increasingly realised [1] that, so long as the banks have an
adequate supply of call money and bills and can immediately
restore their cash reserves by calling from the discount market,
the Bank of England cannot do more than force the bill rate

[1] See especially W. Manning Dacey, 'The Floating Debt Problem',
Lloyds Bank Review, April 1956.

up to Bank Rate. If Bank Rate is raised sufficiently high it will, of course, force up the advances rate to a point where it has a real effect on the demand for loans and also make the banks less anxious to hold securities unless the yield on these rises also ; but Bank Rate may have to rise very high indeed before the rates on advances and long-term securities rise sufficiently to have any substantial effect on investment. Unless a moderate rise in Bank Rate has a very marked psychological effect on the demand for advances and the willingness to invest, the attempt to check excess demand by an increase in Bank Rate alone may prove unnecessarily expensive, for reasons which will be discussed later, from the points of view both of the budget and of the balance of payments.[1]

It is now widely believed that a policy preferable to one of merely forcing the market into the Bank and raising Bank Rate is to starve the banks, not only of cash, but also of call money and bills, thus leaving them with an inadequate ratio of all liquid assets and forcing them to reduce the total of their non-liquid assets. For this policy to achieve its purpose it is not essential that the banks should have a fixed minimum ratio below which they are not prepared to see their liquid assets fall, so long as there is a level below which they are increasingly reluctant to see them fall further. Since the overwhelming bulk of the liquid assets held by the banks consists either of Treasury bills or of loans against the security of Treasury bills, in order to starve the banks of liquid assets it is necessary to starve the whole market of Treasury bills. This will probably involve reducing the total volume of Treasury bills held outside the Bank of England and Government departments by an amount larger than that by which it is hoped to reduce the banks' liquid assets.

---

[1] It may be suggested that it would be possible to avoid this difficulty by limiting the amounts which discount houses can borrow from the Bank of England. Even, however, if such a step were practicable from other points of view, it would not help so long as the banks were large holders of Treasury bills. The Bank of England is lender of last resort to the Government as well as to the discount houses, and if the banks cannot force the Bank of England to create cash by pushing the discount market into the Bank, they can push the Government into the Bank by refraining from renewing their Treasury bills. The only reply the Government could make to this would be a return to compulsion, probably in the form either of a compulsory minimum for the banks' liquid assets ratio or of some system like that of the Treasury Deposit Receipts.

To put the banks in a position where they will want to restrict advances, it is necessary not only that they should be obliged to restrict their total of non-liquid assets, but also that they should not prefer to confine the restriction entirely to investments. In the 1920s the value of the banks' advances was about twice that of their investments, while even in the 1930s it was about 40 per cent higher. It is therefore probable that the approximately equal amounts held to-day represent a much higher proportion of investments than the banks would like, and that, when obliged to reduce their total of non-liquid assets, the banks will normally prefer to concentrate the whole reduction on investments. This preference was clearly shown during the second quarter of 1955, when a reduction of £20 millions in non-liquid assets took the form of a fall of £182 millions in investments and a rise of £162 millions in advances.

To put the banks into a position where they prefer to reduce advances it is necessary to make the disadvantages of selling investments temporarily greater even than those of refusing advances. The only way to do this is to force down prices of securities so far below redemption values that by selling them the banks would not only make a heavy loss on their original cost but, which is much more relevant, would sacrifice a large and certain capital appreciation. Thus, just as a restriction of short-term credit is needed to enable high long-term rates to have their full effects on investment, so high long-term rates are needed in order to make the banks reluctant to sell securities.

Even if the policy of raising long-term rates of interest and of obliging the banks to restrict advances is successfully put into force, its effects on the volume of fixed investment are likely to appear only after considerable delay. Plans and financial arrangements for the construction of highly durable assets are usually made well in advance, and once any appreciable amount of preliminary expenses has been met, the plans can be cancelled or postponed only at a heavy loss. Unless the credit restriction assumes the dimensions of a major financial crisis, existing plans will normally be carried out, and only as the fall in new plans gradually reduces the number of new starts, and as the fall in new starts still more gradually reduces the volume of work in progress, will the higher interest rates and tighter money affect the actual volume of fixed investment.

The delay before the volume of investment begins to fall will be all the longer if the initial tightening of money comes when it has been rising rapidly, and longer still if the rise in investment is partly due, as in 1954–55, to a release of demand (for privately-built houses and offices) after a long period of physical controls.[1] It is thus not surprising that a lag of nearly two years occurred between the initial steps to tighten money towards the end of 1954 and the check to the rise in investment in the second half of 1956.

There can be little doubt that, when the tighter money policy was again introduced at the end of 1954, the authorities expected it to check demand much more quickly than in fact it did. In this expectation they were probably misled by the experience of 1951–52, when a similar policy was followed extremely rapidly by a marked check to demand and a rapid improvement in the balance of payments. The circumstances of 1951–52, however, were very different from those of 1954–1955. In 1951 there was no increase in the volume of fixed investment, and the increased use of resources took the form, to some extent of increased Government consumption of goods and services, but mainly of a very large rise in inventories. In no case would the country have needed to increase stocks on this scale in two successive years, and this natural tendency to slow down the rate of inventory accumulation was reinforced by the fall in prices of many imported commodities as the result of the end of the fighting in Korea. The rise in interest rates and the restriction of advances probably helped to accelerate the fall in demand, but even without it the rate of inventory accumulation would probably have fallen sufficiently to convert the large adverse balance of payments of 1951 into a modest favourable one in 1952.

The position at the end of 1954 was very different. The increased use of resources in 1954 had taken the form largely of a rise in fixed investment, originally in houses but later, and increasingly, in other forms of private fixed investment. Meanwhile, the increases in inventories had been small for the

---

[1] One of the undesirable effects of physical controls is that they make the system insensitive to any other form of control for some time after their removal. The Australian experience of the results of import controls is a case in point.

past three years and, in view of the recent increases in output, the country was probably if anything short of stocks. The tighter money policy therefore had the task, not of merely reinforcing a decline in stock-building which would have occurred in any case, but of checking a strong upsurge of fixed investment in a country short of stocks. In the event it failed to prevent, though it may have moderated, both a substantial increase in inventory accumulation in 1955 and the early part of 1956 and a continued rise in fixed investment, which seems to have continued almost to the end of 1956.

TABLE II

SOURCES AND USES OF INVESTIBLE FUNDS, 1950–56*

(£m. at 1948 Prices)

	1950	1951	1952	1953	1954	1955	Est. 1956
Saving and Depreciation	1697	1761	1740	1952	2164	2317	2420
Capital Grants and Transfers from Abroad	160	69	27	21	9	14	(10)
Total Investible Funds	1857	1830	1767	1973	2173	2331	2430
Less							
Gross Domestic Fixed Capital Formation	1643	1649	1661	1837	2004	2161	2200
Surplus available for Stock Accumulation and Foreign Investment	214	181	106	136	169	170	230
Physical Increase in Stocks	− 186	454	37	95	57	223	110
Balance of Payments on Current A/c.	+ 390	− 251	+ 173	+ 133	+ 156	− 77	+ 120
Errors and Omissions	+ 10	− 22	− 104	− 92	− 44	+ 24	—
Total	214	181	106	136	169	170	230

* Source: National Income Blue Book, 1956. Method of Construction: As for Table VI of Chapter 5. Figures revised to 1961 are given in Table VI of Chapter 8.

Now that the rise in domestic fixed investment seems at last to have levelled off the view is frequently expressed that the financial stringency should be relieved immediately. It would seem, however, that the surplus of saving over domestic fixed investment is still far from sufficient to enable the country to achieve both an adequate level of stock accumulation and a balance-of-payments surplus sufficient to provide long-term capital for the rest of the sterling area, to meet withdrawals from overseas-owned sterling balances and pay off other foreign debts, and to replenish the quite inadequate gold reserves. The size of the balance-of-payments surplus needed to achieve these objectives cannot be put at less than about £350 millions at present prices, to which must be added an average of £150 millions or more for stock accumulation. The surplus of saving over fixed investment at home needs therefore to be something over £500 millions at current prices, or say £400 millions at 1948 prices. As Table II shows, the margin available has been rarely over £200 millions at 1948 prices, and has averaged much less than that. We need to raise this margin to a wholly new level if the country is to avoid a continual recurrence of the crises which have punctuated the post-war period, and until this margin is achieved a resumption of the rise in internal demand can only mean the loss of the precarious stability so far gained.

It may, however, be objected that, just as the tightening of money checks demand only after a long time-lag, so may there be a long interval before a relaxation is followed by an upturn of demand; and that an immediate relaxation is necessary if during the time-lag an unnecessarily large fall in demand and heavy unemployment are to be avoided. Fortunately the danger of an excessive unemployment of resources as the result of an inadequate level of internal demand is much less in a relatively open economy, such as that of the United Kingdom, than in a relatively closed economy, such as that of the United States. In an open economy, just as a large part of any excess of internal demand is reflected, not in rising prices, but in a worsening balance of payments, so a large part of any fall in internal demand will be reflected, not in falling prices or unemployment, but in a more favourable balance of payments. There is some reason for thinking that the United Kingdom has not suffered any serious depression of activity as the result of a purely internal fall in demand for over a hundred years; all have been due, wholly or mainly, to changes in the overseas demand for British exports. There seems a strong case for believing that, as long as demand and activity in the rest of the world remain high, so much of a decline in home demand would fall on imports or be offset by a rise in exports that its effects upon production and employment would be very moderate, especially as soon as restrictions on foreign lending could be relaxed. It seems likely that the very large favourable balances of payments achieved in the years before 1914 were made possible by a sharp decline in domestic fixed investment, particularly in houses, the results of which appeared, not in a rise in unemployment, but in an export boom which was both the cause and the result of a very high level of long-term overseas investment. It can hardly be doubted that the largest conceivable improvement in the United Kingdom's balance of payments could now be absorbed in capital imports by the rest of the world, and would make a very important contribution to both the economic and the political stability of the Sterling Area and the world as a whole.

We have now considered the effects in modern conditions of a tight money policy, operating mainly through a rise in the long-term rate of interest and a restriction of advances. It remains to consider the technical means by which such a policy can be put into force.

The problems facing the whole group of authorities — the Bank of England, the Treasury, the Exchange Equalisation Account, the National Debt Commissioners, and the Government departments — which is now concerned with regulating the supply of liquid assets to the banks are identical in principle with those which used to face the Bank of England in regulating their supply of cash, though there are some techniques which are available to the collective authorities which were not available — or were only vestigially available — to the Bank of England. To begin with, there are very close analogies between the effects of gold movements on the banks' cash ratios under the old gold standard and on their liquid assets ratio under the new. Under the old standard, a loss of gold due to an adverse balance of payments on income account caused a fall in bank deposits held by U.K. residents (presumably mainly on income account), in the clearing banks' balances at the Bank of England and in their cash ratios. To-day the impact effects on deposits are the same, but the gold is now sold, not by the Bank of England, but by the Exchange Equalisation Account and its proceeds are used to buy tap bills from the Treasury, which in turn uses them to redeem tender bills held by the discount market and the banks. Thus, while the cash reserves of the banks are not affected, their total of liquid assets and their liquid assets ratio are reduced. There is, however, one very important difference between the two systems in that, whereas the banks could always convert liquid assets into cash by putting the discount market into the Bank, there is no corresponding mechanism whereby they can convert non-liquid into liquid assets.

Where the loss of gold is due, not to an adverse balance of payments on income account, but either to an excessive export of long-term capital or to the withdrawal of sterling balances invested in securities, the effects under both systems are the same as those described in the previous paragraph, except that the fall in bank deposits occurs mainly in deposits held by U.K. owners on capital account; while if it is due to the withdrawal of overseas balances held in the form of bank deposits, the effects are again the same, except that the fall in deposits occurs in deposits held by overseas residents, so that deposits held by U.K. residents are not affected. Where, however, the overseas balances withdrawn are held in the form of Treasury bills, bank-notes, or balances at the Bank of England (that is to say, in the short-term debts of the monetary authorities), their withdrawal does not affect either the deposits or liquid assets of the banks at all, since the whole of the proceeds of the gold sales are absorbed in the repayment of the foreign-owned Treasury bills or Bank of England debts. Under the old gold standard, only the foreign balances held in notes or in balances at the Bank of England could be withdrawn without affecting the deposits and/or cash reserves of the clearing banks.

A second source of funds from which the Treasury could conceivably make net repayments of tender bills is the budget surplus, which has no counterpart in Bank of England operations under the old gold standard, unless we admit the possibility of its ploughing back large profits to reserve. Unfortunately the possibility of repaying Treasury bills out of a budget surplus is of little practical importance in present circumstances. Much more is needed than a mere favourable balance on ordinary account. The Treasury has also to meet net extra-budgetary expenditure considerably larger than the

usual budget surplus, especially since it assumed the responsibility for the provision of long-term capital for all the
nationalised industries. Even after setting against these expenditures net receipts from sales of National Savings Certificates and other forms of small savings, and sometimes from
Tax Reserve Certificates, only an exceptionally large 'above-
the-line' surplus will provide any margin of cash for the
repayment of other forms of debt. Further, even if such a
margin could be achieved, there would remain the further
difficulty that there are normally several hundred millions of
short- and medium-term Government bonds maturing every
year, by no means all of which are automatically renewed or
converted. Only in the very unlikely event of the above-the-
line surplus plus net receipts from small savings being larger
than the extra-budgetary deficit plus the unconverted portions
of maturing loans would the authorities be relieved of the
necessity of making sales or issues of long- or medium-term
securities if they wished to reduce the floating debt, or even
to prevent it from rising.

It does not matter if the securities sold by the authorities
are new issues or re-sales of securities previously taken up by
Government departments or, more probably, by the Issue
Department of the Bank of England. In fact, the two operations are hardly distinguishable. When an issue of several
hundred millions is made, it is unusual for the whole of it to
be taken up by non-official buyers at the time of issue. A
substantial proportion, frequently the larger part, of the issue
is initially taken up 'inside' and subsequently re-sold gradually
as opportunity offers. The 'departments' pay for their share
of the new issue by surrendering their holdings of a maturing
issue or of tap bills, and as they re-sell the new issue they use
the proceeds either to buy up the next maturing issue or to
subscribe for more tap bills. If we ignore transactions between
the Treasury and the other authorities, the net effect is that
the Treasury makes its issues very largely by selling them
gradually on the market at the price of the day. It is only
these sales to non-official holders that have any economic
significance.

Sales of securities by the authorities to non-official holders
can be divided into two broad types — sales to the banks and

sales to the banks' customers. Of the two, the latter are likely
to be the more important. A sale of securities to the banks of
which the proceeds are used to redeem Treasury bills held by
the banks does nothing directly to reduce deposits, but merely
causes the banks to exchange some of their liquid assets for
non-liquid assets. As it is unlikely that the banks will be
willing to make themselves less liquid unless they have, and
expect to continue to have, a substantial margin of excess
liquidity, such transactions are unlikely in themselves to reduce
their liquid assets ratio to a level which will oblige them to
restrict advances. It is, of course, possible that a reduction
in their liquid assets ratio by such means might be a preliminary
step to reducing it further by other means. Such tactics were,
in fact, used in the funding operation of November 1951,
when the banks were induced to convert nearly £500 millions
of Treasury bills into securities and to reduce their liquid
assets ratio from 39 to 32 per cent; but their subsequent
experience makes it unlikely that they will again co-operate
voluntarily in preparing such a rod for their own backs.

Of greater significance is likely to be the sale of securities
to the customers of the banks. If the proceeds of these are
used to redeem Treasury bills held by the banks, the result is
a fall in their liquid assets without a rise in their non-liquid
assets, and consequently a fall in deposits — presumably
deposits held on capital account — and a rise in interest rates.
Such transactions are quite outside the control of the banks,
and may result in their liquid assets ratio being forced down
to an uncomfortably low level. There is a close analogy between
such a reduction in the banks' liquid assets ratio by means of
sales of securities by the whole group of authorities and a
reduction in their cash ratios by normal open market operations by the Banking Department of the Bank of England
acting alone.

The sale of securities to the public, whether by the Treasury
direct or by the departments, and the use of the proceeds to
redeem Treasury bills held by the market and the banks, affect
interest rates in three ways. In the first place, the original sale
of securities and use of the proceeds, not to buy more securities,
but to pay off bills, tends to cause security prices to fall and
their yields to rise. Secondly, the repayment of bills tends

to cause their yield to fall, especially if it goes far enough to reduce the banks' liquidity ratios below a comfortable level. And thirdly, if the fall in liquidity ratios goes far enough, the banks will be forced either to sell securities, thus causing a further fall in their prices, or to restrict advances, thus forcing some frustrated borrowers to try to raise money on the long-term market.

It is sometimes suggested that the control of credit by means of funding operations is impossible if the securities market is so weak that it cannot absorb any appreciable sales of securities without a heavy fall in prices. But this is to confuse ends and means. In such a case, the ultimate objective of forcing up long-term rates is achieved directly through the primary effect, even though the indirect effects, via the banks, are small. Indeed, such a situation has its advantages in that the rise in rates can be achieved with a minimum addition to the Treasury's future interest obligations. If, however, it is thought desirable, for reasons which will be discussed later, not only to force up long-term rates but also to force down bill rates, there is a technique applicable to all sales on weak speculative markets, whether for securities, commodities, or foreign exchange : to force a sharp initial fall in prices to a level which most potential buyers will regard as below any probable average future level, and then to permit (or cause) them gradually to begin to rise. These tactics are likely to be particularly effective in the securities market, where the result of taxation is to make many operators more interested in capital appreciation than in income.

It is sometimes urged as a criticism of funding policy that for the Treasury to borrow long when interest rates are high involves burdening it with high interest charges for many years. It is, however, extremely doubtful whether the cost of the extra interest burden on that fraction of the long-term debt which it issued during a period of high interest rates, would be as onerous as that of a present rise in the rates paid on the whole of the short-term debt. This doubt is reinforced by the consideration that, whereas by far the greater part of the long-term debt is held by United Kingdom residents, who pay tax, a very large slice of the short-term debt is owned by overseas residents, who do not. Thus the net cost of a rise in long rates is correspondingly reduced as compared with that of a rise in short rates. Again, increased interest payments made to overseas creditors have a directly adverse effect on the balance of payments, while increased payments to local residents do not. Thus, both on budgetary and on balance-of-payments grounds, it seems better, if there is a choice, to raise long-term rates than short.

If it is accepted that a given rise in long-term rates is likely to be as effective in discouraging investment as a very much larger rise in short-term rates, while a rise in short-term rates imposes a heavier net burden both on the budget and on the balance of payments than a corresponding rise in long-term rates, there appear to be good reasons for concentrating any rise in interest rates designed to check investment so far as possible on long rates, with the least possible effect on short rates. It remains to discuss how far the two movements can be dissociated, and how far a rise in short rates is necessary, not for its own sake but as an essential concomitant of a rise in long rates. If there were only two classes of Treasury obligations, one very short and the other very long or irredeemable, the markets for the two might be kept almost completely separate, as indeed they seem to have been before 1914, and the movements in their yields almost entirely independent. To-day, however, there is an almost continuous series of Government obligations, ranging from bills through short and medium bonds to long-dated and irredeemable securities. Thus while, for most holders, long-dated securities are a very imperfect substitute for bills, for a good many buyers short bonds may be reasonably substitutable. Further up the scale, medium bonds may, if the yields are attractive, often be substitutable for short, and long-dated securities for medium. Even the clearing banks, with their rigid definition of what constitutes a liquid asset, might well find their desire to hold bills modified if the bill rates were very low while the yield on short bonds was high; owners of overseas balances and local non-banking holders of bills (whose numbers are probably significant when bill rates are high) have less rigid liquidity requirements and would be much more influenced by the comparative yields of bills and bonds. These, as the gap in the yields widened, would increasingly tend to switch from bills to bonds, this releasing bills to replenish the shortages of the banks. Thus the wider the gap between the rates the greater the volume of funding operations needed to maintain it. What would be the practicable limits to the gap it is impossible to say, but it is unlikely that, in a time of dear money, it would be possible to maintain it at more than 2 per cent, and perhaps at not much more than 1 per cent. It might also be possible, by concentrating sales of securities largely on those with the longest dates and funding not only Treasury bills but also maturing short bonds, to open up and maintain a gap between the yields of short bonds and those of long-dated securities. This would, however, be more difficult, since the banks, if forced to sell securities by shortage of liquid assets, would probably try to minimise their realised losses by selling the shortest-dated bonds in their investment portfolios, thus tending to force down their prices and raise their yields.

In conclusion, there are two further points to be made about the practical operation of the new system. In the first place, if the policy becomes standard practice of enforcing monetary restriction by operating on the banks' supply of liquid assets rather than on their cash, the use of Bank Rate will be deprived of some of its significance, unless quite small changes in it are accepted as formal signals of changes in policy. Thus a rise in Bank Rate from, say, 3 to 4 per cent might well accompany action in the securities market to drive the long rate up from, say, 4 to 5 per cent or even $5\frac{1}{2}$ per cent. Even if the same results could be obtained in the long-term market without a rise in Bank Rate, some rise would then be justified on purely psychological grounds. Secondly, the operation of such a system would be rendered very much easier if a substantial reduction could be achieved in the volume of short bonds maturing each year. It would therefore be wise for the Treasury to take advantage of any 'interinflationary intervals', when rates of interest were relatively low, to press on with the issue of long-term loans in order to buy in or convert, not Treasury bills, but any short-term bonds maturing within the next few years. If the authorities could enter on the task of checking an excessive increase in home demand with the knowledge that no substantial volume of Government securities would mature during the coming year, their task of reducing the volume of the floating debt would be enormously simplified.

CHAPTER 11

THE POSITION OF THE UNITED KINGDOM AS AN EXPORTER OF CAPITAL [1]

DURING the century which elapsed between the end of the Napoleonic War and the outbreak of the First World War the United Kingdom was the world's chief exporter of capital. One estimate puts the cumulative total of British capital exports during this period at almost £4000 millions, and it was largely with the help of imports of capital from Britain that developing countries were able to equip themselves with roads, railways, harbours, docks, public utilities, and the beginnings of manufacturing industries, as well as to develop mines and plantations. From these foreign investments Britain obtained three advantages. She created markets for her exports and sources for the imports of food and raw materials which she needed to support her growing population; she built up an investment income from abroad until it amounted to not much less than 10 per cent of her national income; and she obtained a reserve of marketable foreign assets which were to prove of the greatest help in financing two world wars.

Although the general trend of British capital exports was markedly upward, especially after the middle of the century, the rise was far from continuous. Periods of high capital exports were followed by others when they fell into insignificance. One estimate by A. M. Imlah, of foreign investments throughout the century, and another by J. H. Lenfant, of both home and foreign investments in the period between 1871 and 1913, are shown in Table I. Though the two estimates of foreign investments differ considerably in their absolute levels, they show a close similarity in the size and direction of their fluctuations. From Lenfant's estimates it appears that in

---

[1] The English, Scottish, and Australian Bank Ltd. Research Lecture — 1957. Delivered at the University of Queensland, St. Lucia, on 30th July 1957.

periods of active world trade, such as 1871–75, 1886–90, and
1906–13, foreign investment rose more than total investment,
so that domestic investment fell, while in years of world
depression, such as 1876–80 and 1891–95, foreign investment
fell more than total investment, so that domestic investment

TABLE I

U.K. HOME AND FOREIGN INVESTMENT
BEFORE 1914

(Annual Averages £m.)

	Imlah	Lenfant				
	Foreign Invest-ment	Foreign Invest-ment	Gross Domestic Fixed Investment			Total Invest-ment
			Houses	Other	Total	
1816–20	8					
1821–25	9					
1826–30	3					
1831–35	7					
1836–40	3					
1841–45	7					
1846–50	6					
1851–55	8					
1856–60	25					
1861–65	23					
1866–70	40					
1871–75	74	59	52	85	137	196
1876–80	24	—	68	89	157	157
1881–85	62	35	58	86	144	179
1886–90	86	68	57	80	137	205
1891–95	53	30	61	95	156	186
1896–1900	40	26	86	144	230	256
1901–5	47	25	86	186	272	297
1906–10	145	122	87	150	237	359
1911–13	208	201	74	162	236	437

Sources: A. H. Imlah, 'British Balance of Payments and Export of
Capital, 1816–1913' (*Economic History Review*, 1952). J. H. Lenfant,
'Great Britain's Capital Formation, 1865–1914' (*Economica*, 1951).

rose. Foreign investment was particularly high in the period
just before 1914, averaging about £200 millions a year, or over
8 per cent of the net national income. The equivalent value
of this at to-day's prices would be about £900 millions, while
a similar percentage of national income would to-day amount
to about £1400 millions.

The fluctuating pattern of British foreign investment continued during the inter-war years. During the later 1920s the recovery in world trade brought an active demand for capital from the developing countries, and British exports of long-term capital, mainly to Commonwealth countries, rose to a level which, while below that of 1911–13, was still very substantial. Unfortunately, the overvaluation of the currency involved in the return to the gold standard at the old parity made it impossible, in spite of heavy unemployment, to achieve a balance-of-payments surplus large enough to cover the whole of the long-term foreign investments, and the gap had to be filled by keeping short-term interest rates high enough to attract large short-term balances to London. It was the withdrawal of these balances in 1931, when confidence in sterling was impaired both by an adverse balance of payments and by the banking crises in Austria and Germany, that led to the abandonment of the gold standard and the depreciation of sterling. In the 1930s, on the other hand, the acute world depression destroyed the demand for capital in the developing countries, and new British exports of capital were probably less than the repayments of old debts to Britain. It is these repayments which may account for the greater rise in Britain's gold reserves than in her short-term foreign debts at a time when the balance of payments on income account was barely in equilibrium.

Since the end of the Second World War the economic condition of the world has been such as again to create the most active demand for imports of capital by the developing countries, but the ability of the United Kingdom to satisfy this demand out of her own resources has hitherto been very small. It is true that, as Table II shows, she has been able to provide moderate quantities of long-term capital to other countries in the sterling area, but these have been achieved only by re-exporting capital which she herself has received from overseas. During the first four years after the war an average annual export of long-term capital of £130 millions to the sterling area was made possible only by the receipt of grants and loans from the United States and Canada averaging £416 millions a year, and even so she was obliged to draw heavily on her gold reserve to meet withdrawals of capital by non-sterling countries. Exports of capital during the earlier part of this period were probably stimulated by the cheap money policy of the United Kingdom, and it may be doubted whether in all the countries to which capital was exported during these years the control of the forms which investment might take was as rigorous as in the United Kingdom.

TABLE II

UNITED KINGDOM EXPORTS OF CAPITAL, 1946–56

(£m. at Current Prices)

	Annual Averages			Year
	1946–49	1950–52	1953–55	1956
Balance on Income A/c.	− 177	+ 6	+ 47	+ 210
Defence Aid	—	+ 42	+ 65	+ 23
Balance on Current A/c.	− 177	+ 48	+ 112	+ 233
Net Grants, Loans, etc., from Dollar Area	+ 416	+ 140	+ 25	− 94
Net Loan from International Organisations	+ 4	− 6	− 31	+ 203
Withdrawals from Gold Reserve	+ 39	− 19	− 33	− 5
Export of Capital to non-dollar Area	+ 282	+ 163	+ 73	+ 337
Capital Transactions with non-dollar, non-sterling Area	− 92	− 130	− 53	− 175
Exports of Capital to Sterling Area	+ 190	+ 33	+ 20	+ 162
Changes in Sterling Area Sterling Balances	− 60	+ 129	+ 112	− 19
Net Long-term Investment in Sterling Area	+ 130	+ 162	+ 132	+ 143

Source: Cmnd. 122.

During the next period, from 1950 to 1952, the United Kingdom's own balance of payments reached a precarious equilibrium and with American aid continuing, though on a reduced scale, the country was able to make an average amount of £163 millions available for capital exports of all descriptions to non-dollar countries. Most of this, however, was needed to meet withdrawals by non-sterling countries, and the net amount available for the sterling area averaged only £33 millions a year. Fortunately some countries of the sterling area, and especially certain of the colonial territories, were enabled by high export prices to add substantially to their sterling balances, thus permitting long-term capital exports to be maintained at a substantial rate without drawing on the gold reserve.

In the third period, from 1953 to 1955, Britain managed to achieve a small average export surplus and, with the help of U.S. defence aid and a continued rise in colonial sterling balances, was able approximately to maintain her long-term capital exports and to add to her gold reserves in spite of continued withdrawals by non-sterling countries. Towards the end of the period, however, there appeared a number of indications of future trouble, quite apart from the internal developments which brought about the adverse balance of payments of 1955. Not only had dollar aid ceased but defence aid was rapidly falling, while the colonies were ceasing to add further to their balances, partly in consequence of lower prices for rubber and cocoa, but also as the result of the rapid movement towards self-government in the two largest contributors, the Gold Coast and Malaya. It was obvious that in future Britain would have to rely on her own export surplus to provide not only for her long-term capital exports but also for the repayment of short-term obligations to non-sterling countries, and perhaps to sterling countries also, and for the much-needed augmentation of gold reserve. In 1956, therefore, a great effort was made to achieve a favourable balance of payments large enough to achieve these ends ; the official estimate of the size of the balance needed was put at £350 millions. The effort met with considerable success, and the surplus actually achieved was £210 millions, plus £23 millions of defence aid. But the whole of this surplus was absorbed in meeting the heavy withdrawals by non-sterling countries, caused partly by the Suez crisis, and with the sterling balances of sterling area countries falling slightly instead of rising, it was possible to finance the usual export of long-term capital to the sterling area without drawing heavily on the gold reserves only by borrowing £200 millions from the International Monetary Fund.

Why is it that Britain has been unable, in the post-war period, to provide enough out of her own resources to resume, even on a modest scale, her function of providing long-term capital for the developing countries of the Commonwealth ?

One possible explanation could be that Britain had been too impoverished by her efforts in two world wars to be able to afford to invest abroad even one or two per cent of her national income; and indeed to an observer in 1945 it must have seemed unlikely that for many years to come she would be able to achieve an export surplus of any sort. During the war Britain had suffered direct war damage to a value of well over £2000 millions at present prices, and had in addition been forced to dispense with any maintenance or replacement of capital assets which was not directly needed for the conduct of the war. In addition, stocks, especially of all types of consumption goods, had been very severely depleted. Even if we make allowance for the creation of new capacity for the production of war material, a good deal of which could be adapted for peace-time use, it is difficult to put the net loss of physical capital at less than £2000 or £3000 millions at present prices.

At least equally serious was the net decline in Britain's international capital position. Nearly a third of her long-term foreign investments was sold and debts were incurred more than equal to the remainder, so that the country became, for the first time in its history, a net foreign debtor. Fortunately the remaining investments were largely equities, with a higher yield than the interest payable on the foreign debts, so that there remained a small net income from foreign investments. But in real terms more than three-quarters of her pre-war foreign investment income had been lost, equivalent to a loss of over £500 millions a year at present import prices, or nearly 3 per cent of the national income.

Another very serious loss of real national income was caused by the greater rise, during and immediately after the war, of import prices than of export prices, so that by 1948 it took nearly 20 per cent more exports than in 1938 to pay for a given amount of imports. At present prices and volumes of trade this is equivalent to a loss of national income of about £700 millions a year, or nearly 4 per cent of the national income. In 1951 the sharp rise in import prices brought the loss due to the worsened terms of trade up to nearly £1400 millions or over 7 per cent of the national income, but the terms of trade and the loss of national income have fortunately since returned to about their 1948 levels. Even so, the loss of investment income from abroad and the worsened terms of trade have together reduced national income by something like 7 per cent, to which must be added the fall resulting from the internal loss of capital. In all, it would not have been unreasonable in 1945 to expect that the country would face the post-war period with the initial handicap of a loss something like 10 per cent of its pre-war real income.

Nevertheless, however reasonable the fears about the future poverty of the country may have seemed in 1945, they have in fact proved unfounded. The development which has more than offset the losses described above, and which even the most optimistic would hardly have dared to predict, has been the very remarkable rise in production which has occurred since the war. This rise, which is shown in Table III, may be divided into two phases. In the first, from 1945 to 1948, the rise in production was just about sufficient to offset the loss of national income due to loss of foreign investment income and worsened terms of trade, though income per head of population was still appreciably below the 1938 level. Up to 1948 the rise in output was entirely due to the increase in the number of persons employed, partly as the result of the fall since 1938 in the number unemployed, especially of men, and partly to the rise in the number, especially of women, of those going out to work. Output per person employed was thus no higher in 1948 than it had been in 1938, although, in view of the war-time losses of capital, it may be counted a considerable achievement that it was no lower. Since 1948 the situation has been very different. Of the rise of nearly 26 per cent in production between 1948 and 1956, only about a quarter can be ascribed to the larger number of workers employed, so that there has been an increase of nearly 20 per cent in output per head. This is equivalent to a cumulative increase of over $2\frac{1}{4}$ per cent a year — a rate of increase which, if continued, would double the real national income per head in a generation. This is at least double the average annual rate of increase during the inter-war period, and probably also during the previous quarter of a century; it is also at least as great as the average increase in output per head since the war in the United States. The reasons for this sudden acceleration in the growth of output are complex, but one important factor is certainly the great increase in the share of production taken by the newer industries and sections of industry, many of which expanded greatly under the stimulus of war.   These newer and rapidly expanding industries have naturally found it easier than the older and sometimes declining industries to attract to themselves progressive and enterprising managements, and the average standard of management and its ability to take advantage of the rapid growth of technical knowledge are almost certainly considerably higher than before the war.

TABLE III

GROSS REAL NATIONAL PRODUCT AND GROSS
REAL NATIONAL INCOME OF THE UNITED
KINGDOM, 1946–56

(1938 = 100)

	Total		Per Head of Population	
	Production	National Income	Production	National Income
1946	103·0	96·4	99·5	93·0
1947	103·6	96·9	99·1	92·7
1948	107·0	100·5	101·8	95·7
1949	110·6	104·1	104·8	98·6
1950	113·8	106·1	107·5	100·1
1951	118·1	107·7	111·1	101·3
1952	118·3	109·1	110·8	102·1
1953	122·6	114·2	114·6	106·6
1954	128·2	119·4	119·5	111·3
1955	132·5	123·2	123·2	114·4
1956 (prov.)	134·4	126·2	124·5	117·0

Sources : 'National Income and Expenditure, 1956', Table 12;   Cmnd. 113, Table 2 ;   Author's Estimates.

Until towards the end of 1951 the effects on national income of the rapid rise in production were partly offset by the further worsening of the terms of trade, and even in 1952 the real national income per head of population was only slightly larger than in 1938.   After 1952, however, the rise in production was reinforced by the return of the terms of trade to their 1948 level, and in four years real national income increased by nearly 16 per cent in total and by nearly 15 per cent per head of population, which is now growing only slowly.   With real national income per head of population at 17 per cent above the pre-war level and probably at least one-third above the 1913 level, it is no longer possible to ascribe merely to poverty Britain's inability to achieve a balance-of-payments surplus equal to 2 per cent of the national income.

If Britain's balance-of-payments difficulties during the past few years cannot be ascribed to poverty, the cause must be that, fast as income has risen, home demand has also risen fast enough to absorb the whole, or almost the whole, of the increase. To enquire the reason for this excessive home demand is a question that has no meaning, for all forms of domestic expenditure combine in contributing to the total and it is open to anyone to claim that any one or other of them, by some absolute standard, is too high. It is, however, possible to indicate which forms of expenditure have been growing most rapidly, and therefore which increases have contributed most to the increase in the total. To make this examination possible, in Table IV the real national income has been divided into three parts, according to use : one part used to finance consumers' expenditure, a second for expenditure by public authorities on goods and services (the effects of their transfer payments are already allowed for in consumers' expenditure), and the third part saved.

There are a number of reasons why it would have been reasonable to expect a rise in the post-war period in the proportion of national income used for personal consumption. There has been a very marked redistribution of incomes both before and still more after tax away from the rich and in favour, not so much of the poor, as of the middle income groups with incomes about equivalent to the adult male wage. Since it is generally believed that these groups tend to consume a higher proportion of their incomes than was formerly consumed by the rich, the redistribution of income would seem to be a factor making for the personal consumption of a higher proportion of the national income. Again, at the end of the war many persons were in the possession of unusually large holdings of money and other liquid assets, accumulated not so much as a result of a desire to save as of the inability, in the shortages and restrictions of war-time, to find anything worth while to spend money on. It might have been expected that

TABLE IV

USES OF UNITED KINGDOM NATIONAL INCOME

(At 1948 Market Prices)

| | Consumers' Expenditure | | | | Public Authorities' Expenditure on Goods and Services | | | Saving and Depreciation | | | Gross National Income | |
| | £m. | Percentage of | | | £m. | Percentage of | | £m. | Percentage of | | £m. | Percentage of 1948 |
		Nat. Income	1948	1948 per Head of Population		Nat. Income	1948		Nat. Income	1948		
1938 (partly est.)	8564	73·3	101·1	106·2	1750	15·0	99·3	1373	11·7	90·4	11,687	99·5
1946	8245	73·1	97·3	98·7	2589	23·0	147·0	437	3·9	28·8	11,271	96·5
1947	8519	75·2	100·5	101·0	1773	15·7	100·6	1032	9·1	68·0	11,324	96·4
1948	8471	72·1	100·0	100·0	1761	15·0	100·0	1517	12·9	100·0	11,749	100·0
1949	8616	70·6	101·7	101·0	1915	15·7	108·7	1655	13·6	109·1	12,186	103·7
1950	8824	71·1	104·2	103·3	1899	15·3	107·9	1697	13·7	111·9	12,420	105·6
1951	8782	69·7	103·6	102·4	2048	16·3	116·2	1761	14·0	116·1	12,591	107·2
1952	8730	68·4	103·0	101·3	2273	17·8	129·0	1758	13·8	115·8	12,761	108·6
1953	9098	68·1	107·3	105·4	2310	17·3	131·2	1949	14·6	128·5	13,357	113·6
1954	9512	68·2	112·4	110·1	2293	16·3	130·2	2158	15·5	142·2	13,963	118·8
1955	9800	68·1	115·8	113·1	2256	15·7	128·0	2342	16·2	154·4	14,398	122·6
1956 (prov.)	9859	66·8	116·4	113·2	2294	15·6	130·3	2597	17·6	171·2	14,750	125·6

Sources: 'National Income and Expenditure, 1956', Tables 6, 12, 46, and 47; Cmnd. 113, Table 5; Cmnd. 123, Tables 1 and 6. Figures revised to 1961 are given in Table III of Chapter 8.

the expenditure of these involuntary savings would go to swell still further the total of consumer demand.

However reasonable these expectations, in point of fact the proportion of national income devoted to personal consumption, after an initial rise in 1947, has shown a persistent fall and is now far below the pre-war ratio. In spite of the rise in national income, personal consumption per head of population rose hardly at all between 1947 and 1952, and though during the next three years it rose fairly substantially, giving the public their first real rise in standards of living since the war, the increase was proportionally no greater than that in the real national income, so that the proportion consumed was unchanged. In 1956 the rise in personal consumption was again checked and the proportion of national income devoted to it again fell sharply.

If personal consumption cannot be blamed for the excessive rise in internal demand during recent years, an alternative explanation could be an excessive rise in expenditure by public authorities on goods and services. There are some signs of such a rise in 1949, when the social security programme was introduced, and again, and more markedly, in 1951–52, when heavy additional expenditure was incurred on defence. Since 1952, however, Government expenditure on goods and services has been approximately stabilised in real terms, and has constituted a declining proportion of the rapidly rising real national income. Its 1956 ratio was little more than $15\frac{1}{2}$ per cent, as compared with nearly 18 per cent in 1952, and was about the same as the ratio in 1949 and only slightly higher than the 15 per cent absorbed in 1938. The much higher tax rates ruling now than before the war have been necessitated, not so much by increased expenditure on goods and services as by higher transfer payments, the need for budget surpluses and above all by the redistribution of personal incomes before tax, which have greatly reduced the yield from given rates of direct personal taxation.

The persistent fall in the proportion of national income devoted to personal consumption and the return to its earlier level of the proportion spent by public authorities on goods and services have resulted in a very substantial increase in the proportion saved. Gross saving, which had formed a nearly stable proportion of national income, at 13–14 per cent, since it first recovered in 1948, rose between 1952 and 1956 from 13·8 to 17·6 per cent of a much larger income. This is probably a larger proportion than was achieved at any time during the inter-war period, and is not so very far below the estimated ratio of 21 per cent in 1914, when the distribution of incomes was very different. In net saving the recent rise is even more striking. If we allow depreciation at a rate rising gradually from about 7 per cent of gross real national income in 1938 to about 8¼ per cent in 1956, we find that net saving rose from under 5 per cent of net real national income in 1938 to rather over 6 per cent in 1948–52, and then jumped suddenly to nearly 9 per cent in 1955 and over 10 per cent in 1956. Although net saving in 1956 was still not much over two-thirds of the estimated ratio of 14½ per cent of net national income achieved in 1913, the rise since then in total real national income means that in absolute real terms it was probably rather higher.

The sources of this rise in saving are shown in Table V. The rise from 1947 to 1948 is seen to have been due mainly to the increase in Government saving, achieved by a rise in taxation at a time when Government expenditure was falling ; but the rise since 1951 has been due mainly to a very remarkable revival in personal saving. The causes of this revival are obscure, and indeed its existence was doubted for some time after signs of it began to appear in the national income estimates. The most plausible explanation is that positive personal saving, very largely in the form of increases in life insurance and pension funds, had been substantial and rising steadily ever since the end of the war, but that up to the end of 1951 these positive savings were almost entirely offset by the spending by others of their involuntary war-time savings. It is believed that, as controls on personal expenditure were relaxed or evaded, these involuntary savings were gradually spent and that the process, accelerated by the renewed rise in prices, had largely come to an end by the end of 1951. Thereafter, although positive saving continued to rise only gradually, it ceased to be offset to the same extent by capital consumption, so that net saving took a sudden leap. Of the second steep rise, in 1956, about a third can be accounted for by the restrictions on hire purchase transactions. Most of the remainder,

as welcome as it was unexpected, seems to have been due to
voluntary restraint, especially in the purchase of durable consumption goods.   It is difficult to avoid the impression that,
both in 1952 and 1956, a very slight touch of disinflation contributed to discouraging the demand for durable consumption
goods, not so much by removing the expectation of rising
prices — prices in fact rose appreciably in both years — as
perhaps by bringing some slight uncertainty about the security
of future incomes and so providing a measure of incentive for
keeping resources in liquid form and keeping out of debt.

TABLE V

SOURCES OF SAVING IN THE UNITED KINGDOM

(£m. at 1948 Prices)

	Persons and Unincorporated Businesses	Companies and Public Corporations	Tax Reserves	Public Authorities	Total Savings a Depreciat
1938 (partly estimated)	650	863	52	−192	1373
1946	358	533	−42	−412	437
1947	164	426	264	178	1032
1948	32	735	182	568	1517
1949	129	845	24	657	1655
1950	96	881	128	592	1697
1951	113	705	449	494	1761
1952	548	881	−23	352	1758
1953	652	1060	−30	267	1949
1954	567	1225	120	246	2158
1955	715	1189	30	408	2342
1956 (prov.)	1032	1133	108	324	2597

Sources : 'National Income and Expenditure, 1956', Tables 6 and 12 ; Cmnd.
Table 6. Figures revised to 1961 are given in Table IV of Chapter 8.

In view of the rise in saving between 1952 and 1955, it
follows that the inability of the United Kingdom to provide a
larger margin for foreign investment must have been due to a
rise in home investment.   From Table VI it is clear that the
greater part of this rise was in domestic fixed investment.
This rise in fixed investment occurred in two phases.   In 1952
the new Conservative Government, in fulfilment of its election
pledges, began a campaign to stimulate house-building, partly
by encouraging the local authorities to expand their programmes for building houses to let at subsidised rents, but

TABLE VI
GROSS DOMESTIC FIXED CAPITAL FORMATION IN THE UNITED KINGDOM
(£m. at 1948 Prices)

	Vehicles, Ships, and Aircraft			Plant and Machinery			New Dwellings			Other Buildings, etc.			Total		
	Private Sector	Public Sector	Total	Private Sector	Public Sector	Total	Private Sector	Public Sector	Total	Private Sector	Public Sector	Total	Private Sector	Public Sector	Total
1938	—	—	205	—	—	402	—	—	474	—	—	478	1086	473	1559
1946	—	—	—	—	—	—	—	—	—	—	—	—	—	—	1058
1947	—	—	292	—	—	398	—	—	356	—	—	258	—	—	1304
1948	210	56	266	360	135	495	45	292	337	155	182	337	770	665	1435
1949	211	74	285	355	181	536	54	276	330	188	222	410	808	753	1561
1950	187	70	257	392	208	600	50	273	323	219	244	463	848	795	1643
1951	166	56	222	382	276	658	49	267	316	190	263	453	787	862	1649
1952	162	50	212	336	288	624	76	301	377	173	287	460	747	926	1673
1953	185	57	242	325	307	632	133	360	493	178	306	484	821	1030	1851
1954	200	61	261	379	321	700	187	332	519	211	316	527	977	1030	2007
1955	221	72	293	440	327	767	210	270	480	285	307	592	1156	976	2132
1956 (prov.)	246	76	322	443	329	772	225	237	462	323	320	643	1237	962	2199

Sources: 'National Income and Expenditure, 1956', Tables 46, 47, and 51; and Cmnd. 113, Table 3. Figures revised to 1961 are given in Table V of Chapter 8.

mainly by removing restrictions on private house-building and so releasing a flood of long-frustrated demand. As a result of this change of policy, the number of houses completed rose from the previous level of about 200,000 a year to over 350,000 a year in 1954. The magnitude of the rise in resources employed can be judged from the increase in housing expenditure (at 1948 prices) from £49 millions by private builders and £267 millions by public authorities in 1951 to £187 millions by private builders and £332 millions by public authorities in 1954.

The second phase of expansion in fixed investment did not begin until 1954. In 1952 and 1953 the Government had become increasingly concerned that the rise in investment had been confined entirely to house-building, and that industrial and commercial investment, so necessary for the continued rise in production per head, seemed to be neglected. They therefore took steps, by exhortation, tax remissions and the removal of restrictions, to encourage its expansion. For a long time these measures had little effect, but from about the middle of 1954 a very large and rapid rise began in investment other than housing, which, superimposed upon the existing housing boom, absorbed the whole of the rise in saving and left no increase in the margin for other forms of investment.

For the margin of savings left after the requirements for domestic fixed investment have been satisfied there are two other forms of investment to compete, investment in the form of additions to stocks of raw materials, work in progress and finished goods awaiting sale, and investment abroad, including additions to the gold reserves and the repayment of debts due to foreigners. In the United Kingdom, the physical volume of stocks seems to rise at about two-thirds the rate of production, that is to say, at an average rate of about 2 per cent a year. There are, however, wide fluctuations about this average rate of growth, and the post-war pattern has taken the form of several years of low stock accumulation followed by one in which the rise in stocks is very large. By what is presumably a coincidence, these periods of rapid stock accumulation have occurred since the war at intervals of exactly four years, in 1947, in 1951, and in 1955. As is clearly brought out in Table VII, these variations in the rate of stock accumulation

Table VII

SOURCES AND USES OF INVESTIBLE FUNDS IN THE UNITED KINGDOM

(£m. at 1948 Prices)

	Investible Funds				Gross Domestic Fixed Capital Formation	Surplus Available for Stock Accumulation and Foreign Investment	Use of Surplus	
	Gross Saving	Capital Grants and Transfers from Abroad	Errors and Omissions	Total Investible Funds			Physical Increase in Stocks	Net Foreign Investment
1938	1373	—	—	1373	1559	− 186	—	− 186
1946	437	173	—	610	1058	− 448	− 59	− 389
1947	1032	172	—	1204	1304	− 100	+ 358	− 458
1948	1517	234	− 2	1749	1435	+ 314	+ 175	+ 139
1949	1655	186	− 36	1805	1561	+ 244	+ 62	+ 182
1950	1697	160	− 10	1847	1643	+ 204	− 186	+ 390
1951	1761	69	+ 22	1852	1649	+ 203	+ 454	− 251
1952	1758	27	+ 98	1883	1673	+ 210	+ 37	+ 173
1953	1949	21	+ 117	2087	1851	+ 236	+ 95	+ 141
1954	2158	9	+ 70	2237	2007	+ 230	+ 57	+ 173
1955	2342	12	− 58	2296	2132	+ 164	+ 223	− 59
1956 (prov.)	2597	9	− 92	2514	2199	+ 315	+ 146	+ 169

Sources: 'National Income and Expenditure, 1956', Tables 6, 46 and 47; Cmnd. 113, Table 3; and Cmnd. 123, Table 6. Figures revised to 1961 are given in Table VI of Chapter 8.

caused inverse variations in the balance of payments (*i.e.* in net foreign investment plus changes in the gold reserve), even though the margin of saving (plus foreign aid) over domestic fixed investment was unchanged. Thus in 1951 the margin of savings available for stock accumulation and foreign investment combined was almost exactly the same as in 1950; but the change from a heavy fall in stocks to a very large rise was sufficient to convert a large favourable balance of payments into a very large adverse one, bringing a heavy fall in the gold reserve and a major sterling crisis. In 1955 again, it was the sharp rise in stock accumulation coinciding with a moderate fall in the margin of savings left after providing for the increase in fixed investment which converted a moderately favourable balance of payments in 1954 into an adverse one in 1955 and precipitated another crisis.

While, however, these fluctuations in the rate of stock accumulation have been the immediate cause of three out of the four balance-of-payments crises which have occurred since the war (the immediate causes of the 1949 crisis lay in the rest of the sterling area rather than with the United Kingdom itself), the ultimate cause has been the inadequate surplus of saving left after financing fixed investment at home. In times of subnormal stock accumulation, this margin is enough to provide a balance-of-payments surplus which, while not large enough to provide a really adequate margin, is at least sufficient to prevent serious trouble. But the margin is not large enough to provide for an adequate balance-of-payments surplus in years when the rate of stock accumulation reaches the average, still less in years when it rises above average in order to make up for past under-stocking. To provide for a balance-of-payments surplus of £350 millions a year plus an average rate of stock accumulation, the annual margin of saving over fixed investment needs to be about £520 millions a year at 1956 prices, or rather under £400 millions a year at 1948 prices. In no year since the war has the margin reached this figure. The only two years in which it has even approached it are 1948, when American aid was at its peak, and 1956.

The marked improvement in the balance-of-payments position in 1956, in spite of a rate of stock accumulation which was still above average, can be ascribed mainly to Government policy, though its success has been obscured by the flight from sterling which occurred, largely as the result of the Suez crisis. Ever since the end of 1954, the Government, apart from its 1955 budget, has increasingly directed its efforts towards slowing down the rise in home demand. Part of these efforts has been directed against consumption demand, mainly by means of increases in indirect taxes, by restrictions on hire purchase finance, and by pressure on the banks to restrict personal advances; but the major part has been directed towards slowing down the rise in investment demand by measures designed to restrict the quantity of money and the availability of credit and to raise the rate of interest. It was not until the 1957 budget that any effective effort was made to reduce Government expenditure on goods and services and to increase the level of Government saving.

The efforts to restrict the rise in personal consumption in 1956 had, as we have seen, an effect considerably greater than can be attributed to the direct results of the impediments placed in the way of those who wished to buy durable consumer goods with borrowed money. The measures designed to restrict investment were not quite so successful. Generally speaking, it can be expected that investment will be sensitive to changes in the rate of interest in proportion to the economic and physical durability of the assets created. A piece of rapidly obsolescing industrial equipment might not be introduced unless its owners thought they could see their way to writing it off in five years. With a depreciation rate of 20 per cent and an interest rate of 4 per cent, the total annual cost of ownership would be 24 per cent of the original cost. If the rate of interest is 6 instead of 4 per cent, the annual cost of ownership rises from 24 to 26 per cent. The rise is thus one-twelfth, which would probably not be enough to affect the decision in any but very marginal cases. The position is very different with a highly durable asset little affected by obsolescence, such as a house. Here the interest charge forms the greater part of the annual cost, and changes in it have a correspondingly greater influence on policy decisions. For instance, with an interest rate of 4 per cent, we can probably put the annual cost of ownership of a house at not more than 6 per cent of the capital cost. If the rate of interest now rises to 6 per cent, the annual cost rises from 6

H

to 8 per cent, or by one-third, a proportion which is normally large enough to affect a large number of decisions. Similar considerations apply, though perhaps rather less strongly, to the construction of other classes of highly durable assets with little risk of premature obsolescence, such as blocks of offices and shops. But both these forms of investment, which are those which on principle we should have expected to be checked first by a rise in interest rates, are also those which in the United Kingdom have recently received an exceptional stimulus as the result of the removal of long-standing restrictions. This has released a flood of long-frustrated demand, not only large but also for the time being particularly insensitive to non-physical controls such as a rise in the rate of interest. Indeed, it is one of the strongest arguments against the use of physical controls, at any rate in peace-time, that it is impossible to withdraw them without releasing a demand which is for a long time unusually insensitive to other forms of control. It is noticeable that the construction of houses by public authorities, which had been relatively little restricted in the period before 1952, fell substantially both in 1955 and again in 1956, whereas construction by private builders, which up to the end of 1951 had been very severely restricted, continued to rise in both years, though at a gradually decreasing rate.

The existence of these large unsatisfied demands for private house and commercial building has meant both that the aggregate response of the economy to monetary controls has been slowed down and that a larger share of the adjustment has been borne by industrial investment, which the Government would no doubt have preferred to spare. Nevertheless, in the aggregate, the measures taken have had a very considerable amount of success. The rise in fixed investment from 1955 to 1956 (at constant prices) was barely half the rise from 1954 to 1955 and not much more than a quarter of the rise in saving.[1] It was this that gave a rise in the increased margin of saving over fixed investment which, with the help of some fall in the rate of stock accumulation, was sufficient to convert the balance-of-

[1] Later estimates indicate that the rise in the surplus of Investible Funds over Fixed Capital Investment in 1955–56 was entirely due to an increased rate of growth of Investible Funds and not at all to a fall in the rate of growth of Fixed Investment.

payments deficit of 1955 into a surplus which, though still well below the target, would probably have been enough to end the sterling crisis but for the flight from the pound caused by political events.

What are the prospects for the maintenance and further increase of the 1956 margin of saving over fixed investment and of the balance-of-payments surplus? The signs are by no means all favourable. The effects of increasing the deposits required on hire purchase transactions are temporary, for as soon as consumers have accumulated the necessary additional savings they are in a position to resume their purchases; and there are already signs of an appreciable rise in hire purchase transactions and in the demand for durable consumption goods. It would therefore not be surprising to find at the end of 1957 that the whole of the 1956 rise in personal savings had not been maintained. Again, the improvement in the terms of trade, which so fortunately augmented the real national income in 1956, is not likely to be repeated, and may be succeeded by a move in the opposite direction. On the whole, however, the favourable indications seem to outweigh the unfavourable. If the larger budget surplus provided for in the 1957 estimates can in fact be achieved, the consequent rise in Government saving should go far towards offsetting the fall in personal saving, while a larger rise in production should offset the absence of an improvement in the terms of trade. If the Government persists in its policy of keeping money tight and long-term interest rates high, as it seems determined to do, the total volume of fixed investment seems unlikely to rise further; while if, as is hoped, one effect of the recent modification of the rent restriction acts is to bring about the reappearance of houses to let unfurnished, it may bring a fall in the demand for newly-built houses. And finally, since the increase in stocks in 1956 was still above average, there may be room for a fall in the rate of stock accumulation which would free more of the surplus of saving over fixed investment to augment the favourable balance of payments. On the whole, therefore, there seems to be a reasonable prospect that the balance-of-payments surplus will be at least maintained in 1957 and that, given a continuation of present policy, it may rise to or nearer to the desired level of £350 millions, if not in 1957, at least in 1958.

There remain two questions to answer. The first is whether it is in Britain's own interests to make sacrifices in order to achieve a permanently larger margin of saving over fixed investment and a permanently larger favourable balance of payments. As Table II shows, in 1956 Britain's net exports of long-term capital to the rest of the sterling area reached a figure of £143 millions, in spite of the severe financial stringency and the high rates of interest ruling at home. In view of this, it seems that, so long as the need for capital in the rest of the sterling area remains as urgent as at present, it will be impossible to reduce exports of long-term capital much below the 1956 level without imposing restrictions on the transfer of money from Britain to other sterling area countries, which would mean the end of the sterling area as we know it. Further, if and when the financial stringency is relaxed in Britain, it is reasonable to expect exports of capital to the sterling area to rise. Even to keep them down to their present level would therefore involve either the perpetuation of monetary stringency or the imposition of restrictions on the transfer of money. A condition for the relaxation of monetary stringency without the extension of exchange control to the sterling area is therefore a rise in the favourable balance of payments to a level which would permit a rise in net exports of long-term capital to the sterling area to, say, £200 millions a year.

Nor is this all. We have seen that the rise in sterling area sterling balances has been checked and is likely to be reversed, while it would be only prudent to provide for a continued fall in the balances of non-sterling area countries. It would therefore be prudent to allow for a continued gradual decline of sterling balances. Further, the £200 millions recently borrowed from the International Monetary Fund will have to be paid back during the next few years, while the debt of £125 millions still outstanding to the European Payments Union will also have to be gradually liquidated. In all, therefore, it would be prudent to allow at least £100 millions a year for the repayment of short-term foreign debts. In addition to this, one reason for the vulnerability of sterling since the war to the attacks of foreign speculators has been the quite inadequate size of the gold reserves. It would certainly be in Britain's long-term interest to build these up to a level which would put the stability of sterling out of reach of speculative attacks, and a sacrifice of £50 millions or £100 millions a year of internal expenditure for this purpose would be a wise investment. All in all, the favourable balance of payments necessary to permit a relaxation of financial stringency, without either necessitating the extension of exchange controls to transactions with the rest of the sterling area or imperilling the stability of sterling, cannot be put at less than the Government's estimate of £350 millions, and may well be considerably larger than that.

The second question to be answered is whether a considerably larger favourable balance of payments can in fact be achieved by the restriction of internal demand, or whether the resources so released from domestic use, instead of being used to achieve a larger favourable balance, would merely become unemployed and so be wasted. The relationship between changes in internal demand and changes in the balance of international payments depends on a number of factors, of which the most important is usually the volume of foreign trade in relation to national income. In a wholly closed economy, with no foreign trade, a rise in internal demand is reflected wholly in a rise in money incomes and, if the rise in incomes is greater than the rise in output, in a rise in prices. In a country with a foreign trade, however, only a part of the rise in demand will be reflected in local incomes and prices ; the remainder will be reflected in a rise in imports and/or a fall in exports, leading to a worsening in the balance of international payments. Generally speaking, the more open the system the greater the effect of a rise in internal demand on the balance of payments and the smaller the effect on domestic incomes and prices ; and in a completely open system, with no restrictions on trade, the movement of persons or the transfer of money, and with negligible transport costs, a rise in internal demand will be reflected wholly in the balance of payments and will raise internal incomes and prices only to the same extent that it raises them in the world as a whole. Similarly, while a fall in demand in a closed economy will exercise the whole of its effects on incomes, either through a reduction in income per person employed or through a reduction in the number of persons employed, in a partially open economy it will both reduce internal incomes and improve the balance of payments, while in a completely open system its effects will show themselves almost entirely in a more favourable balance of payments and will reduce domestic incomes only to the same extent that it reduces them throughout the world.

How far any particular country approximates to a closed or open economy is a matter of opinion; but there can be no doubt that the United States, where only about 3 per cent of the national product is exported, approximates much more closely to a closed economy than the United Kingdom, where the proportion of the national product exported is something like 20 per cent. A fall in internal demand will therefore reduce domestic incomes less, and improve the balance of payments more, in the United Kingdom than in the United States. On the other hand, a relatively open economy, like that of the United Kingdom, is extremely vulnerable to changes in the level of demand in the rest of the world, and in fact almost all the serious trade depressions from which the country has suffered during the past hundred years have been caused by falls in the overseas demand for British exports and hardly any (except perhaps the moderate recession which followed the end of the South African War) by a fall in domestic demand. Indeed, it may be doubted whether, in a period of active world trade, and in the absence of a serious over-valuation of sterling, even a deliberate attempt to bring about an internal trade depression by restricting domestic demand would have more than a very limited success, especially after the improving balance of payments had made it possible to throw the London capital market fully open to overseas issues. The resulting rise in foreign investment would go far towards offsetting the fall in home demand and would keep the fall in domestic incomes down to a modest level. There is some reason to think that the years 1906–13 saw a development of this kind. In those years the average level of domestic investment seems to have been lower, and the level of saving higher, than in the preceding quinquennium; nevertheless, so far from experiencing a recession in business, the country enjoyed a major boom as the result of an extremely high favourable balance of payments, made possible by a very high level of foreign lending.

While, however, it is believed that in the United Kingdom a large part of the effects of a reduction in home demand appears in a fall in imports and/or a rise in exports, the process is neither instantaneous nor painless. A decline in the home demand for goods and services has an immediate effect on the level of profits and (probably after some time-lag) on the demand for labour. Some firms which were forced to switch their sales from an easy home market to a more arduous and less profitable foreign market, and others which were not able to make the switch at all, would sooner or later be obliged to discharge labour, which would be able to find other employment only after some delay. There would there-fore be some increase in transitional unemployment. The size of this increase would depend partly on the policies of the trade unions in the still expanding industries, as regards both demands for wage increases and the admission of addi-tional workers; and partly on how far the movement of workers could be facilitated both to other districts and to new types of work. But in view of the great reduction in area specialisation which has occurred in Britain and of the im-provements in travelling facilities, as well as the greater avail-ability of houses to let which is expected to result from the recent modification of the rent restriction acts, there is some reason to believe that, with the co-operation of the trade unions, the total number of unemployed could be kept down to an average level of, say, 500,000, or 2 per cent of the employed population. So low a figure is, however, dependent on the policies of the trade unions; a militant policy of attempt-ing to force up wage rates faster than output, or of resisting transfers of labour, while it could not prevent a determined Government from checking the excess demand, might make the operation very much more expensive in terms of unemploy-ment and loss of output. Even on the most favourable assump-tions, it is not yet clear whether the Government and public opinion are prepared to revise their definition of full employ-ment from 99 to 98 per cent of the working force, though the Government at any rate has recently shown considerable firm-ness of purpose. But I am quite sure that unless the country is willing to pay at least this price it will not be possible either to check inflation or to guarantee the future stability of sterling.

CHAPTER 12

THE LONDON NEW ISSUE MARKET [1]

ALTHOUGH it has only recently been realised that Alice in Wonderland is a major source of information on mediaeval history, it has long been known, on the very best authority, that a detailed acquaintance with Alice is essential for a proper understanding of economic theory. It is, therefore, not without some fear of being thought presumptuous that I venture to say that at this moment I feel a little like Alice herself. You will remember that, after passing through the looking-glass and walking a little in the garden, she was invited by the Red Queen to join in a game of chess in the capacity of a pawn; and that, with the help of much kindness, a great deal of good advice and, at worst, the toleration of her fellow-pieces, she gradually progressed across the board until, jumping her last ditch, she found herself, suddenly encumbered with a crown, undergoing a searching qualifying examination at the hands of her companion queens. So, I, too, after many years of kindness, good advice or, at worst, toleration from my fellow-teachers, having jumped my last ditch and finding myself suddenly encumbered, if not with a crown, at least with a chair, stand here this evening undergoing my examination before my colleagues, some at least of whom were queens before I was even a pawn. I can only hope that, unlike Alice's queens, they will not feel obliged to go to sleep before the examination is completed.

And I think the resemblance can be pushed even a little further. You will remember that, after her examination, Alice proceeded to her castle and that, after a most unsatisfactory dinner, she saw her castle shake, collapse, and vanish into nothingness. So I too, when I get to my castle — part of which is the subject of my lecture this evening — find it, if not threatened with actual dissolution, at any rate dwarfed

[1] Inaugural lecture delivered at the London School of Economics on 5th November 1950. Published in *Economica*, February 1951.

and in danger of being squeezed out of existence by an enormous block of government offices which is sprouting and spreading on all sides of it.

This threatened eclipse of my castle is the more remarkable in that much of it is quite new, and that within the last generation the whole building has been overhauled and renovated almost out of recognition. When, scarcely a generation ago, Lavington wrote his great book on *The English Capital Market*, the substantial use of the new issue market as a means of providing finance for British industry was an extremely recent development. Before 1914 the main business of the London new issue market was foreign investment. Estimates of the annual total of British net investment differ considerably, but if we put gross investment at £550 millions and allow £200 millions, or between 8 and 9 per cent of national income, for the cost of maintaining capital intact, this would leave us £350 millions for net investment. This figure is from £50 millions to £100 millions less than some contemporary estimates, but these seem to allow a quite inadequate margin for depreciation. Even the figures I have suggested mean gross investment equal to over 23 per cent of national income, and net investment of nearly 15 per cent, almost entirely financed out of private saving and probably considerably more than half of it out of personal saving.

Of the estimated total of net national investment at least half, and in some years appreciably more than half, was invested abroad. Since direct private investment abroad, together with net short-term foreign investment, was probably not much greater than the annual amortisation quotas and repayments of existing loans, almost the whole of net foreign investment can be taken as represented by new long-term issues on the London market, which at their peak reached an annual total of about £200 millions. Of net investment at home, on the other hand, only a small proportion — not more than £30 millions or so out of a total of £150 millions or more — was financed through the capital market. The remainder was financed either out of profits ploughed back or out of personal savings invested directly.

The small scale of the new issue market in home securities, and of many of the individual issues, was no doubt the reason

H2

why the great merchant bankers, who were responsible for the
great bulk of the issues on overseas account, took little interest
in it, apart from occasionally sponsoring a large issue of railway
or public utility securities. The issuing of home industrial
securities was in general left to the company promoter or
ad hoc syndicate; and, though there were no doubt numerous
sound issues by reputable companies, only too often the chief
purpose in making an issue was to provide the maximum of
quick profit to promoters and vendors. As Foxwell said in his
famous lecture on 'The Financing of Industry and Trade',
delivered at the Royal Institution in April 1917, in which he
compared British methods unfavourably with those of Germany:

'In the description of German banking just quoted stress
is laid on the important part it plays in the business of issue
and flotation. Here we have one of the most striking contrasts
with English practice. This delicate business, which *we* leave
to the company promoter, is the special care of the banks in
Germany, where the company promoter scarcely exists. The
banks, with their large staff of industrial experts, not to speak
of the many highly trained men they have on their boards of
directors, are able to give the most intelligent examination to
all schemes put before them; and to insist, before they accept
any new proposition, that the necessary provisions are made,
whether as to capital resources, management, or scientific
assistance, to ensure that the undertaking shall have a fair
prospect of success. The company promoter, like Gallio,
cares for none of these things. His concern is simply with the
profits of the promotion. As soon as he has contrived to get
his issue quoted at a premium, and his underwriters have un-
loaded at a profit, his interest in the enterprise ceases. "To
him", as *The Times* says, "a successful flotation is of more
importance than a sound venture."'[1] And again, the facilities
provided by the promoter are 'mere makeshifts, utterly inadequate'.[2] In the temperate words of Lavington, it is not
difficult to see that the promoter's 'methods of operation contain within themselves strong tendencies to overvaluation and
to heavy marketing costs'.[3]

[1] *Economic Journal*, December 1917, p. 514.
[2] *Loc. cit.* p. 510.
[3] F. Lavington, *The English Capital Market*, 1921, p. 213.

If we compare conditions to-day with those of which Foxwell and Lavington wrote we shall find some very remarkable
improvements. These are due partly to the tightening-up of
the law governing new issues. The main outlines of the
present law had already been laid down in the 1908 and earlier
Acts; but the wording of these offered many loopholes to
the unscrupulous, of which full advantage was taken, though
not quite always with impunity, during the new issue boom
of the late 1920s. The more stringent provisions of the present
law fall into three main categories. First, there are those
designed to improve the machinery of the new issue market,
such as those providing for a three-day interval between
advertisement and issue and for making all applications for
new securities firm for three days. Secondly, companies are
now obliged to give much fuller information, both about their
own condition and records and about their recent contracts
outside their usual business, including contracts with vendors,
issuing houses, and others connected with the issue. And
thirdly, it has been made much more difficult for directors
and others to escape responsibility for the accuracy and
adequacy of information published under their authority. Thus
the subscribing public and its advisers are put in a much better
position not only to judge the intrinsic merits of an issue but
also to ascertain if any of those connected with it are making
an unreasonable profit.

Perhaps even more important than are the changes in the
law is the immense extension of the control exercised by the
Stock Exchange over the quality of the securities dealt in on
its floor.[1] Before 1914 the Stock Exchange made no attempt
to restrict or control in any way the right to deal in any security,
whether British or foreign. Only for the fraction of new
issues for which a special settlement was asked, and for the still
smaller fraction for which an official quotation was sought, did
the Committee of the Stock Exchange impose any conditions
whatsoever; and even for these, though its requirements went
in some respects beyond those of the then Companies Acts, it
was in general more concerned with arrangements to ensure a

---

[1] I am indebted for part of the following information to an unpublished
thesis by Dr. N. D. Vandyk on 'Economic Aspects of Company Law Reform,
1908–48'.

reasonably free market in the new securities than with the intrinsic merits of the company or with the adequacy or accuracy of the information provided.

When the Stock Exchange, closed at the outbreak of war, was reopened in 1915, the Government required that trans-actions should be recorded in all securities, whether on the official list or not. Thus it became necessary to publish a Supplementary List, recording bargains in hitherto unquoted securities. In 1921 Stock Exchange regulations were issued covering for the first time the granting of permission to deal and the consequential right to a quotation in the Supple-mentary List. These regulations, though less stringent than for admission to the Official List, provided for the publication of a statement in lieu of prospectus for securities for which no prospectus had been issued.

After the collapse of the 1928 boom, the rules for admission to both lists were greatly tightened up, and thereafter all applications either for permission to deal or for an official quotation were more closely scrutinised, from the point of view not only of the arrangements made to secure a free market, but also of the adequacy of the information to be published and of the records of all persons connected with the issue, whether as vendors, issuers, or underwriters. It is largely to the result of these changes, together, perhaps, with the increased vigilance and efficiency of the financial press, that we can attribute the freedom of the new issue boom of 1937 from the scandals which had marked that of 1928.

By the end of the recent war the distribution of securities between the Official and Supplementary Lists had become largely a matter of historical accident, and it became clear that their continued separation would serve no useful purpose. In 1947, therefore, they were amalgamated, and the distinc-tion between an 'application for permission to deal' and an 'application for an official quotation' was abolished. Thence-forward the conditions for the granting of an official quotation applied to all applications, and indeed were further stiffened up, particularly by the requirements that all applications must have the support of two jobbers and that the profits record must be shown for the past ten years, as against the five years required by the 1948 Companies Act. At the same time the hands of the Council were still further strengthened by the requirement in the same Act that, if it is stated in a prospectus that application for permission to deal will be made to the Stock Exchange, and if that application is either not made or is refused, then all subscriptions to the issue must be refunded in full. This means, in effect, that it is impossible to make an issue to the public without first submitting it to a searching examination by the skilled and experienced officials of the Stock Exchange, in order to ensure that the possibility of the rejection of an application is reduced to the absolute minimum. In considering an application, the Committee on Quotations can take account, not only of the adequacy of the information provided, the intrinsic merits of the issue, the records of the participants, the arrangements made to secure a free market, and the reasonableness of the profits to be made by participants or vendors, but also of the method by which the issue is made. They have, for instance, let it be known that they would not look favourably on an application for a quotation for a privately-placed issue unless a public issue would have been unduly expensive by reason of its small size.

Of at least equal importance with the changes in the law and in the strictness of Stock Exchange regulations are the changes in the organisation of the new issue market. After the 1914–18 war, the rise in prices and the increased levels of taxation, not only of company profits but also of large incomes and deceased estates, obliged companies to supplement private investment and profits ploughed back by large-scale recourse to the market. The results of the new issue booms of 1919–20 and of 1927–28 revealed only too clearly the inadequacy of the old machinery for its new tasks, and public losses from rash, over-expensive and sometimes dishonest flotations were high. But the booms, which revealed the weaknesses of the old system, also helped to bring their remedy. Each of the periods of increased activity in the new issue market saw the establishment of a number of a new type of issuing house, specialising mainly in the sponsoring and conduct of new issues by home industrial concerns, particularly those of smaller size. At the same time certain of the older merchant banks began to find it possible to extend their interests from the shrinking business of making large overseas issues to the growing market for home

issues. In 1945 the two types of issuing house joined forces
to set up an Issuing Houses Association, largely to represent
the interests of issuing houses in discussions with the Capital
Issues Committee and other bodies. The Association has to-
day some fifty-four members,[1] of which rather less than half
may be classified as merchant banks and rather more than half
as members of the new type of issuing house. The contrast
between the origins of the two groups is shown by the fact
that, whereas more than three-quarters of the merchant-bank
members were founded before 1914, only one-sixth of the
issuing houses were in existence before that date. Of the
remainder, five were founded between 1917 and 1921, nine
between 1925 and 1928, and eight between 1932 and 1936 —
all periods of high or expanding activity in the new issue
market for industrial securities.

In the types of business done, the two classes of issuing
house show considerable differences, as the accompanying table
shows. Since the war the new issuing houses have made more
than twice as many issues as the old merchant bankers, but the
aggregate amount of money raised through the merchant
bankers is more than 50 per cent greater, so that the average
size of a merchant banker's issue is more than three times as
large as that of a new issuing house — about £1,000,000, as
compared with about £300,000. It is also noticeable that the
average size of the small proportion of new issues made by
merchant banks founded since 1914 approximates more closely
to that of the new issuing houses than to that of the old merchant
bankers. Thus it would seem that the issuing institutions
established since 1914 tend to specialise on issues by relatively
small companies, while the old merchant banks are interested
mainly in the larger ones.

Issues made by members of the Issuing Houses Association
dominate the market, with well over 80 per cent of all issues
made by issuing houses, both by number and by value. Of
the remaining issues, nearly two-thirds by value are made by
South African mining finance companies, all within their special
field, leaving only a little over 5 per cent for other issuing
houses who are not members of the Association. In addition

---

[1] This, and much of the following information, has been extracted and
compiled from *The Times Issuing House Year Book*, 1949 and 1950.

to issues made by issuing houses, nearly half the total number of issues is made by stockbrokers without the help of issuing houses. The average size of these issues is, however, much smaller than that of issues made by issuing houses, so that by value they amount to only about a third of the grand total of all issues. They consist largely of issues to shareholders only and of Stock Exchange introductions, together with a certain number of Stock Exchange placings, usually of modest size. The number of issues to the public, whether by prospectus or

ISSUE OF INDUSTRIAL SECURITIES, 1946–49 *

	Prospectus and Offer for Sale		Placing and Introduction		Shareholders Only		Total	
	Number	Value (£m.)	Number	Value (£m.)	Number	Value (£m.)	Number	Value (£m.)
Old Merchant Bankers	55	67	111	63	89	128	255	258
New Merchant Bankers	3	6	17	7	6	1	26	14
Other Members of the Issuing Houses Assn.	140	67	269	64	141	34	550	165
South African Finance Companies	3	1	5	1	40	52	48	54
Other Issuing Houses	20	12	49	12	36	9	105	33
Total Issuing Houses	221	153	451	147	312	224	984	524
Stockbrokers	74	44	396	106	359	155	829	305
Total	295	197	847	253	671	379	1813	829

* Issues from April 1946 to December 1949, omitting issues of securities by public authorities and public utilities, bonus issues, and conversion issues. Issues shared by two issuing houses credited to the first named.

Source: Extracted and compiled from *The Times Issuing House Year Book*, 1949 and 1950 editions, with the help of the Economics Research Division of the London School Economics.

offer for sale, made without the help of an issuing house is small, apart from issues by U.K. and Commonwealth public authorities made through the Bank of England or other agents.

The result of this brief examination of the organisation of the market for new industrial issues seems to lead us to the conclusion that the great majority of new public issues, and of the larger Stock Exchange placings, are now sponsored and organised by permanent and responsible concerns which are interested, not so much in maximising the profit they make on any particular operation as in establishing and enhancing their own good name and reputation. It is known that at least the great majority of issuing houses take great care to satisfy themselves about the records and prospects of the companies which approach them for their assistance in raising new capital. No doubt there are occasions when an issuing house, anxious not to let slip an opportunity for profitable business, will agree to sponsor an issue which hardly comes up to its usual standard; or when reckless or dishonest directors, aided perhaps by the unduly restricted view of their functions taken by some auditors, succeed in deceiving the officials of the issuing house and the Stock Exchange, as well as the public. But on the whole it can be said without hesitation that, while no investor can be guaranteed immunity from the inevitable risks of business, still less from the risks of national and international politics, the type of reckless or fraudulent issue which too often disgraced the first three decades of the century is now extremely rare, and that, when it is made, it is unlikely to be made with impunity.

The development of the issuing houses, in fact, seems to have resulted in a system which almost exactly fulfils the recommendations of the Macmillan Committee, that 'relations between finance and industry should be so developed that issuing institutions of first-class strength and repute should vouch to the investor more normally and more fully for the intrinsic soundness of new issues. In this way the investor would be encouraged to support well-vouched issues and be put on his guard against others.' [1] The present system also seems to have most of the advantages that Foxwell claimed for industrial banking, without the disadvantages inherent in the German system, which became so manifest in 1931. The British houses sponsor, but, except to a limited extent in preparation for a new issue, they do not in general themselves finance. They risk their reputations and good names, but not, in general, customers' deposits. Even the severest economic or financial crisis, while no doubt inflicting heavy losses on investors, would not imperil the security of bank deposits or lead to that collapse of bank credit which utterly paralyses the whole economic system.

There is one further addition to the machinery of the new

[1] Cmd. 3897 (1930-31), p. 168.

issue market which has not yet been described. This is the Capital Issues Committee, which is charged under the Borrowing (Control and Guarantees) Act of 1946 and the ancillary Treasury Orders with the duty of passing under review all issues in excess of £50,000. I do not think that the activities of this Committee are particularly relevant to the aspect of the question which is at present under discussion. Its main duties are to prevent, not issues which might lose money for those who invested in them, but those which might perhaps divert resources to uses officially regarded as of insufficient priority or which might facilitate tax evasion. No doubt there are some issues which are both unduly risky and of low social priority, and it may well be that some of the more fantastic issues of the 1928 boom would have been disallowed by a capital issues committee working under present instructions. In conditions as they exist at present, however, it is not very likely that the efforts of the Capital Issues Committee are saving the public from losing money on many unsound issues that have passed the scrutiny both of an issuing house and of the Stock Exchange. From the point of view of the market, the Capital Issues Committee must be regarded mainly as one more factor making for delay in the already lengthy process of bringing out a new issue.

If we take into account the combined effects of the improvements in the law, of the infinitely stricter control on Stock Exchange introductions, of the emergence of the new issuing houses and of the adaptation of the old, I think that it can reasonably be claimed that during the last generation this castle of mine has been so improved and modernised that it is to all intents and purposes a new building. To change the metaphor, the emporium has been rebuilt and re-equipped regardless of expense; in its air-conditioned halls the counters gleam with glass and chromium; the goods for sale are ample in supply and variety, prepared under hygienic conditions, clearly labelled with full descriptions of their contents and attractively displayed; the shop-assistants, scientifically trained and hygienically clothed, stand awaiting business. But where are the customers?

The most superficial glance at the turnover figures of the new issue market reveals that it is doing nothing like the volume of business that it was forty, or twenty, years ago, even in money terms, and still less in terms of money with an unchanged purchasing power. The longest continuous series of new issue figures available is that published by the Midland Bank, which omits not only Government securities and bonus and vendors' shares but also re-sales of long-held shares by existing shareholders and conversion issues. While, however, this series covers only a part of the total activities of the market, it may probably be taken as a reasonable index of the whole, of which, apart from Government and bonus issues, it has in recent years formed about two-thirds.

Excluding the 1948 issue of £100 millions of stock by the British Electricity Authority, which from the point of view of the market should count as a Government issue, the Midland Bank's figures of new issues in 1948 and 1949 totalled £290 millions, or £145 millions a year. The corresponding annual average for the five years ending 1937 was £163 millions, and for the five years ending 1930 £284 millions. Figures for the period ending 1914 are not available on exactly the same basis, but may be put at an average of over £200 millions. If we estimate the present purchasing power of money at roughly half of what it was between the wars and a third of what it was before 1914 we find that the value of the 1948–49 issues was less than half of what it was in the 1930s, about a quarter of what it was in the late 1920s, and less than a quarter of what it had been before 1914. If we express the figures as proportions of national income the fall is even more striking — from nearly 10 per cent before 1914 to 7 per cent in the 1920s, 4 per cent in the 1930s, and less than 1½ per cent in 1948–49.

Very little of the fall between 1913 and 1949 can be attributed (as perhaps can the fall in the 1930s) to an overall decline in the proportion of the national income being saved and invested. We have put net national investment in 1913 at about £350 millions, or nearly 15 per cent of the national income. In 1949, even after making full provision for the cost of maintaining intact in a period of rising prices not only fixed but also circulating capital, net capital formation at home amounted to nearly £1400 millions, or nearly 14 per cent of the national income, and net capital formation at home and abroad to about £1350 millions, or about 13½ per cent of the national income. Thus in 1949 total net national saving and investment amounted to nearly as large a proportion of the national income as it had done in 1913.[1]

A better case can be made for attributing the fall in the importance of the new issue market to the change which has occurred in the origins of the almost unchanged proportion of national saving. While no precise estimates are available, it seems certain that in 1913 at least half, and in all probability more than two-thirds, of the nation's net savings consisted of personal savings, and almost the whole of the rest of business savings, while Government savings were negligible. In 1949, if we can rely on the latest official estimates [2] (who knows what retrospective changes next year's National Income White Paper may bring?), some £700 millions of net savings, or over half the total, were made by public authorities, mainly the Central Government and the social security funds. Of the remainder, over £400 millions, or nearly a third, were made by businesses, and only £200 millions, or less than a sixth, by private individuals. Thus, while the proportion of total savings made by businesses showed little change, more than three-quarters of the savings formerly made by private individuals are now made by the Government.

It is true that there is no precise relation between the volume of net personal savings and the amount available for subscription to new issues. It is probable that a considerable part of the £250 millions of gross savings which were absorbed during the year in paying taxes on capital passed through the capital market on its journey to the tax-collector, and that some part of this no doubt went through the new issue market. It is also true that, while Government and business savings are probably not used on any large scale for subscription to new issues of non-Government securities, they can be made available

[1] If the 1960 National Income Blue Book is to be believed, this paragraph bears little relation to the facts. Since 1950, the official estimate of gross fixed investment in 1949 has been reduced from £2160 millions to £1610 millions, and of net fixed investment from £1185 millions to £682 millions. The estimated value of the physical increase in stocks has also been reduced, from £150 millions to £65 millions. Thus the estimated total of net domestic capital creation in 1949 has been reduced from £1335 millions, or over 13 per cent of net national income, to £745 millions, or less than 7½ per cent.

[2] Cmd. 7933. All estimates of saving in 1949 have since been drastically reduced, but it remains true that net savings of public authorities in that year constituted more than half the total of all net saving.

to supplement the savings of private investors by purchases or repayment of old securities or by purchases of privately owned assets. Thus during 1949 some £200 millions of medium- or long-term debt seems to have been either redeemed or bought in by the National Debt Commissioners, while, in addition, some £200 millions of payments were made by the Government during the year on account of recompense for war damage and other capital transfers, of which some considerable part no doubt went to individuals. On the other hand, a large part of the investible funds of private individuals is ultimately invested otherwise than through the new issue market — in houses or farms, in private companies or other firms, or in other countries. All these conflicting influences may cause changes in the total of new capital issues to differ widely from changes in the total of personal net savings. Nevertheless, it is difficult to avoid the belief that these considerations merely modify rather than destroy the impression that there is a real connection between the volume of personal saving and the volume of new issues, and that it is to the fall in personal savings from perhaps nearly 10 per cent of the national income in 1913 to barely 2 per cent in 1949 that the decline in new capital issues from 10 per cent to 1½ per cent of national income must be mainly attributed.

There is some reason to believe that the customers of the new issue market have not only fallen in number but also changed in type. Considerable attention has recently been drawn to the fact that the shrunken annual total of net personal saving is now more than equalled by the annual increase in the funds at the disposal of institutional investors. There is, of course, no necessary connection between the annual growth of funds at the disposal of building societies, life insurance companies, and other investment institutions and the part they play in deciding the ultimate use of those funds; for in so far as they use them to buy existing securities or other assets from personal holders they transfer back to individuals the responsibility for deciding what, if any, forms of capital creation these funds are ultimately to finance. Thus in 1949 the amounts advanced by building societies to finance the actual construction of new buildings were almost certainly considerably less than the £50 millions or so repaid to them as instalments under existing mortgage contracts, so that more than the whole of the year's increase of £115 millions in their total of outstanding mortgages must have been used to finance the purchase of existing houses, thus passing back to the sellers, mainly individuals, the responsibility for re-investing the proceeds. Similarly, it would have been possible for the life insurance offices to return the whole of the £190 millions [1] by which their funds increased in 1949 into the hands of personal investors by using them exclusively for the purchase of existing securities.

There is, however, other evidence to show that institutional investors are now playing a larger relative, if not absolute, part in the new issue market. Before 1914 some 90 per cent of all issues, other than issues to shareholders, were made by prospectus or offer for sale, and only about 10 per cent by placing. By 1938 the proportion of Stock Exchange placings had risen to 50 per cent, and since the war it has risen to nearly 75 per cent. Since the average size of prospectus issues and offers for sale is a good deal larger than that of placings, the increase in terms of value is rather less marked, but even so the value of placings has recently been well over half the total of all issues other than to shareholders. The switch to placings would no doubt have been even more marked but for the Stock Exchange ruling that these must be confined to the smaller issues. It is probably largely as a result of this ruling that two large issues have recently been placed privately without application for a Stock Exchange quotation.

It is well known, and is confirmed by a study of lists of shareholders, that Stock Exchange placings are mainly taken up by large investors, principally institutions, and that only the fraction of the issue made available through the Stock Exchange is available for the personal investor. This system is convenient to both sides. The small numbers of investors with whom the issuing house or broker has to deal and the absence of sub-underwriting costs reduce the expenses of the issue, while the buying institutions have the opportunity of acquiring their securities in blocks of convenient size, usually of £5000 or more. Blocks of this size of the securities of small companies, on which the yields are generally higher, could not

---

[1] *Economist*, 18th November 1950, p. 847.

easily be obtained by purchases on the Stock Exchange without disturbing the price. It is true that these blocks of securities of small companies are less marketable than securities of larger companies, but life insurance offices have little need to concern themselves with marketability so long as the yield of the securities they hold remains satisfactory.

Thus the increasing prevalence of Stock Exchange placings, together with the fact that these are largely taken up by institutions, indicates the increasingly important part played by institutions in providing a market for new issues. The importance of the part still played by the individual investor should not, however, be underestimated, for more than 40 per cent of the value of all new issues consists of issues to shareholders only, of which a much larger proportion than of placings is probably taken up by individuals. At a guess I should put the proportion of total new issues still going to personal investors at not less than half.

We therefore find that, while the organisation of the new issue market for industrial securities has been improved out of all knowledge during the past generation, it is now catering for a demand which is both far below that which it is organised to supply and is also largely of a type which needs the protection of the new safeguards less than did its original customers. How far is this condition desirable, and how long is it likely to continue?

To deal with the less important development first, I do not consider the increased relative importance of institutional investment as on the whole undesirable. It is true that the securities taken up by institutions through Stock Exchange placings seem to consist largely of debentures and preference shares. But the reason for this seems to be at least as much the unwillingness of existing owners of small companies to part with control as any reluctance on the part of the institutions to supply risk capital. The recent accounts of many life insurance companies, for instance, show no evidence of any reluctance to increase their holdings of ordinary shares: though since these are presumably largely obtained by purchases in the market they probably consist mainly of the shares of larger companies, which alone can normally be obtained through the market in blocks of adequate size without disturbing prices. From the personal investor's point of view, the important part played by institutions, with their staffs of experts, provides additional safeguards, not only for the investor who entrusts his savings to their care, but also for the private investor who finds himself a fellow shareholder or debenture-holder with them ; for the institutions are far better equipped than he is to stand up against boards of directors both for their own rights and for his.

The fall in the total business of the new issue market, on the other hand is, I think, a pity. The great danger to our present national economy is rigidity — a tendency to keep on running in its accustomed ruts instead of breaking away and exploring new paths. In the past the greatest new developments have frequently come from the growth of new firms and new industries, often to the great discomfort of those already established. But for new firms and new industries to grow they must have access to capital, and this is facilitated by the existence of a large and active market, where the newcomer may compete on equal terms with the old and well established. The possibilities for a new and efficient firm to obtain the capital it needed to enable it to grow were greatest when there were a large number of substantial private investors looking for investment opportunities and when a firm could plough back freely the exceptional profits its exceptional efficiency enabled it to make. To-day the position is very different from this. The place of the private saver has very largely been taken by the state, which is naturally prone to give priority for such capital as it can spare from housing or other social investment to basic industries, whether nationalised or not. The proportion of the national income saved in the form of business profits ploughed back may not be very different from what it has been in several previous periods ; but there is a world of difference between savings made out of lightly taxed profits earned in the face of strenuous competition and the same amount of savings made out of profits that have been easily earned but heavily taxed. In the first case only the efficient can make profits, but if they make them they keep them ; in the second case profits depend more on being allowed a due share of materials and of the market than on any particular excellence of management, and such profits as are left after tax are shared much more equally between the more and the less efficient. Thus the exceptionally efficient firm is starved of the new capital which would enable it to realise its full potentialities, while the less efficient firm is able to continue to exist with every outward appearance of success.

It is difficult to be very optimistic about any substantial and continued expansion in the near future in the volume of business on the London new issue market. It is, of course, always possible for a temporary improvement, such as that which occurred in the autumn of 1950, to develop as the result either of an improvement in confidence — or a decrease in liquidity preference, if you prefer the current jargon — or of an influx of funds from abroad which is allowed to expand the volume of bank deposits. But neither of these developments — unless, indeed, they lead to a worsening of our balance-of-payments position — does anything in conditions of full employment to make more resources available on which to spend the proceeds of new issues. Their effects are in themselves purely inflationary, and they cannot continue for long without either intensifying the tendency towards a rise in domestic prices or checking the improvement in our balance of payments.

Until recently it appeared that it might be possible for the authorities to increase the rate of their purchases or repayments of long-term Government debt and so make more money available for institutions and persons to re-invest through the market. This hope was based partly on the gradual fall in war-damage payments and other capital transfers and partly on the increased rate of saving by the social security funds. But now the news of the impending cessation of Marshall Aid coupled with the prospect of greatly expanded expenditure on armaments makes it likely that the Government will have less rather than more funds available for the repayment of debt, and that total investible funds in the capital market may therefore tend rather to diminish than to increase. If so, the Government will have to look to other means for balancing the national savings and investment budget without inflation. It seems likely that it will first look, as indeed it is at present looking, to a still further expansion of business savings. If by reason of a breakdown in wage restraint this policy should fail, there are only four other courses open to it if inflation is to be avoided — an increase in Government saving through higher taxes or reduced non-military expenditure; an increase in personal saving, mainly in the middle- and lower-income groups, enforced by renewed controls on consumption; a decrease in non-military investment by stricter controls on capital formation; and a general discouragement of investment by a restriction of the quantity of money and a rise in rates of interest. Of these possible courses, the enforcement of more stringent controls on capital investment seems the likeliest; and it is too much to expect that the brunt of them will fall on capital formation by public authorities or nationalised industries. This would mean that demand for new capital through the market would be reduced to match the reduced supply, and that inflation would be avoided at the expense of a still further fall in the business of the new issue market.

Only in the very long run is it possible to be even moderately optimistic about an expansion in the market's activity. While it is unlikely that net personal savings will expand spontaneously while taxation is as heavy as at present, and while it is also unlikely that any Government, of whatever political complexion, would bring about any large and rapid reduction in public expenditure and in taxation, it may perhaps be possible to hope that Government expenditure may some day begin to rise more slowly than the national income, so that the present immensely high ratio of taxation to income may begin to decline. If the benefits of tax reductions are distributed among all income groups, and still more if they are concentrated on those taxes which are at present paid mainly out of capital, we may perhaps see the beginning of a rise in gross saving and of a fall in capital consumption combining to produce an increase in net savings available for investment. If these modest hopes are justified, the next generation may perhaps see the institutions of the London capital market dealing with a volume of business more commensurate with the improvements which this generation has seen in its organisation and capacity.

POSTSCRIPT (May 1961)

The concluding paragraphs of the foregoing paper, written in the autumn of 1950, are a good example of the fallibility of human foresight, although on this occasion, exceptionally, the event proved better than the expectation.

The expectation of 1950, that any expansion in the business of the London new issue market was likely to be small and slow, was falsified mainly as the result of two unforeseen developments. The first of these was the sharp acceleration, from 1952 onwards, in the rate of increase of the real national income, from an average of less than 2 per cent a year between 1946 and 1952 to one of over 3½ per cent from 1952 to 1960. The acceleration of the rate of rise of real national income after 1951 was due partly to an increase in the rate of rise of output from an average of barely 2½ per cent a year from 1946 to 1953 to one of 3 per cent a year from 1953 to 1960, but more to the change in the trend of the terms of trade, which since 1951 has caused real income to rise faster than output, whereas up to 1951 a substantial part of the rise in output was offset by the worsening terms of trade.

The other main cause of the increase in new capital issues seems to have been the remarkable recovery since 1951 in personal saving. This has occurred mainly in three discontinuous rises, in 1952, 1956, and 1960, separated by periods of stationary or falling saving :

GROSS PERSONAL SAVING *
(£m.)

Average 1948–51	1952	Average 1953–55	1956	Average 1957–59	1960
38	416	509	959	926	1464

* Including depreciation, but excluding stock appreciation.

While the timing of the increases in personal saving may have been wholly or partly determined by special factors, such as the exhaustion of involuntary war-time savings in 1952 and hire-purchase restrictions in 1956 and 1960, there can be little doubt that the general rise in saving since 1951 is associated with the acceleration of the rise in real personal incomes after tax. Between 1946 and 1951, when aggregate real personal incomes after tax rose by an average of less than 1 per cent a year, gross personal saving rarely exceeded 1 per cent of incomes. From 1951 to 1960, on the other hand, real personal incomes after tax rose by an average of over $3\frac{1}{2}$ per cent a year, and people seem to have saved about a fifth of their additional real incomes. The proportion saved of total expendable incomes therefore rose from less than 1 per cent in 1951 to $4\frac{1}{2}$ per cent in 1955, nearly 6 per cent in 1959 and over 8 per cent in 1960. Almost entirely as the result of the rise in personal saving, the proportion of gross national income saved has risen from $15\frac{1}{2}$ per cent in 1951 to $19\frac{1}{2}$ per cent in 1960.

Up to 1954 the increase in personal saving seems to have been used almost entirely to finance an increase in housebuilding. Thereafter, much of it became available for financing increased industrial investment. The result, as can be plainly seen in the accounts of nearly 3000 quoted public companies analysed by the National Institute for Economic and Social Research and later by the Board of Trade, is a marked rise both in the total of industrial fixed investment and in the proportion of investment financed by new capital issues:

SOURCES AND USES OF FUNDS OF NEARLY 3000 PUBLIC COMPANIES

SOURCES				
	Average 1949–54		Average 1955–58	
	£m.	Per cent of Total	£m.	Per cent of Total
Internal finance	639	76	895	69
New long-term capital	136	16	305	24
Other	64	8	89	7
Total	839	100	1289	100
USES				
	Average 1949–58		Average 1955–58	
	£m.	Per cent of Total	£m.	Per cent of Total
Fixed investment	452	54	912	71
Other	387	46	377	29
Total	839	100	1289	100

The effects of the increase in the proportion of an increased amount of industrial investment financed by new capital issues are seen in the Midland Bank's figures of new issues on the London capital market. These show new issues by all quoted U.K. companies as rising from an average of £131 millions a year in the period 1951–54 to £258 millions a year in the period 1955–59. Although overseas issues have remained very small, the machinery of the London new issues market has therefore been much more fully used in recent years than seemed likely in 1950.

The benefits of the increased volume of new issues appear to have gone particularly to the largest issuing houses, the merchant banks. This is probably because much of the increase has been due to large issues by large companies, which did not need to go to the market at all during the earlier period. Although the following table has been prepared on a slightly different basis from that covering the years 1946–49, published on p. 229, it is probably sufficiently similar in coverage to provide a reasonably fair comparison:

NEW ISSUES OF INDUSTRIAL SECURITIES, 1954–57 BY TYPE OF ISSUER

	Prospectus and Offer for Sale		Stock Exchange Placing and Introduction		Shareholders Only		Total	
	No.	Value £m.	No.	Value £m.	No.	Value £m.	No.	Va £
Merchant Banks	45	362	172	188	248	487	465	10
Other Issuing Houses	28	35	236	43	95	61	359	1
Stock Brokers	66	32	282	124	573	477	921	6
Total	139	429	690	355	916	1025	1745	18

Sources: Extracted and compiled from the 1958 edition of *The Times Issuing H Year Book* with the help of the Economics Research Division of the London Scho Economics.

CHAPTER 13

THE ECONOMIC FUNCTIONS OF
THE STOCK EXCHANGE [1]

THE emergence of man from a condition of primitive poverty and his development of advanced and complex societies have been due, more than to anything else, to his accumulation of productive assets. For this accumulation two things are necessary : first, the ability and willingness of people to consume less than their incomes — that is to say, to save ; and secondly, their willingness to tie these savings up in specific forms which will facilitate future production — that is to say, to invest. Investing savings in specific productive assets inevitably involves risks. These are of two sorts : first, the risk that, even if the investment turns out as well as expected, the owner may come to want something else more, but be unable to obtain it because he cannot sell his existing asset — that is to say, the risk of illiquidity ; and secondly the risk that, even if he can sell it, he will get less back than he paid for it, either because it is now expected to yield less income than was originally hoped, or because other people now attach a smaller capital value to a given income — that is to say, the risk of capital loss.

The function of a market in productive assets or titles to productive assets is to reduce these risks, either by offsetting them against each other or by enabling those best fitted to specialise in bearing them. The risk which it most obviously reduces is the risk of illiquidity — the risk of being permanently stuck with an asset you now want less, and of being unable to exchange it for an asset you now want more. In the absence of a market, anyone who is likely to want an asset in the future must produce it himself, or at least seize any accidental opportunity which may come along of buying it, and hold it, perhaps for a long time, until he needs it. Similarly, anyone who happens to own an asset which he wants to get rid of may have to wait a long time, or indefinitely, before he can

[1] Lecture delivered to the Institute of Bankers, April 1954.

exchange it for another or for money. Thus the difficulty and risk of becoming an owner are increased, and people will be unwilling to invest in productive assets unless the prospective yield is very high. Instead, they either do not invest at all or invest in non-productive assets, such as a hoard of precious metals or jewels, if these are more readily exchangeable.

A second advantage of a market is that it facilitates a greater degree of specialisation between those who provide the savings and those who do the actual investing. If there is an active market in a type of asset, its current value will be well known and the risk of lending against it as security less than the risk of lending against unmarketable assets. Owners will therefore be able to borrow more of the cost of the asset and so increase their specialisation in risk-bearing, while the lenders will be taking a much smaller share of the risk and so increasing their specialisation in the mere provision of capital.

In fully organised markets this specialisation of function can be carried still further. Even after borrowing a considerable proportion of the cost of a productive asset, the investor must still provide a considerable proportion himself and remain both a provider of capital and a risk-bearer. He can, of course, arrange to convert certain types of risks, especially risks of physical accidents, into small annual costs by means of insurance ; but there remain other risks which cannot be insured against, of which one of the most important is the risk of changes in the market prices of assets. In the absence of a suitably organised market the owner of the asset must bear these risks himself, and so combine the rôles of owner (or investor) and risk-bearer (or speculator). In some organised markets, however, owners of certain kinds of assets can get rid of nearly all the risk of loss due to changing prices by a process known as 'hedging'. As soon as he can do this, he can borrow a much larger proportion of their cost, and so specialise almost entirely on the function of investment, leaving others to specialise on providing capital or on risk-bearing. This process of specialisation is carried a good deal less far on the Stock Exchange than in certain other markets, and before dealing specifically with stock exchanges I propose to examine the working of the process in one or two other and more fully developed markets.

Let us first look at the organised produce markets, which can come into existence wherever there is a large trade in a commodity which is both storable and can be sold by description. Such commodities include many metals, grains, and commercial fibres, as well as certain other materials, such as rubber. On these markets we find at least two main types of contract — a contract for the sale and purchase of goods actually on the spot, for immediate payment and delivery; and a contract for the sale and purchase of goods at a price now fixed, but to be delivered and paid for in some future month, usually from three to twelve months ahead. These forward contracts enable a buyer to ensure supplies at a price now fixed, thus in turn enabling him to quote firm prices well ahead; they also enable a seller to know what he will get for his produce at some future date, whether he holds it now on the spot, holds it somewhere else, or merely hopes to buy it or produce it. Though the contract is made at a price now fixed, no money needs to pass until delivery is made, apart from any deposit by way of guarantee according to the rules of the exchange.

If the seller holds goods already on the spot, it will pay him to sell forward rather than for immediate delivery only if the forward price is sufficiently above the spot price to make it worth his while; that is to say, if the excess of the forward price over the price for immediate delivery is enough to cover the costs of holding — storage costs, insurance, and interest on the money locked up. If, however, his goods are not on the spot, supplies for immediate delivery may well fetch a better price than supplies for delivery at a future date, and the seller may be willing to accept a forward price well below the spot price rather than take the risk of what the spot price will be by the time his supplies arrive.

If the only sellers were those who actually owned or had contracted for stocks, and the only buyers were of stocks for actual use, sales could be carried through only to the extent that there was an identity between genuine supply and genuine demand. If either buyers or sellers were in a temporary majority, either they would have to offer unusually favourable terms in order to induce their counterparts to sell or buy earlier than they had intended, or some members of one side or the other would be unable to deal. Prices would, however, have to fluctuate much less violently if a slight rise or fall attracted sellers or buyers who did not wish actually to deliver or receive stocks, but who expected to reverse their bargains at a profit as soon as the temporary disequilibrium between genuine buyers and sellers was reversed. These short-term speculators, who buy forward goods they do not need or sell forward goods they do not own, provide the service of filling up the temporary gaps in the market due to a temporary preponderance of genuine buyers or sellers. Sometimes, however, the gaps are not merely temporary but may persist for months, as, for instance, would happen if farmers wanted to sell their grain as soon as it was harvested, but millers wished to buy it only as they wished to use it. Someone would have to buy it and hold it until the millers wished to buy. But if those who specialise in storing grain do not wish to take the risk of its price falling while they hold it, the gap can be filled only if someone else will come along and take over the risk. To fill this gap is the function of the long-term speculator.

The ability of holders to sell forward to speculators, who hope to re-sell at a profit before they have to take delivery, not only permits the emergence of a specialist class of grain-storers but enables the owners of the grain sold forward to borrow a very large proportion of its cost from specialist providers of finance, very often the banks. But the specialist holder will be prepared to continue to hold only on one condition — that the price at which he sells forward is sufficient to cover not only the current cost of buying but also all storage, insurance and interest charges, plus a margin of profit for himself. If the speculators come to the opinion that the forward price is too high and therefore sell or refuse to buy forward, the forward price will fall until its margin over the spot price is too small to cover the carrying costs. It then becomes more profitable for holders of grain to sell for immediate delivery than to carry stocks. Spot sales rise and the spot price falls until the necessary margin between spot and forward prices is restored. Meanwhile the fall in the spot price has made the commodity cheaper and brought about increased consumption, so that the total amount carried forward from the present to the future is reduced. Thus the speculators, by selling forward, have caused the holders to sell more for immediate consumption and have reduced the amount carried forward from the present to the future. If, conversely, they had bought more forward, they would have made it unusually profitable to buy spot, hold, and sell forward, so raising spot prices, reducing consumption and causing more to be carried forward. Thus the long-term speculators give a lead to holders about whether they should buy or sell and so increase or reduce the amount carried forward. If speculators who buy forward, the so-called 'bulls', are right in their belief that supplies will be more wanted in the future than in the present, they will cause supplies to be moved from times of relative plenty to times of relative scarcity. They will therefore, like the Joseph who caused grain to be carried over from the seven fat years to the seven lean years, be benefactors of humanity as well as makers of profits. If, conversely, they are right in believing that the future will be a time of greater plenty than the present and, by selling forward, prevent supplies from being carried over unnecessarily, they are similarly benefactors as well as profit-makers.

On the other hand, if speculators are wrong and cause stocks to be carried from times of scarcity to times of plenty, or prevent them from being carried from times of plenty to times of scarcity, they will harm the rest of the world as well as lose their own money. The argument for having these risks carried by specialists is that specialists are able to devote more attention to the study of conditions likely to affect the future demand and supply of the commodities they deal in. If in fact they do not do so, they are likely to do far more harm than good. There is a strong case for the encouragement of speculation by skilled professionals ; there is none for speculation by ignorant amateurs.

In the foregoing discussion we have been considering the case of a commodity of which only a single grade is quoted on the exchange. For commodities with a number of quoted grades we find a rather more complicated system, under which a contract for a future month, though made in terms of a standard grade, can be satisfied by the delivery of any one of a number of specified grades, with appropriate price adjustments in accordance with a schedule fixed by the exchange

I

authorities. Such a contract is called a futures contract, and a holder on the spot, instead of selling forward the actual grade he has in stock, sells a future. He thus enters into a separate contract in a generalised commodity, the price of which can be expected to move roughly parallel with that of the grade he holds. This separate contract, constituting a risk which will almost certainly operate in the opposite direction to his existing risk, is called a 'hedge'. It will normally be reversed before maturity and is hardly ever satisfied by delivery. By dealing in futures, holders or prospective buyers can cover their risks almost as completely as if they sold or bought forward the actual grade they held or wanted.

Another market in which the speculative and investment functions can be clearly separated is the foreign exchange market. When this market is functioning normally, it is possible to deal in the chief currencies of the world not only spot but also for future delivery. We find here the same rule for an equilibrium relationship between spot and forward prices that we found in the produce exchanges : that is, that the forward price equals the spot price plus the cost of carrying. But whereas the cost of carrying a stock of produce is always positive, the cost of carrying a stock of foreign exchange may be either positive or negative ; for the holding of a stock of foreign exchange enables the holder to invest it on short term in the foreign centre, and so earn a rate of interest which may be sufficient to offset, or more than offset, the interest he is paying or might have earned at home. Thus the equilibrium forward rate will be above the spot rate only when the foreign short-term rate of interest is below the home rate, while when the foreign interest rate is above the home rate the foward rate will tend to be below the spot rate. Speculators, by buying a foreign currency forward and forcing up the forward rate, can make it exceptionally profitable for investors to buy it spot and sell it forward, thus raising the spot rate ; or, by selling it forward and depressing the forward rate, they can make it unprofitable to buy spot and sell forward and so can depress the spot rate. Thus here again speculators, by operating in the forward market, can affect the operations of investors and through them the prices for immediate delivery.

In the light of these principles, which we have been able to observe clearly in the fully developed produce and foreign exchange markets, let us examine the economic functions of the Stock Exchange. The assets dealt with on a stock exchange are titles, not to stocks of commodities or to stocks of foreign currencies, but either to shares in the ownership of productive enterprises or to debts (usually long-term debts) owed either by governments and other public authorities or by productive enterprises. Its most obvious function is to increase the liquidity of the owners of these assets by enabling them to buy and sell freely. If a security can be sold for cash at short notice, its owner can afford to hold a larger proportion of his assets in the form of shares or long-term loans and a smaller proportion in cash or short-term loans. In the absence of a market, not only may there be a long delay before the asset can be sold, but there will be great uncertainty about the price that it will realise and therefore difficulty in raising a loan against it. If, in the absence of a stock exchange, productive enterprises wished to raise capital either by the issue of shares or on long-term loans, they would have to offer much higher yields to offset the disadvantages of illiquidity and increased uncertainty; alternatively, they would have either to bear increased risk themselves by borrowing entirely on short term, or to restrict their investment to what they could finance out of their own resources.

Arising out of this function, the stock exchange performs a second which is perhaps even more important. It enables investors, by expressing, through their purchases and sales, their preference for certain types of existing securities, to facilitate the issue of some types of new securities and to discourage others. Thus, by their demand, they can largely determine into which directions the new savings of the community shall flow.

For a stock exchange properly to perform its function of increasing the liquidity of investors, it must fulfil two basic conditions: first, it must be possible for investors to buy or sell any quoted securities with a minimum of delay; and secondly, it must be possible for them to buy or sell in considerable quantities without moving the price seriously against them. These conditions are probably more difficult to fulfil on a stock exchange than on a produce market; for whereas on a produce market there are always ultimate consumers who must buy and producers who must sell, on a stock exchange there are relatively few compulsory sellers, apart perhaps from executors who have to sell to meet death duties, and still fewer compulsory buyers, for it is always possible to hold cash for a time. Further, whereas on a produce market the number of grades dealt in is relatively small, stock exchange transactions cover an enormously larger number of separate securities, some of which are dealt in only very infrequently. If, therefore, prospective buyers and sellers are to be able to deal without delay and without seriously disturbing prices, there is an even greater need than on produce markets for a class of short-term speculators who will step in to fill the gap left by temporary disparities between investment buying and selling of particular securities.

In all stock markets there is therefore an important function fulfilled by short-term speculators, who take advantage of the temporary price fluctuations caused by accidental disparities between the number of investors who wish to buy and sell particular securities on any particular day, and by so doing reduce the magnitude of the price fluctuations which would otherwise occur and enable investors to deal freely. But the London Stock Exchange is unique in providing a large body of short-term speculators actually built into its basic organisation. Ideally the jobbers, aided by the system of fortnightly accounts, should be able to provide an automatic counterpart to any investor who wished to buy or sell, taking securities on to their books whenever the investment supply temporarily exceeded the demand and releasing them again when the demand again exceeded the supply, with the minimum of fluctuation in their prices. At one time, for the more actively traded securities, the London Stock Exchange probably did actually approximate to this ideal. In the less active securities, however, it is probable that it has never been possible to be sure of dealing without delay. For these the jobber has probably always had to act rather like the specialist on the New York Stock Exchange, recording orders in his book to be carried out only when he can find an investor who is willing to deal in the opposite direction at a satisfactory price. But in recent years it is probable that there has been a growing reduction in the effectiveness with which jobbers can fulfil their function of providing a free market. This is largely because death duties and high rates of surtax have prevented the accumulation and maintenance of sufficient capital to enable them to take large risks; and probably also because the high rates of transfer tax have discouraged investors from changing their investments as frequently as they used to and so have reduced the total flow of business in the market. As a result, there is a growing proportion of transactions in which the jobber is prepared to act, in effect, only as an agent; while even in the more actively traded securities the quantities that can be bought or sold on a single day without affecting the price appreciably are probably much smaller than in earlier decades.

While the London Stock Exchange's advantage over others in providing specialised short-term speculative services is probably less marked than formerly, it has, unlike some others, never made any serious attempt to provide or facilitate specialised long-term speculative services. It is extremely difficult to be a pure long-term speculator on the London Stock Exchange; it is also impossible, or almost impossible, to be a pure investor, owing to the absence of hedging facilities. If a speculator believes that the price of a security will be higher six months or a year hence than it is now, the only way he has of backing his judgment is to buy the security, pay for it and hold it — in other words, he has to combine the functions of investor and speculator (and often to find much or all of the capital himself). Similarly, an investor cannot buy and hold a long-term security without himself bearing the risk of a fall in its market price while he is holding it — he is obliged to be a speculator as well as an investor. Thus it is that investors who do not wish to take risks of capital depreciation are obliged to confine themselves to the short-term debts of undoubted creditors, such as the Government, or to deposits in the banks, the savings banks, or the building societies, and cannot make their savings available for the use of productive industry.

Before the war there did exist a type of contract which enabled a speculator to undertake fairly long-term risks without also becoming an investor, and some degree of hedging facilities for the investor who wished to avoid risk.[1] But the option contract was a very expensive way of hedging. Since the buyer of an option to sell at the present price at a future date had the right to choose whether to exercise it or not, an option was naturally expensive. An option to sell at a future date (or 'put' option) might well cost something like 10 per cent of the market price. Thus an investor could protect himself against a fall in the price of his security only at the immediate cost of a tenth of its price; while if its price rose by more than 10 per cent the profit on the securities he held would be greater than the cost of the option and he would still make a speculative profit. There were no means by which he could obtain a real hedge, sacrificing the whole (or almost the whole) of his potential speculative profit in exchange for being relieved of the whole (or almost the whole) of his potential speculative loss.

It would be very interesting to see the effects of the introduction of a genuine hedging contract on the London Stock Exchange, whereby an investor could give up his chance of a capital gain in order to be relieved of the risk of a capital loss. Such a contract could take the form of the sale and purchase of a security for delivery in three, six, or twelve months' time at a price now fixed (though only by a coincidence at the same as the present price for immediate delivery). Such a contract would, of course, give rise to many technical difficulties — problems of share splitting, bonus issues, rights issues on bonus terms, and many others. It would also probably be necessary for the Stock Exchange authorities, not merely to give permission, but to provide an elaborate machinery for ensuring the fulfilment of contracts such as exists in many produce exchanges — the provision of margins, arrangements for keeping the margins up to date at weekly or daily settlements, and so on. But if these technical difficulties could be overcome, I am sure that arrangements for the making of firm contracts for future delivery would have a very good chance of greatly improving the ability of the Stock Exchange to fulfil one of the basic functions of all

---

[1] Option dealings on the London Stock Exchange were resumed in October, 1958.

organised markets — the opportunity for greater specialisation between the functions of providing capital, investing it, and bearing the risks of investment.

If such a contract were possible, no doubt at first only in the most active securities, what would be its effect ? If effective hedges were in fact available, it is clear that many investors who cannot now accept risks would be able to invest in stock exchange securities for the first time, or to transfer their capital from safe to higher-yielding though riskier investments. If such an investor could buy a security spot and sell it again for delivery in, say, twelve months' time, he would know exactly what he would be able to get for it next year. The only risk he would be taking would be that the interest or dividend payment for the year might not come up to expectations. Such institutions as charities and pension funds would be able to invest in securities which now they would shrink from. Banks and other financial institutions could safely lend a much higher proportion of the value of a pledged security if it were safely hedged. Thus, provided that a sufficient number of long-term speculators were available to provide the counterparts to the necessary hedges, there is no doubt that a great deal of capital which is now confined to 'safety-first' investments could be attracted into the finance of business enterprises.

The development of a specialist class of long-term risk-bearers would have another advantage. The only type of pure speculation which can now exist is very short-term speculation, mainly within the period of a single account and rarely extending for more than two or three accounts. Such short-term speculation is inevitably, and rightly, concerned with filling temporary gaps between investment demand and investment supply rather than with the long-term prospects of particular securities. Short-term speculators are therefore less interested in the underlying facts of the situation than in what the investing public is likely to do in the near future. Thus, as Keynes has complained, they try to guess, not what is going to happen in the real world, but what investors are likely to think about what is going to happen. Thus, instead of the speculators giving the lead to investors, as they do in other markets, in the stock markets the pure speculators look

to the investors for a lead. If the investor happens to be able
to combine that rôle with that of a good long-term speculator
this will do no harm. If in fact the investor makes himself
well informed about the present position and prospects of
every security he buys or sells, the speculator, by watching his
actions, will in fact be operating, though at second-hand, in
accordance with the situation in the real world. But unfortunately by no means all investors are well equipped to act
also as long-term speculators. In particular, many are apt to
follow the current trend of prices and to buy when they think
prices are rising and to sell when they think they are falling,
sometimes with little regard to long-term prospects. If this
can happen, it can follow that the short-term speculators can
initiate a price movement which becomes magnified and continued by the effect it has on the operations of investors. We
thus get the possibility of the development of a vicious circle
— the market rises or falls because the short-term speculators
think that investors are going to buy or sell, and investors
buy or sell because the market is rising or falling. Thus a
movement which may have little or no relationship with the
long-term prospects of the securities concerned can be prolonged, and the speculators can make profits, not by guiding
investors into the most profitable concerns, but by misleading
them and then getting out before their wrong leadership is
discovered. The remedy for the possibility of such developments is not fewer pure speculators but more — the supplementation of the existing short-term speculators by a body
of long-term speculators, who would act less on what they
expected investors to do in the near future and more on expert
judgment of the long-term prospects of the securities in which
they dealt.

If the facilities were made available for entering into long-
term speculative and hedging stock exchange contracts, what
are the chances of a class of expert long-term pure speculators
growing up to take advantage of them ? It is no argument
against the possibility to say that no such class now exists, for
hitherto the conditions in which it could develop have not
existed. But it seems quite possible that, given the technical
facilities, the profession of long-term stock market speculator
would prove a profitable one for the right man. While even

the most careful and expert study of the underlying economic and political data is rarely of much help in making predictions about movements in stock market prices during the next week or month, it is a good deal more likely to be of assistance in estimating what is likely to happen over the next six months or year. If then it is true that those who are able and willing to give time and thought to a careful study of the underlying data are likely to be more often right in the long run than many of those who merely happen to have money to invest, a specialisation of function between the two would benefit both. A man who found he had a flair for estimating future prospects would be able to operate on a far larger scale with a given capital than he could if he had to fulfil the function of investor as well as that of long-term speculator ; while the man with capital but little desire to back his own (or other people's) judgment about the future could avoid the risks of capital loss by hedging his investment through a forward sale.

It is, of course, true that a man who tried to set himself up as a long-term speculator with a limited capital and who went at all seriously astray on the average of his expectations would very soon find himself out of business, and that, especially in the early days of the experiment, the financial mortality-rate among those who were trying to find out whether or not they had a talent for estimating the future would be high. But there seems reason to believe that in due course the advantages of specialisation would be found to be as high in this field as elsewhere, and that there would grow up a body of expert long-term professional speculators (often, of course, institutional speculators) who, by a combination of natural ability and expert knowledge, would prove themselves better at judging future prospects than the average of those who at present are obliged to combine speculation with investment. These specialist speculators would therefore combine the rendering of a public service with the making of a sufficient income for themselves to prefer their new occupation to any other open to them.

If we can assume both that the necessary facilities for forward contracts can be provided and that a sufficient number of long-term speculators appear to provide counterparts for

12

those investors who wish to hedge against capital losses, it is interesting to examine the effects to be expected on the price structure of the market.

An investor who buys an irredeemable Government security and sells it twelve months forward at the present spot price is taking no more risk of a capital loss than if he had bought a one-year Government bond. If, however, the current yield on irredeemable bonds is 4 per cent and on one-year bonds 2 per cent, he will greatly increase his income by selling the one-year bond, buying the irredeemable security, and selling it forward. The initial effect of opening the forward market would therefore be a fall in the demand for short-dated securities, a rise in the spot demand for long-dated securities, and a rise in their forward sales. The price of short-dated securities will tend to fall, the spot price of long-dated securities to rise, and their forward price to move to a discount on their spot price. There are an infinite number of ways in which a final equilibrium between the prices could be reached, depending on the various possible shifts in demand and supply in response to the changes in price and yield, but one possible equilibrium arrangement would be for the yield on one-year bonds to rise to $2\frac{1}{2}$ per cent, the yield on irredeemable securities to fall to $3\frac{3}{4}$ per cent, and the one-year forward price of the irredeemable security to be at $1\frac{1}{4}$ per cent discount on the spot price. The safe yield to the investor (apart from questions of tax, which will be considered later) would then be $2\frac{1}{2}$ per cent on both types of security. Incidentally, since the spot price of the irredeemable security would rise to $106\frac{3}{4}$ and the forward price to nearly $105\frac{1}{2}$, the long-term speculators would have done quite well in spite of the development of a forward discount. It should be noted that a buyer at the present forward price can expect a profit of $1\frac{1}{4}$ per cent provided that spot prices remain unchanged over the coming year.

For a variable-dividend security, or a fixed interest security where there is thought to be some chance that the next year's interest payment will not be made, or made in full, the equilibrium relationship between the spot and forward prices cannot be calculated exactly, for the investor, while safe from any loss of capital in excess of the forward discount, is still bearing the risk of variations in one year's dividend or interest. It can, however, be said that whenever the expected income yield for the coming year, fully discounted for risk and uncertainty, is in excess of the yield on a safe one-year bond, the forward rate will tend to stand at a discount on the spot rate. Only when no income is expected from the investment during the coming year, or when its amount, after discounting for risk and uncertainty, is below the safe one-year rate, will the equilibrium level of the forward price be above the spot price.

In practice, the concept of any clear equilibrium relationship between the spot and forward price of securities is blurred by the effects of taxation. For investors who either pay no tax on income, such as charities, or who both pay tax on realised capital gains and are allowed tax relief on realised losses, such as banks and finance companies, the equilibrium relationship remains as above. But for investors who paid tax on income received from securities while obtaining no relief for the capital loss incurred in selling forward at a discount, the equilibrium rate of discount would be smaller. If, for instance, an investor pays income tax on his marginal income at a rate of 50 per cent, the net yield to him of a one-year bond with a gross yield of $2\frac{1}{2}$ per cent is $1\frac{1}{4}$ per cent, and an on irredeemable security yielding $3\frac{3}{4}$ per cent it is $1\frac{7}{8}$ per cent. The highest rate of discount at which it would pay him to buy the long-dated security and sell it forward would therefore be $\frac{5}{8}$ per cent, whereas it would pay a bank or a charity to buy spot and sell forward at a discount of anything up to $1\frac{1}{4}$ per cent. For a surtax-payer the equilibrium level of discount is still lower — $\frac{5}{16}$ per cent if his marginal rate of tax is 15s. in the £, $\frac{1}{16}$ per cent if it is 19s. Unless, therefore, the tax regulations allowed the capital loss on forward sales to be deducted from the gross income yield for purposes of tax, the benefit to investors from the ability to hedge by selling forward would be mainly, if not entirely, confined to non-taxpayers and finance institutions. On the other hand, high tax-payers might find it well worth while to buy non-yielding securities and sell them forward at a premium.

If forward trading in individual securities were tried and

proved successful, it might be possible to take a further step towards specialisation, and therefore efficiency, in stock exchange speculation. We have seen how, by means of a futures contract, some produce exchanges provide the means of dealing in a generalised commodity as well as in particular grades. It would hardly be possible for a stock exchange to achieve this result in the same way, by allowing the seller of a standard security to satisfy his contract by delivery of any one of a number of other securities with appropriate price adjustments, for the diversity of price movements between different securities, even within a closely related group, is likely to be much greater than between different grades of the same commodity. It might, however, be possible to achieve a very similar result by permitting forward contracts in whole collections of related securities — in effect, in index numbers. It would be possible to satisfy such a contract by delivery (though this would rarely, if ever, occur in practice) if the seller transferred to the buyer a specified amount of each of a number of specified securities, as laid down in regulations made (and no doubt frequently revised) by the exchange authorities. In the vast majority of cases, of course, the contract would be reversed before it matured.

Such a contract would enable long-term speculators to adopt one of two main types of specialisation. On the one hand there would be those who were experts on the general prospects of broad classes of securities, and on the other those who, while less concerned with general prospects, had specialist knowledge of the individual securities within the group. If such a contract existed, an investor would have the choice either of obtaining a complete hedge against capital loss by selling his own securities forward, or of covering himself only against the effects of a general movement by selling forward the index number for the whole group of securities of which his own formed a part; while a speculator who had bought a particular security forward could sell the index number and so protect himself against a general fall in prices, while continuing to bear the risk of a fall affecting only his particular security. Since the type of knowledge which enables its possessor to form a judgment on the general prospects for a whole industry is often very different from that which enables him to judge the efficiency of a particular concern, contracts which enabled speculators to concentrate on the particular type of judgment they were best fitted to make would increase their efficiency and therefore the reliability of the service they could offer to the community.

CHAPTER 14

COMPANY PROFITS AND THEIR DISTRIBUTION SINCE THE WAR [1]

CONDITIONS in which British businesses have been operating since the war are quite unlike any known before. The last ten years, with the most temporary and local interruptions, have been years of continuous boom, with demand for most products and nearly all types of labour almost continuously in excess of supply, with rapidly rising real national income and still more rapidly rising money national income, and with a continuous tendency towards inflation, slowed, but never entirely checked, by high taxation and, more recently, by restrictions on the quantity of money. It is therefore natural that a number of enquiries [2] should recently have been made into the effect which these conditions of unprecedented boom and unprecedented rates of tax have had on the conduct of British business.

The first question which enquirers have asked is whether one effect of the continuous boom has been to raise business profit margins. Unfortunately the question is complicated by the fact that since the war the concerns and industries included within the scope of the definition 'private industry' have been continuously changing under the influence of successive measures of nationalisation and de-nationalisation, while the bulk of the concerns now included under the heading of 'public corporations' were included under 'companies' in the pre-war figures. An attempt has therefore been made, with the help of information most kindly provided by the Central Statistical Office, to separate out among the pre-war companies those that have not since been nationalised, and so obtain roughly comparative figures for companies both before and after the

---

[1] Published in *District Bank Review*, June 1955. Figures revised to April, 1961.

[2] Especially by David Walker 'Some Aspects of the Taxation of Companies' ('Manchester School', January 1954), and by Nicholas Kaldor, 'The Economic Effects of Company Taxation' (paper delivered to the Manchester Statistical Society, March 1955).

war. Throughout this article, therefore, the 1938 company figures exclude those of companies which were subsequently nationalised.

As a starting-point we can, as shown in Table I, get a rough idea of changes in the profitability of companies by relating gross company trading profits to the gross domestic

TABLE I

GROSS COMPANY TRADING PROFITS

	Gross Trading Profit	Total Domestic Income before providing for Depreciation and Stock Appreciation	Gross Trading Profit as a percentage of Total Domestic Income
	£m.	£m.	
1938	580	4,870	11·9
1948	1798	10,582	17·0
1949	1848	11,140	16·6
1950	2131	11,969	17·8
1951	2488	13,287	18·7
1952	2185	13,666	16·0
1953	2318	14,501	16·0
1954	2583	15,616	16·5

product before and after the war. Unfortunately the only pre-war year available, 1938, was a year of fairly severe business recession, in which profits were probably lower than in the previous two or three years.

From the preliminary enquiry we get the impression of very large increases in the profit margins of business since before the war. This first impression is, however, considerably modified if we consider not gross trading profits, but net trading profits after providing for the maintenance of capital physically intact. The difficulty of estimating the cost of maintaining fixed capital intact has been largely removed by the recent work of Mr. Redfern,[1] from which it appears that, because prices of capital goods have risen more than other prices since before the war, the proportion of the national income needed to maintain fixed capital intact is considerably greater than before the war. Mr. Redfern does not attempt to classify his results by type of

[1] Philip Redfern, 'Net Investment in Fixed Capital in the United Kingdom, 1938-53' (Paper delivered to the Royal Statistical Society, January 1955).

ownership, but his classification by industry and type of asset is such that it is possible to make rough estimates of depreciation at replacement cost on the fixed assets owned by companies.

To obtain estimates of net profits, we must also exclude inventory profits and losses — that is to say, those profits or losses which are due to changes in the book values of inventories of unchanged size. Thus in 1938, which was a year of falling prices, we must add back inventory losses, while in most post-war years we have to make substantial deductions for inventory profits. If we thus make allowance for keeping both fixed assets and inventories physically intact before arriving at net profits, we get the following result:

TABLE II

GROSS AND NET COMPANY TRADING PROFITS

	Gross Trading Profit	Depreciation at Replacement Cost	Stock Appreciation or Depreciation	Net Trading Profit	Net Domestic Product at Factor Cost	Net Trading Profit as a percentage of Net Domestic Product at Factor Cost
	£m.	£m.	£m.	£m.	£m.	
1938	580	−127	+60	513	4,589	11·2
1948	1798	−296	−200	1302	9,367	13·9
1949	1848	−302	−170	1376	10,013	13·7
1950	2131	−332	−440	1359	10,348	13·1
1951	2488	−372	−465	1651	11,472	14·4
1952	2185	−427	+22	1780	12,592	14·1
1953	2318	−461	+44	1901	13,411	14·2
1954	2583	−501	−53	2029	14,338	14·1

While taking net profits instead of gross reduces the scale of the rise in profits margins since before the war, it still leaves us with a rise of something like 30 per cent over 1938, though the rise over an average of the years 1936–38 would be smaller. The picture can be made still more precise if we check these results with the figures (in Table III) which the annual reports of the Commissioners of Inland Revenue give of the ratio of gross profit to turnover in various industries. Unfortunately the latest figures available refer to profits returned in the financial year 1952–53, which mean profits actually earned mainly in 1951. Similarly, the pre-war figures for 1938–39 refer to profits earned in 1937, which was a more profitable business year than 1938.

These figures give the impression that, while gross profit margins increased moderately in most lines of business (we can exclude Drink and Tobacco, where turnover was greatly

TABLE III

GROSS COMPANY PROFITS AS A PERCENTAGE
OF TURNOVER

	1938–39 (1937)	1952–53 (1951)
Mining and Quarrying (not coal)	18·1	19·2
Treatment of non-metalliferous mining products (not coal)	14·5	15·1
Chemicals and Allied Trades	12·1	11·4
Iron and Steel	11·0	13·8
Non-ferrous metals	7·6	10·3
Shipbuilding and non-electrical engineering	11·1	14·6
Electrical engineering and electrical goods	13·5	14·5
Vehicles	9·3	9·9
Metal Goods	13·1	15·8
Precision Instruments, Jewellery, etc.	3·5	11·9
Cotton	5·5	11·8
Wool	5·5	7·5
Other Textiles	7·1	13·2
Leather and Fur	2·8	9·7
Clothing	6·2	7·4
Food	6·4	7·1
Drink	13·0	10·5
Tobacco	8·8	3·7
Wood and Cork	8·1	9·7
Paper and Printing	11·4	17·6
Other Manufacturing	10·3	11·1
Building and Contracting	5·1	7·1
Road Transport	18·9	16·4
Other Transport and Communication, Storage (excl. Railways and Shipping)	22·9	17·0
Distribution (wholesale)	3·7	5·1
do. (retail)	5·9	6·4
Entertainment and Sport	11·3	13·6
Other Services	7·4	10·5

inflated by taxation), the really large increases were confined mainly to those industries, particularly the textile industries, which had been seriously depressed before the war. Taken in conjunction with the figures for net trading profit given in Table II, it can probably be said that, for most industries

TABLE IV
COMPANY PROFITS AND THEIR DISTRIBUTION
(£m.)

	1938	1948	1949	1950	1951	1952	1953	1954
Net Trading Profits (from Table II)	513	1302	1376	1359	1651	1780	1901	2029
Other Income (net)	263	460	433	569	575	492	572	673
Total Profit	776	1762	1809	1928	2226	2272	2473	2702
Less Interest paid (gross of Tax)	114	117	113	121	131	162	178	183
Net Profit before Tax	662	1645	1696	1807	2095	2110	2295	2519
Less Tax paid	204	857	1008	1008	1006	1235	1203	1140
Change in Tax Reserves	−7 197	+118 975	−43 965	+70 1078	+396 1402	−41 1194	+19 1222	+145 1285
Net Profit after Tax	465	670	731	729	693	916	1073	1234
Dividends paid (net of Tax) Preference	63	64	57	57	55	54	56	57
Ordinary	247	217	215	221	232	226	261	290
Change in Dividend Reserves	+5 315	−21 260	−5 267	+29 307	−3 284	+36 316	+12 329	+70 417
Net Company Saving	150	410	464	422	409	600	744	817

which were doing well before the war, net profit margins, after providing for the maintenance of capital intact, were not much greater in post-war years than they had been in 1937, though a few, especially those depressed before the war, were doing a great deal better, and nearly all were doing appreciably better than in the relatively depressed year, 1938.

Let us now turn to an examination of changes, not in the size of company profits, but in their distribution. Here, as will be seen from Table IV, the changes are dramatic.

The most obvious of the changes in the distribution of net profits before tax which has occurred since before the war is the enormous increase in the proportion going to the Treasury and the enormous fall in the proportion going to the share-holder.

This is made clear by the figures recorded in Table V. In 1938, of the net profit before tax, 31 per cent was paid in taxation (of which 1 per cent was withdrawn from tax reserves),

TABLE V

PERCENTAGE DISTRIBUTION OF COMPANIES'
NET PROFITS BEFORE TAX

	1938	1948	1949	1950	1951	1952	1953	1954
Taxes paid	31	52	59½	56	48	58½	52½	45
Additions to Tax Reserves	− 1	7	− 2½	4	19	− 2	1	6
Preference Dividends paid (net of Tax)	9½	4	3	3	2½	2½	2½	2
Ordinary Dividends paid (net of Tax)	37½	13	13	12	11	11	11	11½
Additions to Dividend Reserves (net of Tax)	1	− 1	—	2	—	2	½	3
Additions to Companies' Reserves	22	25	27	23	19½	28	32½	32½
	100	100	100	100	100	100	100	100

48 per cent was paid in net preference and ordinary dividends or added to dividend reserves, and 22 per cent added to the companies' own reserves. Since the war, the proportion going in taxation (including changes in tax reserves) has increased in all years to well over 50 per cent, in some years to nearly 60 per cent, and in one year (1951) to nearly 70 per cent. Except

in 1951, this increase was wholly at the expense of net preference and ordinary dividends, whose combined share of net profits at one time fell to 13½ per cent and even after the slight increases of the last year or two, received only 16 per cent in 1954. Except in 1951, the proportion going to the companies' own saving has been maintained at well above the pre-war figure.

The fluctuations since the war in the proportion of net profits taken in, or set aside for, taxation have not in the main

TABLE VI

COMPANIES' DEPRECIATION

(£m.)

	1948	1949	1950	1951	1952	1953	1954
Depreciation allowed for Tax:							
Annual Allowance	208	220	247	254	287	303	364
Initial and Investment Allowances	95	185	227	238	111	104	157
Total allowed for Tax	313	405	474	492	398	407	521
Estimated Depreciation at replacement cost	296	302	332	372	427	461	501
Annual Allowance as percentage of depreciation at replacement cost	70	73	74	68	67	66	73
Total Allowance as percentage of depreciation at replacement cost	106	134	143	132	93	88	104

been due to changes in rates of tax, but rather to the fluctuations in the relationship between true profits after maintaining capital intact, as calculated in Tables II and IV, and accounting profits as calculated for purposes of taxation. The difference between the two is not in the main due to inadequate depreciation allowances. While for the whole country these have, according to Mr. Redfern's calculations, been little more than half the actual annual cost of maintaining fixed capital physically intact, their inadequacy has been most marked for public corporations, public authorities, and house-owners. From Table VI it will be seen that for companies by themselves the addition of the 40 per cent Initial Allowance appears to have made depreciation allowances more than adequate for the years 1949–51, while, even after the withdrawal of the 40 per cent allowance, their inadequacy in 1952 and 1953 was not very large. With the introduction of the Investment Allowance in 1954 total depreciation allowances for companies seem to have been again brought into line with replacement costs, at least for the time being.

Mr. Redfern himself calculates that, for many of the fixed assets owned by companies since the war, depreciation at original cost does not amount to much over half the total of depreciation at replacement cost. On the other hand, if we compare our estimates of depreciation at replacement cost with the normal annual depreciation allowances calculated at original cost for tax purposes, before the inclusion of the initial and investment allowances, we find that the allowances are in most years equivalent to more than 70 per cent of replacement cost, only falling below 70 per cent in years during and immediately following periods of particularly rapid price increases. The apparent discrepancy between these and Mr. Redfern's proportions is probably accounted for, at least in part, by the fact that Mr. Redfern used the straight line method of depreciation, while, for tax purposes at least, most British companies use the diminishing balance method, which gives a much heavier weight to the more recent purchases. In a period of rapidly rising prices, the diminishing balance method of calculating depreciation gives considerably higher depreciation allowances and a considerably lower taxable profit than the straight line method.

While the complaints about inadequate depreciation allowances for companies seem to have had a less firm basis than had been supposed, a really serious degree of over-estimation of profits and of over-taxation has occurred through including in profits the rise in the value of inventories due entirely to changes in prices. For a company to continue to operate efficiently, it is no less necessary to keep circulating capital than fixed capital physically intact, and to include in taxable profits the rise in the book value of an inventory of unchanged size is to tax receipts which are needed to maintain capital intact. It is largely the check to the rise in prices which occurred after 1951, and the consequent disappearance of the fictitious element of stock appreciation in taxable profits, that account for the fall in the proportion of true profit which has had to be paid or set aside for tax, from 67 per cent in 1951 to 57 per cent in 1952, 54 per cent in 1953 and 51 per cent in 1954.

It has been this fall in the proportion of true profit taken in taxation during the recent period of relatively stable prices which has been the main reason for the easier financial position of most companies. While some part of the larger share of profits remaining after tax has gone towards increasing ordinary dividends — Mr. Walker's contention that these are unaffected by the level of taxation is clearly not completely defensible — the greater part has gone to increasing the companies' own savings, which in 1953 and 1954 received about 32 per cent of net profits before tax, as compared with not much over 25 per cent in earlier years and only 20 per cent in 1951. The increase in company saving since before the war, as shown in Table IV, is however not nearly so great as is suggested in the paper read by Mr. Kaldor, who reaches the conclusion that 'net savings of companies in the non-nationalised industries were ten times as large, in the average of 1951–53, as in 1938; so that, even allowing for a threefold rise in the price of capital goods, net capital savings available for expansion were over three times as great in the latter period as in the former'.

The difference between Mr. Kaldor's conclusions and those reached here is due, not to any difference of opinion about actual facts, but to differences about what is meant by 'net savings of companies'. To reach his conclusion Mr. Kaldor includes in net saving two elements which are excluded here, inventory appreciation and changes in tax (and dividend) reserves. He takes a year, 1938, of falling prices and heavy inventory losses, and compares it with a period, 1951–53, which contained large inventory profits. Thus in spite of the fact that he is purporting to calculate net savings — that is to say, saving available for expansion after providing for maintaining capital intact — he is in fact arriving at an amount which in 1938 was considerably smaller and in 1951–53 considerably larger than that which was available for expansion after maintaining capital physically intact.[1]

---

[1] Since the above was written I have been informed by Mr. Kaldor that the failure to correct the figures for stock appreciation (as distinct from tax

The second point is more arguable. It is true that reserves set aside by a company to cover taxes which it will not need to pay until the following year are available for meeting the company's expenditures in the current year: it is also true that so long as profits are maintained tax reserves will not fall, and the money so set aside remains permanently at the company's command. But the same is true of many other forms

TABLE VII

NET COMPANY SAVING

(£m.)

	1938	1948	1949	1950	1951	1952	1953	1954
Mr. Kaldor's Definition	88	707	596	961	1267	573	757	1085
Adjustments for:								
Stock Appreciation	+ 60	− 200	− 170	− 440	− 465	+ 22	+ 44	− 53
Changes in Tax Reserves	+ 7	− 118	+ 43	− 70	− 396	+ 41	− 19	− 145
Changes in Dividend Reserves	− 5	+ 21	− 5	− 29	+ 3	− 36	− 12	− 70
Alternative Definition	150	410	464	422	409	600	770	817
Index for Capital Goods Prices	100	239	243	250	276	306	309	308
Net Saving at 1938 Prices:								
Mr. Kaldor's Definition	88	296	246	384	459	187	245	352
Alternative Definition	150	172	191	169	148	196	249	265
Indexes of Real Saving:								
Mr. Kaldor's Definition	100	337	280	436	521	213	279	400
Alternative Definition	100	115	127	113	99	131	166	177

of delayed payment, including trade debts; and it is not suggested that an increase in these should be included as part of the company's saving. It is, of course, not altogether fair to group tax reserves with trade debts as current liabilities of the company, for if the company should go into liquidation on the day after the date of its balance sheet, or if it should incur a sufficiently heavy loss in the ensuing year, the tax debt, unlike a trade debt, would be wholly or partly extinguished. On the other hand, if in the following year the company fails to make a profit while yet avoiding a loss, the

reserves) in his estimate of 'real savings' was due to a slip in the preparation of the figures and not to any difference of view as to the appropriate definition of 'real savings'; the figures will be corrected in the published version of his lecture.

amount standing to the credit of the tax reserve will have to be paid out to meet tax liabilities. Surely therefore tax reserves should not be considered as on a par with a company's own capital, but should be regarded as at least a contingent liability, even though a rise in them may come in extremely useful in emergency to meet current payments, especially when, as in 1951, the cost of replacing inventories is rising rapidly.

The difference between the effects of these contrasting definitions is clearly brought out in Table VII.

It will be seen that Mr. Kaldor's definition shows net company saving at a maximum in 1951, a year of great financial

TABLE VIII

GROSS AND NET FIXED CAPITAL FORMATION BY COMPANIES
(£m.)

	1938	1948	1949	1950	1951	1952	1953	1954
Gross Fixed Capital Formation	200	554	592	645	646	648	691	806
Less Depreciation at Replacement Cost	127	296	302	332	372	427	461	501
Net Fixed Capital Formation	73	258	290	313	274	221	230	305
Net Fixed Capital Formation at 1938 Prices	73	108	120	125	100	73	74	99
Index of Real Net Fixed Capital Formation by Companies	100	148	164	171	137	100	101	136

stringency, with a heavy fall in subsequent years, which were years of increasing financial ease. The alternative definition has the opposite effect.

While company savings, even on the strictest definition, have in real terms recently been running at not far short of 50 per cent above the 1938 total, the figures in Table VIII provide confirmation that net domestic fixed investment by companies has recently been lagging.

The fall since 1950 in net fixed capital formation in this country by companies may be attributed partly to the effects on the statistics of the nationalisation of the iron and steel industry, but also to the effects of changes in Government policy, perhaps especially the dropping of the 40 per cent initial allowance in 1951 and the introduction of credit restriction in 1951–52. Mr. Redfern's figures, however, make it clear that, even in 1952 and 1953, net investment in industrial buildings, and still more in plant and machinery, was well above the 1938 level, while there had been a very heavy fall in commercial buildings. Investment recovered slightly in 1954, and there are signs that this will be accelerated in 1955. It should also be remembered, in assessing the significance of

TABLE IX

TOTAL DOMESTIC CAPITAL FORMATION BY COMPANIES
AND ITS FINANCE
(£m.)

	1938	1948	1949	1950	1951	1952	1953	1954
Net Fixed Capital Formation	73	258	290	313	274	221	230	305
Change in Size of Stocks	+60	+212	+49	−24	+426	−62	+66	+195
Total Net Capital Formation	133	470	339	289	700	159	296	500
Net Saving by Companies	150	410	464	422	409	600	770	817
Net Capital Transfers	—	64	55	54	32	32	42	25
Companies' Own Resources	150	474	519	476	441	632	812	842
Excess of Resources over Net Capital Formation at Home	+17	+4	+180	+187	−259	+473	+516	+342
Changes in Tax and Dividend Reserves	−2	+97	−48	+79	+393	−5	+31	+215

the fall in investment since 1950, that the mere replacement of worn-out or obsolete fixed capital usually implies an improvement in quality, so that even with net investment at zero it would be reasonable to expect a continued rise in productive capacity.

From Table IX it may be gathered that investment in the physical expansion of stocks and of work-in-progress, while fluctuating violently, has since 1948 averaged about £140 millions in a year, or about half the amount of net fixed capital investment. It has been mainly in years of rapidly rising stocks that symptoms of capital shortage for companies have been most apparent.

The existence of a surplus of financial resources at the disposal of companies as a whole over their investment needs in this country does not necessarily imply that the majority of industrial companies are in a position to finance themselves without outside help. Many companies are financial companies of one kind or another, which normally expect to invest their savings in the securities of other companies or of the public sector, and others have large interests overseas which they need to expand out of their savings. Nevertheless, it is difficult to believe that, in most post-war years, and especially since 1952, it has been shortage of capital which has constituted the chief brake on investment by companies.

To summarise our comparison of the financial position of United Kingdom companies since 1948 with what it was before the war, we find that net profit margins, after full provision for maintaining capital physically intact, are probably not much, if any, higher in most of those industries which were already prosperous before the war, though they are very markedly higher in industries which were previously depressed. Of these net profits, however, the Government takes a greatly increased share, which rose from 30 per cent in 1938 to nearly twice that figure in 1948–50, and to nearly 70 per cent in 1951, when, owing to the big rise in the cost of replacing inventories, the excess of taxable profits over true profits was unusually large. Since 1951, chiefly as the result of the check to the rise in inventory prices, the Government's share of true net profits has fallen back to about 51 per cent.

The rise in the Government's share of profits has not been at the expense of company savings, the share of which rose from 22 per cent in 1938 to 25 per cent or more in 1948–50 and then, after a fall in the exceptional year 1951, to 32 per cent in 1953 and 1954. It has been more than wholly at the expense of net dividends, whose share of profits fell from 47 per cent in 1938 to a minimum of $13\frac{1}{2}$ per cent in 1951. The reduction since then in the effective tax burden has not, however, been wholly without effect on dividends, for net ordinary dividends, plus dividend reserves, have risen from 11 per cent to $14\frac{1}{2}$ per cent of net profits. Even after this rise, however, gross ordinary dividends in 1954 had a purchasing power of only 75 per cent of what they had in 1938, while, after deducting tax, ordinary dividends were worth less than 60 per cent of their 1938 value. In spite of the rise in company saving, investment in this country by companies has recently been down to the pre-war level, though it is now rising again.

Is the system thus outlined, in which shareholders receive only a minute fraction of the profits earned by the companies they own, and where aggregate market values of all the issued securities of a company may be worth much less than the value of the business as a going concern, or even than the break-up value of its assets, one which is likely to prove stable?

Both Mr. Walker and Mr. Kaldor say no. Mr. Walker expects that, as businesses or their assets change hands at their market prices, their loan and share capitals will gradually be brought into line with the value of their assets and 'the percentage of profits distributed will rise to something approaching the 1938 level'. It is difficult to believe that Mr. Walker is serious in this prophecy. We must, of course, take 'the percentage of profits distributed' to mean gross distribution, before tax; but even so, this would involve an increase in gross dividend and interest payments from the £900 millions actually paid in 1954 to nearly twice that amount, leaving (on the 1954 figures for profits) less than £900 millions for tax payments and company saving combined. Such an increase would be possible (at unchanged rates of tax) only on two assumptions — an enormous increase in company capitalisation in the form of loans (interest on which would, of course, not be liable to profits tax) and a very large fall in company savings. If we assume, as a limiting case, that the whole of the increase in distributions over the 1954 level consisted of interest on debts, raising this item from under £200 millions to over £1000 millions, we should still have to reduce company saving from the £817 millions actually achieved in 1954 to about £500 millions in order to meet the tax payments of over £450 millions (exclusive of tax deducted from dividends) which would still be due.

While, however, we must regretfully dismiss Mr. Walker's hopes (in the absence, of course, of drastic further tax reductions) as a dream, there is good reason to expect that some modest steps may be taken in the direction he indicates. Whether or not under pressure from threats of 'take-over' bids, there is clearly scope for some further increase in ordinary dividends, at least so long as there is no accelerated rise in inventory prices to cause a rise in effective rates of tax on true net profits. At 32 per cent of net profits, recent appropriations to reserve are clearly still generous, and a further rise in the share of net ordinary dividends to, say, 15 per cent of profit does not seem unreasonable. This, together with a continued rise in the absolute level of company profits as a result of increasing production, might well in a propitious political climate give ordinary shareholders a further increase of perhaps 20 per cent or so in real terms in their gross receipts over the next few years, plus, of course, any extra addition to net receipts as the result of any fall in tax rates. Even so, the purchasing power of their gross dividends, and still more of their net dividends, would still remain below the 1938 level.

Mr. Kaldor's argument is different. He rightly points out the effect which profits tax has on widening the gap between earnings per share and dividends per share, and considers that, while this gap has hitherto been opened wholly or mainly by depressing dividends, in due course it will lead to a rise in earnings. This is because companies, finding that the addition of tax to dividends makes the total annual cost of new share capital very high, will not be willing to make new share issues except when the earnings yield on new investment is also expected to be unusually large. The increased cost of annual payments on new issues will tend to discourage the growth of such new businesses as find that they are unable to finance expansion entirely out of ploughed-back profits. Thus competition with established businesses will be reduced and the earnings yield on capital will tend to rise. Mr. Kaldor regards this potential development as undesirable, and is therefore in favour of the removal of profits taxes. As, however, this would leave the ordinary shareholder as a main ultimate beneficiary of a full-employment economy, he proposes that an alternative means of skimming off his profits should be sought in a capital gains tax.

It is difficult to say just how important in practice are the disadvantages for the economy as a whole which Mr. Kaldor attributes to the profits tax, or whether his proposed alternative (which he does not discuss) might not have effects, especially on the free working of the capital market and on the further growth of the tax avoidance industry, which would be even more undesirable. But if he is right in believing that profits tax is an important factor in making it more difficult for new and growing firms to establish themselves in competition with established companies, surely it is not the possible widening of the profits margin — the consequence of reduced competition — which is most to be feared ? A much more dangerous effect of the present system of full employment, excess demand, and drastic taxation, is not that it may enable companies to enjoy profit margins that are too large, but that it may reduce the incentive to try to make them larger. When conditions are such that only the remarkably inefficient or unlucky can fail to survive, while the highly efficient are deprived of the power of, and incentive for, the extremely rapid growth which has characterised so many efficient businesses in the past, it is only too likely that directors will find it both possible and convenient to maximise something other than profits, and minimise something other than costs. This will mean, not only that production will rise more slowly than it might have done, but that things will be produced that are less needed, instead of those that are needed more, and will be produced with costs and prices higher than would otherwise have been necessary. The real cost of excessive business taxation may well be, not higher profit margins, but higher costs and an intensified tendency towards inflation.

POSTSCRIPT (September, 1961)

The forecast, made in 1955, of a substantial rise in ordinary dividends over the next few years had to wait a long time for fulfilment. According to the continuation of Table IV,[1] ordinary dividends after tax, plus increases in dividend reserves,

---

[1] The 1961 National Income Blue Book makes considerable retrospective alterations in the 'Companies' Appropriations Account' (Table 26). To make comparisons possible with subsequent years, revised figures for 1954 have been included in the continuation of Table IV.

TABLE IV (*Continued*)
COMPANY PROFITS AND THEIR DISTRIBUTION
(£m.)

	1954 (Revised)	1955	1956	1957	1958	1959	1960
Net Trading Profits	2049	2249	2229	2376	2334	2521	2712
Other Income (net)	786	720	816	870	1004	953	988
Total Profit	2835	2969	3045	3246	3338	3474	3700
Less Interest paid (gross of Tax)	183	223	284	322	344	318	366
Net Profit before Tax	2652	2746	2761	2924	2994	3156	3334
Less Tax paid	1140	1232	1168	1269	1321	1300	1118
Change in Tax Reserves	+145 1285	+8 1240	+136 1304	+14 1283	−88 1233	−157 1143	+347 1465
Net Profit after Tax	1367	1506	1457	1641	1761	2013	1869
Dividends paid (net of Tax)							
Preference	57	63	63	62	61	65	69
Ordinary	290	333	350	368	386	480	604
Change in Dividend Reserves	+70 417	+17 413	+17 430	+27 457	+21 468	+181 726	+25 698
Net Company Saving	950	1093	1027	1184	1293	1287	1171

rose only from £360 millions in 1954 to £407 millions in 1958, or by 13 per cent. This was a little less than the rise of 14 per cent in prices of consumption goods, so that in real terms appropriations to ordinary dividends fell slightly.

The absence of any rise in real dividends between 1954 and 1958 was due to the combined effects of a number of factors. Largely as the result of action taken in the period 1955–57 to check the over-rapid rise in incomes, gross domestic product rose by less than 7 per cent between 1954 and 1958, as compared with a rise of nearly 9 per cent between 1952 and 1954. In addition, the proportion of net national income going to net trading profits fell from 14·1 to 12·7 per cent. As a result, company profits before tax rose more slowly than prices, and in real terms fell by 1 per cent in terms of consumption goods and by 5 per cent in terms of capital goods.

With a fall in the proportion of profits taken in tax from 48 to 41 per cent, profits after tax did better than this, rising by 29 per cent in money terms and 13 per cent (or 8½ per cent) in real terms. But ordinary shareholders did not benefit from this increase, for their share in profits after tax fell from 26 per cent in 1954 to 23 per cent in 1958, while the share going to company reserves rose from 69½ to 73½ per cent. Net company savings in 1958, at £1293 millions, were thus 36 per cent higher in money terms and 14 per cent higher (at capital goods prices) in real terms than in 1954.

In 1959 all the factors unfavourable to a rise in dividends were reversed and expectations of a substantial rise were at last realised. Between 1958 and 1959 real gross domestic product rose by over 5 per cent, and the proportion of net national income going to net company trading profits recovered from 12·7 to 13·2 per cent. In consequence, net company profits before tax rose from £2994 millions to £3156 millions, or by 5½ per cent. In the same year there was a surprisingly sharp fall in the proportion of profits required for tax, from 41 to 36 per cent, so that profits after tax rose from £1761 millions to £2013 millions, or by 14 per cent. Finally, the proportion of profits after tax put to reserve fell from 73 to 64 per cent. The combined affects of these changes was to increase ordinary dividends after tax (including a large increase in dividend reserves) from £407 millions to £661 millions, or by 62 per cent. As the rise in prices was negligible, the rise in real terms was almost as large. Even after this increase, ordinary dividends after tax were equal to only about 3¼ per cent of net national income, as compared with 5½ per cent in 1938. As real national income in 1959 was about 60 per cent higher than in 1938, ordinary dividends after tax still had slightly less aggregate purchasing power than in 1938.

From 1959 to 1960 real national product again rose by over 5 per cent, while the share of net national income going to net company trading profits recovered further to 13·4 per cent, and the rise in net profit before tax was again 5½ per cent. The proportion of net profit appropriated for tax, however, showed a very sharp rise, from 36 to 44 per cent, and net profit after tax fell from £2013 millions to £1869 millions. The greater part of this fall was reflected in net company saving, which absorbed only 62 per cent of net profit after tax, as compared with 64 per cent in 1959, and appropriations to ordinary dividends fell only from £661 millions to £629 millions.

As the result of the increase in the share of profits after tax going to ordinary dividends from 26 per cent in 1954 to 34 per cent in 1960, net company saving rose over the seven years by only 23 per cent in money terms and by less than 4 per cent in real terms (at capital goods prices). The rise in net company saving of £221 millions was quite inadequate to cover the rise of £529 millions in net company fixed investment, and this deficiency, together with the abnormal increase in inventories in 1960, explains the need for companies to obtain greatly increased amounts of finance both from the long-term capital market and from the banks.

It is difficult to explain either the exceptional fall in the proportion of profits required for tax in 1958–59 or the exceptional rise in 1959–60. The movements seem much too large to be accounted for either by changes in tax rates, or by changes in the difference between real and taxable profits. It would not be surprising if both the exceptional fall in taxation in 1959 and the exceptional rise in 1960 were retrospectively adjusted in subsequent estimates.

As regards the future, it would seem that the more favourable conditions created in 1959 have already come to an end. The checking of resurgent inflationary pressures is necessitating measures which will operate largely through an initial reduction in the share of national income going to company profits, and probably also in a further increase in the share of company profits taken by taxation. At the same time, credit conditions are likely to make it difficult and expensive for companies to obtain as much finance as they would like from outside sources. Even with a much-reduced rate of inventory accumulation, companies may be obliged, in order to meet their investment programmes, to re-expand the share of profits placed to reserve and to reduce the share going to dividends. While in the long run there is no reason to doubt that the upward trend in real national income will continue to be reflected in rising real company profits and dividends, there may well be a considerable pause (though not, it may be hoped, as long as that from 1954 to 1958) before the next substantial rise.

K

CHAPTER 15

THE REAL INCIDENCE OF PERSONAL TAXATION [1]

THERE is a general impression that direct taxation on personal incomes, which during the war was raised to the highest level deemed bearable even under conditions of the greatest emergency, has since the war been greatly reduced for all levels of income. In reality, as will be shown, the reductions in tax rates have not meant anything like a corresponding alleviation of the real tax burden, for the reason that the persistent inflation of all money values has steadily been pushing large numbers of people into higher income brackets, subject to higher rates of tax.

On the face of it, the reductions in rates of taxation have been impressive. The standard rate of income tax has been reduced from 10s. in the pound to 8s. 6d. without any corresponding increase in surtax. Earned income relief has been increased from one-tenth of the first £2000 to two-ninths of the first £2025. The single allowance has been increased from £100 to £140, the married allowance from £150 to £240, and the child allowance from £45 to £100. The effect of these and other concessions can be seen in Table I on page 283, and Chart I, which show the changes in the proportions of income before tax paid in income tax and surtax by a married man with two children at a number of different levels of money income.

These make it clear that for the family man with a wholly earned income the proportions of tax paid on all levels of money income have fallen very substantially since the war. Tax on an income of £600 a year has fallen from 20 per cent almost to nothing. On £1000 a year it has fallen by almost three-quarters. On £2000 a year it has been reduced by almost a half, and even on £10,000 a year the fall is over 10 per cent.

The reductions in rates of tax on other classes of taxpayers,

[1] Published in *Lloyds Bank Review*, January 1957.

though less than for the family man with a wholly earned income, have still been substantial. For instance, a married man with two children and an income of £600 a year derived wholly from investments would have paid 25 per cent in tax in 1945–46 and only 5 per cent in 1956–57. A single man with the same income, but wholly earned, would have paid 13 per cent in 1956–57, as against 24 per cent in 1945–46. At

CHART I

PERCENTAGE OF MONEY INCOMES PAID IN
INCOME TAX AND SURTAX

(Married Man with Two Children)

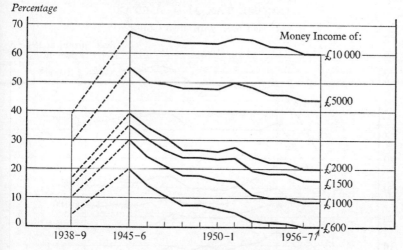

£2000 a year the reduction would have been from 42 to 30 per cent for the family man with an investment income and from 40 to 27 per cent for the bachelor with an income wholly earned. At £10,000 a year the corresponding changes have been from 68 to 62 per cent and from 68 to 61 per cent respectively.

Tax on Real Incomes

Unfortunately, further examination shows, as has been mentioned above, that these apparent reductions in the tax burden are partly or wholly illusory. During a period of rising prices, a man who succeeds in increasing his income before tax by an amount just enough to offset the rise in the cost of living, so that his *real* income before tax remains constant, is continually tending to move into higher tax brackets. With a system of progressive taxation, he will therefore pay in tax a constantly increasing proportion of a constant real income, even if rates of tax are not raised.

This tendency for rising prices to lift constant real incomes into higher tax brackets has during the last ten years gone far towards offsetting the benefits of lower rates of tax. The net

CHART II

PERCENTAGE OF REAL INCOMES PAID IN
INCOME TAX AND SURTAX

(Married Man with Two Children)

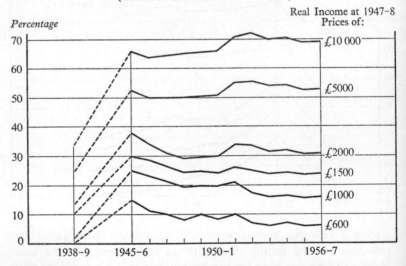

results of the opposing tendencies are set out in Table II, and Chart II which show the proportions paid in tax — also by a married man with two children and a wholly earned income — at different levels of real income corresponding to the money incomes shown in Table I for the year 1947–48.

This table shows a very different picture. To provide the same purchasing power as £600 in 1947–48, an income would have to rise from £536 in 1945–46 to £917 in 1956–57. On this constant real income, the proportion paid in tax has fallen, not from 20 per cent almost to zero, but from rather over 15 per cent to just under 7 per cent or by about 55 per cent. On higher real incomes the reduction in the tax burden becomes progressively smaller. On the equivalent of £1000 a year in 1947–48, the proportion paid in tax has fallen from rather over 25 per cent to somewhat less than 17 per cent, or by 35 per cent. On the equivalent of £2000 a year, it has fallen from 37½ to 31½ per cent, or by 16 per cent. On the equivalent of £5000

TABLE I

PERCENTAGE OF MONEY INCOMES PAID IN
INCOME TAX AND SURTAX

(Married Couple with Two Children. All Earned Income)

	£600	£1000	£1500	£2000	£5000	£10,000
1913–14	3·0	3·7	3·7	3·7	5·8	5·8
1938–39	3·7	10·2	13·5	16·3	28·3	38·6
1945–46	20·2	30·1	35·1	38·8	55·2	67·8
1946–47	14·0	24·1	30·3	34·0	50·8	64·7
1947–48	10·6	21·4	26·7	31·3	49·7	64·1
1948–49	7·7	18·0	24·0	27·0	48·0	63·3
1949–50	7·7	18·0	24·0	27·0	48·0	63·3
1950–51	6·5	16·9	23·2	26·4	47·8	63·2
1951–52	5·8	16·3	23·8	27·3	49·7	65·3
1952–53	2·2	11·2	19·7	24·0	48·3	64·7
1953–54	1·8	10·2	18·4	22·6	46·2	62·4
1954–55	1·8	10·2	18·4	22·6	46·2	62·4
1955–56	0·5	8·5	16·6	20·7	43·9	60·0
1956–57	0·5	8·5	16·6	20·7	43·9	60·0

a year, the proportion paid in tax has remained unchanged at 53 per cent, while on larger incomes it has actually risen. At the £10,000 (1947–48) level, for instance, the payment in 1945–1946 was 66 per cent on £8950, while in 1956–57 it is 68½ per cent on £15,288.

Other classes of taxpayers have fared even less well. For instance, on the £600-equivalent level, if the same taxpayer had an income derived wholly from investments he would have paid 22 per cent in 1945–46 and 16 per cent on the same real income in 1956–57; while if his income had been wholly earned but he himself had been single he would have paid 32 per cent in 1945–46 and 20 per cent in 1956–57. The falls in average tax rates would thus have been only 27 per cent and 38 per cent respectively, as compared with 55 per cent in the case shown in Table II. Similarly, at the other end of the scale, a married man with two children and a wholly investment income equivalent to £10,000 a year in 1947–48 would have paid 66½ per cent in 1945–46 and 71 per cent in 1956–57, while the single man with an income of similar size but wholly earned would also have paid 66½ per cent in 1945–46, rising to 70½ per cent in 1956–57. Thus the increases in both cases would have been about 7 per cent, as compared with an increase of 4 per cent for the married man with two children and a wholly earned income.

In all cases, however, average rates of tax on real incomes below £2000 a year in 1947–48 have been appreciably reduced since 1945–46, while above the equivalent of £5000 a year they have risen. It is also noticeable that in 1956–57, after five years of Conservative Governments, the proportions paid on real incomes equivalent to £2000 a year and over in 1947–48 are higher than during the years between 1947 and 1951, when a Labour Government was in office. The exclusion of the higher real incomes from most or all of the benefits of reduced direct taxation since the war may well give rise to difficulty if any future Government should find it necessary again to increase it. The choice would have to be made between exempting the higher real incomes from the increase, which might be politically difficult, and raising the proportions of such incomes taken in taxation above the level which was regarded as possible even in time of war.

In a year in which prices rise, it is necessary only to leave tax rates unchanged in order to increase the proportions paid over in tax of unchanged real incomes at all levels. This is clearly shown in Table II in the results for the years 1949–50, 1954–55, and 1956–57, when rates of tax remained unchanged while the proportions paid increased. Thus highly progressive rates of tax have tended to provide a partial check to inflation by raising, without the necessity for any increase in tax rates, the proportion going to the Government of a constant real national income. When the real national income is rising as well as prices, the effect is, of course, all the greater.

The extent to which the effect of rising prices increases the tax burden on constant real incomes can be seen even more clearly if we contrast the percentages of various levels of real

TABLE II

PERCENTAGE OF REAL INCOMES PAID IN
INCOME TAX AND SURTAX
(Married Couple with Two Children. All Earned Income)

	Money Income 1947–48 £600		Money Income 1947–48 £1000		Money Income 1947–48 £1500	
	Equivalent Income	% Tax	Equivalent Income	% Tax	Equivalent Income	% Tax
	£		£		£	
1913–14	235	0·8	392	2·0	588	2·8
1938–39	368	—	613	4·3	920	10·0
1945–46	536	15·4	895	25·4	1340	30·3
1946–47	564	11·6	940	23·2	1410	28·9
1947–48	600	10·6	1000	21·4	1500	26·7
1948–49	648	8·4	1080	19·2	1620	24·5
1949–50	666	9·4	1110	19·7	1665	24·8
1950–51	690	8·4	1150	19·3	1725	24·6
1951–52	750	9·7	1250	21·1	1875	26·5
1952–53	828	7·4	1380	17·8	2070	25·1
1953–54	840	6·3	1400	16·7	2100	24·0
1954–55	864	7·3	1440	17·2	2160	24·5
1955–56	882	6·2	1470	16·2	2205	23·5
1956–57	917	6·9	1529	16·7	2293	24·0

	Money Income 1947–48 £2000		Money Income 1947–48 £5000		Money Income 1947–48 £10,000	
	Equivalent Income	% Tax	Equivalent Income	% Tax	Equivalent Income	% Tax
	£		£		£	
1913–14	784	3·7	1960	3·7	3,920	5·8
1938–39	1225	13·0	3065	24·0	6,130	33·5
1945–46	1790	37·5	4470	53·3	8,950	65·9
1946–47	1880	33·3	4700	49·8	9,400	63·5
1947–48	2000	31·3	5000	49·7	10,000	64·1
1948–49	2160	29·1	5400	49·8	10,800	65·0
1949–50	2220	29·4	5550	50·1	11,100	65·3
1950–51	2300	29·7	5750	50·8	11,500	66·0
1951–52	2500	33·4	6250	55·5	12,500	70·5
1952–53	2760	33·3	6900	56·2	13,800	72·2
1953–54	2800	32·0	7000	54·4	14,000	70·0
1954–55	2880	32·5	7200	54·8	14,400	70·3
1955–56	2940	31·0	7350	53·0	14,700	68·3
1956–57	3058	31·5	7644	53·4	15,288	68·6

income which would have been paid in tax in 1956–57 if tax rates and allowances had remained as they were in 1947–48 with those which were actually paid then and those which are actually paid now. If rates and allowances were the same in 1956–57 as they were nine years before, a married man with two children and a wholly earned income with the same purchasing power as £600 in 1947–48 would be paying nearly 20 per cent

TABLE III

RISING PRICES AND THE POTENTIAL RISE IN TAX
(Married Couple with Two Children)

1947–48		1956–57				
			Tax at 1947–48 Rates		Tax at 1956–57 Rates	
Income £	Tax as % of Income	Equivalent Income £	Tax as % of Income	Change since 1947–48 as % of Income	Tax as % of Income	Change since 1947–48 as % of Income
600	10·6	917	19·9	+9·3	6·9	−3·7
1,000	21·4	1,529	27·0	+5·6	16·7	−4·7
1,500	26·7	2,293	34·3	+7·6	24·0	−2·7
2,000	31·3	3,058	40·1	+8·8	31·5	+0·2
5,000	49·7	7,644	58·7	+9·0	53·4	+3·7
10,000	64·1	15,288	73·3	+9·2	68·6	+4·5

of his income in tax, as compared with 10·6 per cent in 1947–48. At the £1000 a year equivalent income the increase would be smaller — from 21·4 to 27 per cent, or 5·6 per cent of income, as against 9·3 per cent for the equivalent of £600. With higher incomes the increase again becomes larger, but even at the equivalent of £10,000 a year the rise is only 9·2 per cent of income, or barely as large proportionally as at the £600 a year level. In actual fact, of course, effective tax rates on incomes up to the equivalent of £1000 a year have been so reduced that the proportions paid in tax have fallen substantially in spite of the rise in money incomes. Above this level there is a progressive fall in the net benefits from tax reductions, until at the equivalent of £2000 a year they are only just sufficient to offset the money rise; thereafter the effects of the reductions in tax rates fall progressively below those of the rise in money incomes.

THE DISTRIBUTION OF INCOMES

The effect of rising prices in increasing the proportion paid in tax on constant real incomes is, however, only one of the factors affecting the proportion of an unchanged total of real personal incomes yielded by constant rates of tax. There is also another which, though on balance less important than the first, substantially modifies its effects. This is the tendency which has continued since before the war and still persists for the proportion of total personal incomes received by the higher income groups to fall, even before tax. This second factor pulls in the opposite direction, by reducing the proportion of incomes paying the higher tax rates and increasing the proportion paying lower rates.

Information on the distribution of personal incomes is much less full than on rates of tax, and estimates are given in the National Income Blue Books for only five years : 1938, 1949, 1953, 1954, and 1955. Of these, only unrevised estimates of distribution are available for 1953 and 1954, though the changes in the totals are small. Further, the estimates for 'attributable' incomes exclude such items as interest on life insurance funds and increases in pension funds, which are included in the total of personal incomes but cannot be allocated to particular income groups. The total naturally excludes benefits, in cash or kind, which fail to find their way into tax returns at all levels of income. How far the inclusion of these would modify the conclusions drawn from the published estimates must be a matter of opinion.

The distribution of personal incomes is not set out in the National Income Blue Books in a form immediately suitable for the present purpose, since incomes before and after tax are divided into income groups which vary greatly in size from year to year. However, by fitting an appropriate curve, it is possible to interpolate aggregate incomes before and after tax for groups of constant size.

The results for incomes before tax are submitted in Table IV. It is estimated that the 100,000 largest incomes in the country were those above £2070 a year in 1938 and £3850 a year in 1955. The table shows that the share of aggregate

K2

(attributable) personal income received by this group fell from
11·7 per cent of the total before tax in 1938 to 7·1 per cent in
1949, and again to only 5·3 per cent in 1955. Similarly, the
million largest incomes were those above £450 in 1938 and

TABLE IV

DISTRIBUTION OF PERSONAL INCOMES BEFORE TAX *

Income Range	1938 %	1949 %	1953 %	1954 %	1955 %	1955 Range of Income Covered † £
(1) 1st 100,000	11·7	7·1	5·8	5·8	5·3	*3850 and over*
(2) 2nd ,,	3·6	2·9	2·6	2·4	2·4	*2700–3850*
(3) 3rd ,,	2·6	2·2	1·9	1·9	1·8	*2150–2700*
(4) 4th ,,	2·0	1·8	1·5	1·6	1·5	*1825–2150*
(5) 5th ,,	1·6	1·6	1·4	1·3	1·3	*1625–1825*
(6) 1st 500,000	21·5	15·6	13·2	12·7	12·3	*1625 and over*
(7) 2nd ,,	6·3	5·9	5·2	5·3	5·1	*1175–1625*
(8) 1st million	27·8	21·5	18·4	18·0	17·4	*1175 and over*
(9) 2nd ,,	8·2	8·3	8·0	7·9	7·8	*910–1175*
(10) 3rd ,,	6·0	6·4	6·4	6·3	6·4	*800–910*
(11) 4th ,,	5·1	5·5	5·8	5·9	5·7	*730–800*
(12) 5th ,,	4·5	5·0	5·4	5·4	5·3	*680–730*
(13) 1st 5 millions	51·6	46·7	44·0	43·5	42·6	*680 and over*
(14) 2nd ,,	16·8	20·5	21·2	21·8	22·6	*510–680*
(15) 1st 10 millions	68·4	67·2	65·1	65·3	65·2	*510 and over*
(16) Remainder	31·6	32·8	34·9	34·7	34·8	*under 510*
Total Incomes	100·0	100·0	100·0	100·0	100·0	

* The table covers only attributable personal income (see text).

† *Range of income covered in 1938:* (1) £2070 and over (2) 1260–2070 (3) 970–1260
(4) 795–970 (5) 685–795 (6) 685 and over (7) 450–685 (8) 450 and over (9) 300–450 (10)
238–300 (11) 205–238 (12) 184–205 (13) 184 and over (14) 123–184 (15) 123 and over
(16) under 123.

Range of income in 1949: (1) £3200 and over (2) 2190–3200 (3) 1770–2190 (4) 1465–
1770 (5) 1290–1465 (6) 1290 and over (7) 875–1290 (8) 875 and over (9) 635–875 (10) 532–
635 (11) 468–532 (12) 418–468 (13) 418 and over (14) 290–418 (15) 290 and over (16) under
290.

£1175 in 1955. The share of the whole of this group declined
from 27·8 per cent in 1938 to 21·5 per cent in 1949 and 17·4
per cent in 1955. What of the counterpart of this movement?
If the share of one section has declined, that of some other
section or sections must obviously have risen. In fact, the

largest share of the increase seems to have accrued, not so much to those with the lowest incomes as to those in the middle range — the second five million group. This comprises the stratum with incomes between £123 and £184 in 1938 and between £510 and £680 in 1955. The proportion of total income going to this group increased from 16·8 per cent in 1938 to 20·5 per cent in 1949 and 22·6 per cent in 1955.

The share of those with incomes below the first ten millions increased from 31·6 per cent in 1938 to 32·8 per cent in 1949 and 34·8 per cent in 1955 ; but part of this rise was due to an increase in their number from probably well under 15 millions in 1938 to 15·5 millions in 1949 and 16·2 millions in 1955. The relatively small rise in the share of the lowest income groups, in spite of the exceptionally large proportional rises in the earnings of women and juveniles, is probably attributable to the fact that these groups include many pensioners and others whose incomes have not risen proportionately with the cost of living.

The shift since 1938 in personal incomes before tax away from the higher income groups towards the middle groups has probably been caused mainly by the fall in incomes derived from investments and rent. These fell from over 22 per cent of total personal incomes in 1938 to little more than half that proportion in 1949 and 1955. The most important cause of this fall in real investment incomes has probably been the effect of inflation in reducing the real incomes derived from all forms of fixed interest investments, and even more drastically those from the ownership of rent-controlled houses. The fall in the real incomes from the ownership of rented farm property has frequently been only a little less marked, while even holders of ordinary shares have on the average suffered a loss of something like 25 per cent in their real incomes before tax since 1938, in spite of some recovery since 1949.

Contributory causes of the fall in the share of personal incomes going to the highest groups seem to have been the reduced share taken by incomes of self-employed persons, in spite of some net rise in farmers' incomes, and the slower rise per head in salaries, especially the higher salaries, than in wages. It seems likely that the higher salaries would have risen faster if taxation had been lower at the margin, since the very high rates of marginal taxation have probably induced some employers to seek alternative methods of remuneration. It therefore seems possible that lower marginal rates of tax on high salaries might actually have provided a larger tax yield than the present high rates.

CHANGES IN REAL INCOMES BEFORE TAX

The magnitude of the changes in the distribution of incomes before tax becomes even more apparent if we convert

TABLE V

CHANGES IN REAL INCOMES BEFORE TAX,
ADJUSTED FOR CHANGES IN PRICES, 1949 = 100

Income Range	1938	1949	1953	1954	1955
1st 100,000	164	100	87	87	88
2nd ,,	123	100	94	94	100
3rd ,,	115	100	91	94	93
4th ,,	111	100	94	97	100
5th ,,	104	100	94	97	97
1st 500,000	137	100	90	91	93
2nd ,,	105	100	95	99	101
1st million	128	100	92	94	95
2nd ,,	98	100	103	106	110
3rd ,,	93	100	106	110	116
4th ,,	90	100	112	119	121
5th ,,	88	100	114	120	124
1st 5 millions	109	100	101	104	107
2nd ,,	81	100	110	119	129
1st 10 millions	101	100	103	108	114
Remainder	95	100	113	118	124
Total Incomes *	99	100	107	111	117

* This table refers only to attributable incomes; the corresponding figures for non-attributable income are 82, 100, 102, 113, 119.

money incomes into *real* incomes measured at 1949 prices, using for the purpose (as in Table II) the National Income Blue Book index of market prices for consumers' expenditure. The results of these calculations are presented in Table V. They show that, in real terms, the aggregate purchasing power of the 100,000 highest incomes fell *before tax* by nearly 40 per cent between 1938 and 1949 and by a further 13 per cent between 1949 and 1953, subsequently recovering very slightly (to 88 per cent of the 1949 level) in 1955. The remainder of the first million suffered a loss of real income of 11 per cent between 1938 and 1949 and of a further 6 per cent between 1949 and 1953, but have since recovered nearly to the 1949 level.

On lower real incomes, the gains become progressively larger, both between 1938 and 1949 and between 1949 and 1955, until they reach a maximum with the second five millions. This is the group receiving between £123 and £184 in 1938 and between £510 and £680 in 1955. For this section, the increase in real income is 29 per cent since 1949 and 59 per cent since 1938. Those with incomes below this level probably show little or no rise in average real income per head between 1938 and 1949, and a rise of rather under 20 per cent thereafter.

Effects of Income Redistribution on Tax Yields

This very remarkable redistribution of personal incomes before tax accounts for an apparent anomaly in the figures for the yield of personal income tax and surtax, which are set out in Table VI. As was shown in Table II, tax rates on constant levels of real income have doubled, or more than doubled, since 1938. Nevertheless, the proportion of total (attributable) personal income paid in tax has risen only from 7 per cent to just over 10 per cent, or by 44 per cent. In addition, we must take account of the rise in the total of such incomes, amounting to 18 per cent. The combined effect of these two factors is that the real yield of tax on personal incomes has risen by 70 per cent, from £614 millions to £1042 millions measured at 1949 prices—still very far short of the increase in tax rates.

If, with the same increase in aggregate real personal incomes, the distribution of that income had remained the same in 1955 as in 1938, the rise in the real yield of income tax and surtax on personal incomes would have been not 70 per cent but something like 160 per cent. The yield would have been approximately £1600 millions at 1949 prices and over £2000

TABLE VI
TAX ON PERSONAL INCOMES

(a) Percentage of Incomes paid in Tax					
Income Range	1938 %	1949 %	1953 %	1954 %	1955 %
1st 100,000	38·2	57·6	57·2	57·5	55·8
2nd ,,	19·7	35·6	35·2	36·0	35·4
3rd ,,	16·0	31·4	27·6	28·6	27·7
4th ,,	15·1	29·2	24·6	25·9	22·6
5th ,,	12·5	27·5	22·7	24·3	20·6
1st 500,000	28·3	43·5	41·2	41·7	39·9
2nd ,,	8·8	22·2	16·2	17·9	16·5
1st million	24·0	37·7	34·1	34·7	33·1
2nd ,,	2·8	12·6	12·3	12·4	12·1
3rd ,,	1·5	10·6	9·6	9·1	9·5
4th ,,	0·4	8·7	8·2	7·3	6·7
5th ,,	0·4	7·5	6·5	6·0	6·3
1st 5 millions	13·5	22·8	19·8	19·7	18·8
2nd ,,	—	6·0	3·3	4·5	5·0
1st 10 millions	10·3	17·7	14·5	14·6	14·0
Remainder	—	0·7	2·2	2·6	2·7
Total tax paid	7·0	12·1	10·3	10·4	10·1

(b) Percentage of Total Tax contributed by Income Groups					
Income Range	1938 %	1949 %	1953 %	1954 %	1955 %
1st 100,000	63·8	33·7	32·4	30·1	29·5
2nd ,,	10·1	8·5	8·8	8·3	8·6
3rd ,,	5·9	5·8	5·2	5·1	4·8
4th ,,	4·2	4·3	3·7	3·9	3·4
5th ,,	2·9	3·5	3·1	3·2	2·7
1st 500,000	87·0	55·9	53·2	50·6	49·0
2nd ,,	7·8	10·8	8·4	8·9	8·2
1st million	94·8	66·7	61·6	59·5	57·2
2nd ,,	3·3	8·7	9·8	9·2	9·4
3rd ,,	1·3	5·6	6·0	5·6	6·0
4th ,,	0·3	4·0	4·8	4·1	3·7
5th ,,	0·3	3·1	3·5	3·2	3·5
1st 5 millions	100·0	88·1	85·7	81·6	79·8
2nd ,,	—	10·0	6·9	9·2	11·0
1st 10 millions	100·0	98·1	92·6	90·8	90·8
Remainder	—	1·9	7·4	9·2	9·2
	100·0	100·0	100·0	100·0	100·0

millions at 1955 prices. This compares with the actual yield of £1042 millions at 1949 prices and £1340 millions at 1955 prices.

The greater part of the difference is accounted for by the loss of taxable capacity in the first 100,000 incomes. These, in spite of a doubling of tax rates, actually paid only £307 millions in tax in 1955, as compared with £392 millions in 1938, the tax being measured in both cases at 1949 prices. Had their share of income before tax remained as in 1938, they would have paid something like £800 millions at 1949 prices, or over £1000 millions at 1955 prices, compared with the actual payment in that year of £390 millions. It therefore seems that the very high rates of tax which have been in force since the war cannot be attributed entirely to increased Government expenditure. It is not unreasonable to say that they have been occasioned also by the loss of taxable capacity in the higher incomes, a loss which, with highly progressive rates of tax, is offset only to a small extent by the rise in the lower incomes. If income distribution before tax were to-day the same as it was in 1938, the present total yield from taxes on personal incomes could be obtained with tax rates about one-third lower all round.

CHANGES SINCE 1949

The effects on tax yields of the changes in income distribution since 1949, while much smaller than those since 1938, have been similar in tendency. With the same total personal income and tax rates as in 1955, but with a 1949 distribution of incomes before tax, the yield of personal income tax and surtax would have been some £200 millions higher than in fact it was, of which some £150 millions would have come from the highest 100,000 incomes. The trend was still continuing in 1955. In 1949 the 100,000 highest incomes, with 7·1 per cent of total income before tax, contributed 33·7 per cent of total tax collected. In 1953, with 5·8 per cent of total income, they contributed 32·4 per cent. In 1954, the share of total income going to this group further declined to 5·5 per cent and their share of total tax collected to 30·1 per cent, while in the following year their share of income dropped to 5·3 per cent and

their contribution to the total tax collected to 29·5 per cent.
For the first million incomes the movement was similar :

First Million Incomes		
	Share of Total Income	Share of Total Tax Collected
	%	%
1949	21·5	66·7
1953	18·4	61·6
1954	18·0	59·5
1955	17·4	57·2

REAL INCOMES AFTER TAX

Even if the distribution of income before tax had remained
unchanged, the great rise in rates of tax since 1938 would, of
course, have caused a very large fall in the real value after tax
of the highest incomes. In spite of a postulated rise of 20 per
cent *before* tax, the aggregate real incomes *after* tax of the first
100,000 would have fallen by 40 per cent or more. In actual
fact, however, the effects of taxation on the highest incomes, as
shown in Table VII, have been overshadowed by the fall in
the total of those incomes *before* tax.

For the first 100,000, the higher rates of tax merely converted a fall in real incomes of 46 per cent before tax into one
of 62 per cent after tax. It is on the ranges of incomes between
£910 and £3850 that the higher tax rates have had their
relatively greatest effect. The rise in taxation increased the
loss of the remainder of the first half million (those with gross
incomes in 1955 between £1625 and £3850) from 15 per cent
before tax to 26 per cent after tax ; the loss of the second half
million (those with incomes between £1175 and £1625) was
increased by higher taxation from 4 to 12 per cent ; and for
the second million (drawing incomes in 1955 between £910
and £1175) a potential gain of 12 per cent before tax was
almost entirely eliminated by taxation. At lower levels, the
effects of tax increases again become relatively unimportant.
For the largest gainers before tax, the second five millions, the
higher tax rates have merely reduced a gain of 59 per cent

TABLE VII
CHANGES IN RETAINED INCOMES, ADJUSTED
FOR CHANGES IN PRICES, 1949 = 100

(a) Changes in Income Groups					
Income Range	1938	1949	1953	1954	1955
1st 100,000	239	100	88	87	92
2nd ,,	153	100	95	94	100
3rd ,,	141	100	96	98	99
4th ,,	133	100	100	102	110
5th ,,	126	100	100	101	106
1st 500,000	174	100	94	94	99
2nd ,,	123	100	102	105	109
1st million	157	100	97	98	102
2nd ,,	109	100	104	106	110
3rd ,,	102	100	107	112	118
4th ,,	98	100	113	120	124
5th ,,	95	100	115	122	126
1st 5 millions	122	100	104	108	112
2nd ,,	86	100	113	121	130
1st 10 millions	110	100	107	112	119
Remainder	96	100	112	115	122
Total Incomes	105	100	109	114	120

(b) Percentage of Total in Income Groups					
Income Range	1938 %	1949 %	1953 %	1954 %	1955 %
1st 100,000	7·8	3·4	2·8	2·6	2·6
2nd ,,	3·1	2·1	1·8	1·8	1·8
3rd ,,	2·3	1·7	1·5	1·5	1·4
4th ,,	1·8	1·4	1·3	1·3	1·3
5th ,,	1·6	1·3	1·2	1·1	1·1
1st 500,000	16·6	10·0	8·6	8·3	8·2
2nd ,,	6·1	5·2	4·9	4·8	4·7
1st million	22·7	15·2	13·5	13·1	12·9
2nd ,,	8·6	8·2	7·8	7·7	7·6
3rd ,,	6·4	6·5	6·4	6·4	6·4
4th ,,	5·4	5·8	6·0	6·1	6·0
5th ,,	4·8	5·3	5·6	5·7	5·6
1st 5 millions	47·9	41·0	39·3	39·0	38·5
2nd ,,	18·1	21·9	22·7	23·3	23·9
1st 10 millions	66·0	62·9	62·0	62·3	62·4
Remainder	34·0	37·1	38·0	37·7	37·6
	100·0	100·0	100·0	100·0	100·0

before tax to one of 52 per cent after tax, while for the remainder a gain of about 19 per cent per head is reduced to one of 16 per cent.

How far the two conflicting tendencies, of inflation to raise tax yields and of income redistribution to lower them, will continue to operate in the future depends largely on how successful are the present attempts to check the rise in prices. If prices can be stabilised, or the rapidity of their rise greatly reduced, Chancellors will no longer be able to rely on rising money incomes to provide them with increasing proportions of constant real incomes. Hence they will no longer be able to make inexpensive bids for popularity by reductions in tax *rates* which do not in fact do more than prevent the real burden of taxation from rising. On the other hand, since the fall in the share of the higher income groups has been due largely to rising prices, their stabilisation would also be likely to slow down the process of income redistribution or even bring it to an end. It seems likely, however, that the process of redistribution would tend to slow down even if prices continued to rise. This could be partly because maturing fixed-interest securities can now be re-invested to yield a higher income, partly perhaps as an effect of modifying or abolishing rent-restriction. Most of all it could be because investors and others, as they come increasingly to anticipate continuously rising prices, will increasingly seek out means for ensuring that their money incomes rise at least part of the way with them.

POSTSCRIPT (May, 1961)

CHANGES IN TAXATION SINCE 1956–57

During the five years between 1956–57 and 1961–62 there were four major reductions in direct taxation of individuals. By the first, in 1957, the earned income allowance of two-ninths was extended, for income tax only, to incomes between £2000 and £4000 a year and of one-ninth to incomes between £4000 and £10,000; by the second, in 1959, the standard rate of income tax was reduced from 8s. 6d. in the pound to 7s. 9d.; by the third, in 1961, the earned income reliefs previously allowed for income tax were extended to surtax; and by the fourth, also in 1961, a special earned income allowance of up to £2000 was introduced for purposes of surtax. The combined effect of the last two measures was to exempt from surtax altogether all wholly earned incomes below £5000 a year, substantially to reduce surtax payments on earned incomes above that level, and to reduce the rates of surtax payable on the investment part of a partly earned income. In addition, in 1957 children's allowances were increased for children between 11 and 16, and further for children over 16, while the excess of total personal allowances over the single allowance was made deductible for purposes of surtax as well as of income tax.

Since the average annual rise in prices was much less than in earlier periods, the benefits received by taxpayers from these reductions in rates were much less illusory than those from earlier reductions, and there were substantial falls in the proportion paid in tax at all levels, not only of earned money incomes but of earned real incomes. The extent of these reductions is shown in the last four columns of Table I. It will be observed that in 1961–62 the proportions paid in tax

TABLE I

PERCENTAGES OF INCOMES PAID IN INCOME
TAX AND SURTAX

(Married Couple with Two Children under 11. All Earned Income)

	Constant Money Incomes			Constant Real Incomes					
				1956–57		1961–62		Rate of Tax in 1961–62 as % of Rate of Tax in	
	1947–1948	1956–1957	1961–1962	Equivalents of 1947–48 Incomes*	% Paid in Tax	Equivalents of 1947–48 Incomes*	% Paid in Tax	1947–1948	1956–1957
£									
600	10·6	0·5	0·4	869	6·0	925	6·3	59·4	105·0
,000	21·4	8·5	7·7	1,448	16·0	1,542	13·0	60·7	81·2
,500	26·7	16·6	15·1	2,170	23·2	2,314	20·4	76·4	87·9
,000	31·3	20·7	18·8	2,896	30·5	3,084	22·8	72·8	74·7
,000	49·7	43·9	26·5	7,240	52·8	7,710	33·4	67·0	63·3
,000	64·1	60·0	38·8	14,480	68·5	15,420	52·0	81·0	76·0

* The price index used for converting money incomes to their 1947–48 equivalents has been ;htly revised.

were substantially lower than in 1947–48 for all levels of
earned real incomes, the reductions ranging from 40 per cent
of the 1947–48 ratio for the equivalent of £600 in 1947–48
to 19 per cent for the equivalent of £10,000.

THE DISTRIBUTION OF INCOMES

The most recent year for which the distribution of personal
incomes can be estimated (from Table 22 of the National
Income Blue Book, 1960) is 1959. It is surprising to find that,
in spite of the relaxation of rent restriction and more liberal
dividend distributions by companies, the distribution of
personal incomes before tax was a good deal more equal in
1959 than it had been in 1955. In 1959 the proportion of all
attributable personal incomes received by the first half million
(those with incomes above £1930 a year) was 11·5 per cent,
as compared with 12·3 per cent in 1955 and 15·6 per cent in
1949, while the first million (with incomes over £1400 a year)
received 16·2 per cent, as against 17·4 and 21·5 per cent.
While the downward trend in the proportion going to the
highest income groups was thus a continuation of that of
earlier years, there was a marked change in the beneficiaries
from the redistribution. Whereas in earlier years the largest
gainers were the middle income groups (the second five
millions, with incomes between £625 and £825 in 1959),
between 1955 and 1959 this group suffered a reduction in its
share of the total, from 22·8 to 21·6 per cent, and the beneficiaries of the shift in distribution were the lower groups, and
particularly the two lowest groups, with incomes below £460
in 1959, whose share of the total rose from 18·5 per cent in
1955 to 20·8 per cent in 1959. Only a very small part of this
increase can be accounted for by the rise in their number from
11·2 millions in 1955 to 11·35 millions in 1959.

The effects of this shift in distribution of personal incomes
are shown very clearly in the changes in real incomes before
tax (last column but one of Table II). It is estimated that the
real incomes before tax of the first million rose by 2·7 per
cent between 1955 and 1959, of the first five millions by 6 per
cent, and of the second five millions by 5·3 per cent. In
contrast, real incomes before tax of the third five millions are

TABLE II
DISTRIBUTION OF INCOMES AND CHANGES IN REAL INCOME, 1955–59*

	Income Range		Percentage Distribution of						Real Incomes in 1959 as percentage of Real Incomes in 1955	
			Income Before Tax		Tax Payments		Income After Tax			
	1955	1959	1955	1959	1955	1959	1955	1959	Before Tax	After Tax
1st 100,000	3850+	4450+	5·3	4·8	29·8	24·4	2·6	2·6	100·5	110·3
2nd ,,	2700–3850	3150–4450	2·4	2·3	8·7	7·1	1·7	1·7	102·8	108·5
3rd ,,	2150–2700	2540–3150	1·8	1·7	5·1	4·8	1·4	1·4	105·4	105·7
4th ,,	1825–2150	2180–2540	1·5	1·5	3·9	3·6	1·2	1·2	108·5	109·4
5th ,,	1625–1825	1930–2180	1·3	1·2	3·1	2·4	1·1	1·1	103·4	109·0
1st 500,000	1625+	1930+	12·3	11·5	50·7	42·3	8·1	7·9	102·9	109·0
2nd ,,	1175–1625	1400–1930	5·1	4·7	8·2	7·1	4·7	4·4	102·3	103·2
1st million	1175+	1400+	17·4	16·2	58·9	49·4	12·8	12·3	102·7	106·8
2nd ,,	910–1175	1080–1400	7·6	7·6	8·2	8·9	7·6	7·5	110·8	109·3
3rd ,,	810–910	950–1080	6·5	6·2	4·8	5·9	6·6	6·2	106·6	104·0
4th ,,	750–810	875–950	5·9	5·7	3·7	4·5	6·1	5·8	107·0	105·0
5th ,,	710–750	825–875	5·3	5·1	3·0	3·6	5·6	5·3	106·2	104·4
1st 5 millions	710+	825+	42·7	40·8	78·7	72·3	38·8	37·1	106·0	106·1
2nd ,,	515–710	625–825	22·8	21·6	11·6	13·4	24·0	22·6	105·3	104·0
3rd ,,	360–515	460–625	16·0	16·8	6·7	9·5	17·0	17·6	116·4	114·5
4th ,,	220–360	295–460	10·5	11·6	3·0	4·5	11·3	12·4	122·6	121·2
Remainder†	50–220	50–295	8·0	9·2	—	0·3	8·9	10·3	128·5	128·1
Total	50+	50+	100·0	100·0	100·0	100·0	100·0	100·0	110·9	110·7

* 1955 figures slightly revised.   † 6,200,000 in 1955 ; 6,350,000 in 1959.

estimated to have risen by 16·4 per cent, of the fourth five millions by 22·6 per cent, and of the remainder by 28·5 per cent, or more than 25 per cent per head.

The changes in the estimated distribution of incomes before tax are modified, though only slightly, by the effects of taxation. These were twofold. On the one hand, the reductions in tax rates reduced the proportions of some incomes paid in tax, especially those in the higher groups, which increased least before tax. On the other hand, the combination of higher prices and higher real incomes brought many of the lower incomes so far into higher tax groups that, in spite of lower tax rates, they paid both a higher proportion of all taxes paid and a higher proportion of their incomes before tax. As a net result, the proportion of all incomes paid in tax went up slightly, from 10 to 10·2 per cent, in spite of the reduction in tax rates. Of total tax payments, the proportion paid by the first million incomes fell from 58·9 to 49·4 per cent, while that paid by the next four millions rose from 19·8 to 22·9 per cent, and by the remainder from 21·3 to 27·7 per cent. The fall in the proportion of income paid in tax by the first million incomes meant that their share of total income after tax fell only from 12·8 to 12·3 per cent, while the fall in the share of the next four millions was accentuated, with a decline from 26 to 24·8 per cent, as compared with one from 25·3 to 24·4 per cent before tax. The decline in the share of the second five millions was also slightly greater after than before tax, but for the lower groups combined tax changes made practically no difference to the rise in their share. A similar impression is made by the estimates of changes in real incomes after tax. The rise in real incomes was very much increased by tax changes for the highest 500,000 incomes, especially for the highest 200,000, slightly increased for the second 500,000, and slightly reduced for the remainder. Apart from an exceptional gain of over 9 per cent by the second million, the gain of 9 per cent in real incomes after tax made by the top 500,000 is not again equalled until we come to the increases of 14½ per cent for the third five millions, 21 per cent for the fourth five millions, and about 25 per cent per head for the remainder. These last three groups are the only ones in which the increases in real incomes exceeded the national average rise of 10·9 per cent before tax and 10·7 per cent after tax.

While it should be recognised that official estimates of income distribution, especially in the lower half of the range, are highly tentative and liable to revision, it is thought unlikely that they are so wildly wrong as to render fictitious the impression of a substantial trend towards greater equality of incomes, and of rapidly rising real incomes towards the bottom of the scale. One cause of this trend seems to have been the rapid rise in this period of incomes derived from national insurance benefits and other grants from public authorities. Income from these sources appears to have risen between 1955 and 1959 by 46 per cent in money terms and 32 per cent in real terms, as compared with rises in total attributable incomes before tax of 23 per cent in money terms and 11 per cent in real terms. The rise in social security benefits does not, however, seem to account for more than about half the increase in the share of real income before tax going to the lowest groups. If the apparent facts of this increase are even approximately correct, they represent a major step towards the reduction of poverty.

CHAPTER 16

AN ECONOMIST'S APPROACH TO THE FUNCTIONS OF INDUSTRY[1]

ACCORDING to the dictionary, there are two possible meanings which can be attached to the word 'function' as used in the title of this paper. The first meaning is 'what Industry is actually doing', and the second 'what Industry ought to be doing'. An economist, as such, is concerned only with the first of these meanings. His job, like that of all scientists, is to observe facts and events and to attempt to establish causal relationships between them, in the hope that he may thereby be able to develop generalisations which may, in turn, conceivably enable him, in particularly favourable conditions, to predict with some hope of success the future results of known events. His only liking should be accuracy, and his only dislike a non-sequitur.

The chances of an economist making successful predictions are, of course, much smaller than are those of most natural scientists. For the facts and events he has to observe, being the results of human actions, are far more numerous and far more complex than those with which most natural scientists have to deal; and further, since most of his data refer to the combined effects of the actions of very large numbers of people, he cannot normally make experiments under artificially simplified conditions. Such simplifications as he can make — and very great simplification is necessary, for it is obviously quite impossible either to observe or to work with the millions of variables of which his raw data are composed — must in general be hypothetical, arbitrary, and subjective. He can only hope that, in choosing his simplifications, he will be lucky enough to select the two or three variables — or, if he is a mathematician, perhaps the six or even twelve — which in the particular case under consideration are so important that they

[1] Paper prepared for Seminar on Problems in Industrial Administration, London School of Economics, March 1951.

will outweigh the millions which have to be neglected and will enable him to give a prediction more accurate than a random guess.

The economist's proper approach to the functions of industry can therefore be only one of enquiry. If a stranger stops one and asks if he is going the right way, it is rarely possible to answer intelligently until one has found out where it is he wants to go. There are, of course, times when there is a very strong presumption that he cannot possibly be going the right way about reaching his destination, whatever it may be. If, for instance, you meet him going up a passage which leads only to the foot of a down escalator, it is a fair guess that he is going the wrong way — though of course he may be going back to look for a parcel he has lost or may even enjoy running up a down escalator. Even more certainly, if you encounter a motorist who is accelerating with his handbrake full on, or a government of a country with full employment which is trying to reduce the cost of living while expanding the quantity of money, you may be able to say that, whatever he is trying to do, he is unlikely to achieve it. But the occasions when an economist finds a business man in such a situation, when he can advise without knowing the objective sought, are probably not very frequent.

Unfortunately, the economist cannot ask every business man what his aims are; if he could, he would very often not receive a clear answer; and even if he did receive nothing but clear answers, the extreme complication of the picture revealed would probably defeat his powers of analysis. He is therefore often driven to make simplifying assumptions; and provided that he remembers that the assumptions are only assumptions, and do not necessarily reflect real life, he may sometimes be able to draw useful conclusions. One such possible assumption is that business men wish to maximise their profits; another, that they wish to maintain a certain optimum balance between their different forms of assets. No doubt, it would be possible to find others — a business man whose objective at the moment is a seat in the House of Lords; or a quiet life; or a business within easy reach of a good golf-links; or to produce the world's most beautiful lead soldiers. On the obtaining of some of these objectives an economist's experience may enable his advice to be of use, on others not. But, except perhaps where an industrialist is pursuing two or more objectives which are clearly incompatible, the only attitude an economist can take to what he is doing is to observe it.

But economists, like other scientists, are also men, which means that they cannot help making judgments of their own and becoming interested in the function of industry in the second sense of the word — what industry ought to be doing. Now if we are asked by an enquirer, not 'Am I going the right way?' but 'Where ought I to go?' there are three possible criteria for the answer. The first is what the adviser thinks will benefit himself; the second is what the adviser thinks will be good for the advisee; and the third is what the adviser thinks the advisee will prefer. Thus, for instance, I can recommend the questioner to go to the boarding-house I keep myself; or I can recommend him to go to a temperance hotel; or I can say that I think he will like the George & Dragon best. While very few of us would admit that we are influenced by the first of these criteria, it is not easy for any of us to give advice which is directly contrary to our own interests. Thus, however much university teachers may favour a reduction in general Government expenditure, it is unusual to find one who considers that the University Grant stands high on the list for cutting. Again, the fact that university teachers do not suffer seriously from unemployment in depressions, and receive salaries which are adjusted only slowly to changes in the cost of living, may have something to do with the fact that they tend to be opposed to inflation in favour of 'sound money'.

While this natural bias towards self-interest is probably common in greater or less degree to all of us, there is an active difference between those who support the second of the criteria mentioned and those who support the third — between those who want to make other people do what they think is good for them, and those who want to help other people to achieve their own ends. On the whole, I think the majority of economists fall into the latter class. Perhaps it is because, in their professional capacities, they have to try to find out what people are wanting to do that they take an additional step and begin to want to help them to do what they want. But in so doing they have, of course, stepped over the line between the scientific and the ethical, and their opinions about the validity of this criterion are of no more value than those of anyone else.

The criterion is not necessarily a hedonistic one. It is true that for a man who knows what he wants any extension of freedom of choice increases his chance of increasing his satisfaction. The more shades of stockings there are, for instance, the more likely it is that any particular buyer will get exactly the shade she wants. But it may very well be that people who do not know just what they want may feel an increase in the range of their choice not as a pleasure but as a responsibility. It is true that they can frequently obtain professional advice, sometimes free of charge; or they may save themselves trouble by choosing to abandon part of their freedom, as when they prefer to go on a conducted tour instead of travelling on their own. But the choice of which advice to follow, or of whether to go on a conducted tour at all or, if so, which, still remains the responsibility of the consumer, which he may not always welcome. Nevertheless, it is my own belief that the only way to learn to exercise responsibility is by having to exercise it; and that a nation where the maximum of responsibility for choice is borne by the individual citizens is one which is more stable, more adult and, in the long run, happier than one in which people merely do what they are told, however wise the instructors may be.

Even when we accept as our criterion the general extension of freedom of choice, we have to solve other problems before we can translate it into policy. We are at once brought up against the difficulty that to extend freedom of choice for one may limit it for another, and that the attempt to secure complete freedom for everyone is necessarily self-frustrating. If, for instance, we attempt to reduce the limitations on choice due to poverty by transferring income from one man to another, we necessarily also reduce the freedom of choice of the one from whom income is taken. This does not mean that we should not do it, for we may hold, by a political judgment, that the gain is more important than the loss. But at least we see that it is not a net gain, and that it would be still better to make someone richer without having to make anyone else poorer.

Again, to extend the range of choice open to a man in his capacity as producer will probably entail a curtailment of the freedom of other producers, or of consumers, or both. If he is free to expand his output and lower prices, he may very well curtail the opportunities of other producers. If he is free to raise prices by restricting output, he will curtail the opportunities of consumers. How are we to choose between these conflicting interests ? Whose freedom are we to limit in order to extend that of others ?

I think we must look for the answer by trying to find those extensions of opportunity which are generally compatible with each other, and giving them preference over those which are not. Each of us may become better off in one of two ways — by greater plenty of the things we want to buy and by greater scarcity of the things we want to sell. But only by the first of these ways can we all succeed in our objectives ; for a scarcity of what we have to sell means a scarcity of what someone else wants to buy, and a scarcity of what they want to sell means a scarcity of what we want to buy. If all of us choose to reduce output it is inevitable that most of us, and possibly that all of us, will find our other freedoms of choice correspondingly curtailed.

If, on the other hand, we exercise our freedom of choice in the direction of expanding output our ends are not necessarily conflicting, and it is probable that most of us, and possible that all of us, will find our other freedoms of choice expanded. How far there will be exceptions to the general improvement will depend on how far it is possible to shift resources from producing those goods and services which as a result of the general increase in output are in relatively less demand into producing those which are in relatively greater demand. The greater the mobility of resources, the more widely will the benefits be shared.

If it is desired to help the minority who, because they find it difficult to move, are worse off as a result of a general increase in output, the help should be given, not in the form of enabling them to stay where they are without loss, but of helping some of them to move into the production of things which are now in relatively greater demand.

It is therefore only by looking at the problem entirely from the point of view of our interests as consumers, and ignoring our interests as producers, that we can hope to render internally consistent our objective of a general widening of the area of choice. In other words, the function (in the second sense) of industry is to serve the consumer, by increasing the quantity of its output, by adapting it continuously in accordance with his changing wants, and by attempting to anticipate his still unrealised wants by offering him a continually increasing variety from which to choose. So far as I can see, it has no other functions.

Both for enabling producers to discover what the consumer's wants really are, and for inducing him to do his best to supply them, no machinery has yet been invented to beat the price system operating in a competitive market. In such a market, that firm will make the largest profits which most correctly follows, or better still anticipates, changes in consumer demand. It is perhaps for this reason that economists have tended to take profit maximisation as the obvious simplification of a producer's objectives, for in a competitive system it is only the producer who maximises his profits who is acting as a faithful servant of the consumer. Otherwise he is producing less than he might of what the consumer wants most, whether because his total production is less than it might be, or because he is producing some things that the consumer wants less in place of things which the consumer wants more. (Profit maximisation does not mean, of course, the mere maximisation of short-run profits, which might prove most wasteful in the long run. Probably the best definition is the maximisation of the discounted present aggregate value of all expected future profits.)

It is only under conditions of competition that profit maximisation is an indication that the best possible service is being provided for consumers. Where any really substantial degree of monopoly exists it is possible for the producer to increase his profits by restricting output either in quantity or variety, or alternatively to relax his efforts and enjoy a quiet life without being penalised by reduced profits or by losses. Wherever monopoly conditions exist, there is a very strong presumption that industry is not doing all it could to fulfil its function.

In conclusion, it may be remarked that Governments frequently intervene to prevent industry from serving the consumer as well as it could. Governments inevitably have to express those consumers' demands which can only be expressed collectively — the demands for defence and for law and order are the most obvious ones. But to-day Governments frequently insist on making collective demands which could perfectly well have been expressed individually, and on taxing consumers to finance the supply of some things when they would have preferred to spend the money on others. Sometimes such action is excused by the plea of income re-distribution; this, however, is not justified, because income redistribution can be better achieved by paying money to the beneficiaries and allowing them to spend it in accordance with their own preferences. The giving of benefits in kind can be justified only if we adopt the criterion which I rejected earlier in this paper — that other people should have what we think is good for them rather than what they want. A similar objection can be made about giving people goods or services at subsidised prices rather than giving them the corresponding money to spend at their own discretion. I am afraid there is nothing that industry can do about this, for an attempt to adjust production to what demand would have been if consumers had been left to formulate it for themselves would hardly be likely to be successful. It can only continue to obey the demand, as affected by Government action, and assume that the collective wants so formulated do in fact represent the real priorities of the consumers concerned.

There are other ways also in which governments interfere with industry's ability to serve the consumer. It is no doubt possible to make a case for controlling sales to the public of firearms, poisons, and habit-forming drugs, but it is difficult to see why, if a man happens to lose his handkerchief after six o'clock in the evening, any retailer who remedied his need by selling him another should be regarded as committing a crime. It may be desirable to control the sale of spirits as if they were poisons, but does it really add to the well-being of consumers to prevent cafés from selling light wines or beer? Is it really injurious to consumers that a man should help country-dwellers to visit the local town by starting a new bus service that he thinks will yield him a profit? If we once accept the principle that the sole function of industry is to serve the consumer, it also throws some light on the functions of governments.

CHAPTER 17

OUTPUT, INFLATION, AND GROWTH

THE PROBLEM STATED

THERE have been few periods in British history when economists have found the situation more perplexing than they do at present, or were more divided in their views. At the moment of writing (July 1961) the country seems to be threatened with its fourth major balance-of-payments crisis since the war. Like its predecessors in 1947, 1951, and 1955,[1] the present adverse balance of payments on current account is accompanied by symptoms of internal inflationary pressure, and in particular by more rapid rises in wages and other incomes than in output. Why is it that this country cannot run prosperously for more than a very few years without getting into trouble?

In face of these difficulties, economic commentators have produced a wide variety of diagnoses and an even wider variety of prescriptions. Some, concentrating their attention on the balance-of-payments difficulties, have advocated import restrictions, devaluation of sterling, or a 'floating pound'. Others have laid the blame on the trade unions for forcing up wage rates, and have deduced that what is needed is a 'wages policy' to prevent wages from rising faster than output per head. Others again have observed that inflationary pressure and rising prices have been most in evidence, not in periods when output has been rising rapidly, but after the rise has been slowed down or checked; and they have deduced from this that what we need to do is to keep output rising as rapidly as possible in all circumstances. They condemn as self-frustrating any action to restrain demand and slow down the rise in incomes, since such action usually has the effect of also checking the rise in output.

[1] The crises of 1949 and 1957 were crises of international confidence rather than the result of current weakness in the balance of payments on income account.

In the analysis attempted here, an alternative interpretation is put forward. This, though much over-simplified, seems to be internally consistent, and also to fit the facts of recent years better than some of the interpretations previously advanced.

I

THEORETICAL ANALYSIS

Productive Capacity and its Utilisation.—The first step is to break down any change in the volume of output into two component parts : a change in the level of productive capacity and a change in the proportion of that capacity currently in use. The significance of a given rise in output cannot be appreciated unless we know whether it was accompanied by a rise or a fall in the margin of unused resources. For instance, a rise of 3 per cent in output during a year may represent a 2 per cent rise in productive capacity plus a 1 per cent rise in the proportion of capacity employed; or it may represent a rise of 3 per cent in capacity with no change in the proportion of capacity employed; or a rise of 4 per cent in productive capacity with a fall of 1 per cent in the proportion employed. Until we know which of these possible situations exists, we cannot make any useful diagnosis of the situation.

The Margin of Unused Capacity and the Rise in Incomes.— The next step in the argument is to make the assumption, which appears to have considerable statistical confirmation,[1] that, at any rate in conditions of near-full employment,[2] the most important factor in determining the rate of rise in money incomes is the proportion of productive capacity currently employed.[3] If we accept this assumption, it follows that, in any given system at any given time, there must be some

[1] See A. W. Phillips, 'The Relation between Unemployment and the Rate of Change of Money Wage Rates in the U.K., 1861–1957', *Economica*, November 1958; R. G. Lipsey, 'The Relation between Unemployment and the Rate of Change in Money Wage Rates in the U.K., 1862–1957; A Further Analysis', *Economica*, February 1960; L. A. Dicks-Mireaux and J. C. R. Dow, 'The Determinants of Wage Inflation : United Kingdom, 1946–56', *The Journal of the Royal Statistical Society*, 1959.

[2] A system is defined as working at full capacity when a further increase in demand brings no further increase in output.

[3] A second factor affecting the rate of rise in money incomes is probably the rate of rise in output. It seems likely, however, that at levels approaching full employment this factor is less important than the size of the margin of

margin of unused capacity at which money incomes will rise at an annual rate equal to that of the growth of productive capacity. If the margin of unused capacity can be permanently stabilised at just this level, with the rate of rise in actual production kept equal to the rate of rise in productive capacity, we have, in a closed system, the necessary conditions for long-term price stability, since output and incomes will always rise at the same rate.

Long-term and Short-term Price Stability.—While, however, these conditions are the only ones in which price stability will be permanent, it is quite possible for prices to remain stable for a limited period even with a margin of unused resources smaller than that postulated above. This can be achieved by allowing output to rise faster than productive capacity and running down the margin of unused capacity. So long as this process can continue, incomes can also rise faster than productive capacity without rising faster than output. Let us put the growth of capacity at 3 per cent a year, and the proportion of unused capacity needed to prevent incomes from growing by more than 3 per cent a year at 5 per cent. Let us start from a position where the proportion of capacity in use is 96 per cent, so that the margin or unused capacity is only 4 per cent, and let us assume that in the recent past output has been rising at 3 per cent a year. Since the margin of unused capacity is less than 5 per cent, money incomes have been rising by more than 3 per cent a year. Let us say that they have been rising at 4 per cent a year, so that prices have been rising by 1 per cent a year.

Let us now take steps, by stimulating demand, to increase the rate of growth of output to 6 per cent a year, at the cost of a further reduction in unused capacity. At first the rise in output will be faster than the rise in incomes, and the rise in prices will stop. As, however, the margin of unused resources is absorbed, the rise in incomes will be accelerated, while as output approaches full capacity its rate of increase will decline. After a period of stability, which may last a year or more,

---

unused capacity, unless, perhaps, output is increasing extremely fast. When, however, the margin of unused capacity is very large, its exact size is probably less important, and changes in the rate of rise in output may well be more important as a cause of income change.

incomes will again be rising faster than output, and the rise in prices will be resumed. Once full capacity is reached, and the rise in output has to slow down to 3 per cent, the disparity between the rate of rise in incomes and the rate of rise in output is likely to become large and the rate of rise in prices consequently rapid. Thus a year of rapid growth of output with stable prices will have been bought at the cost of a great intensification of inflationary pressure and a great acceleration in the rise of prices after the end of the year. Any equilibrium between a rise in incomes and a rise in output obtained by reducing the margin of unused capacity below the long-term equilibrium level is inevitably unstable and temporary.

Just as the penalties for allowing incomes to rise faster than capacity may be postponed, at the cost of a subsequent increase in their severity, so long as output can rise faster than capacity, so are the benefits of measures taken to check the rise in incomes also postponed so long as the rise in output continues to be checked. Let us assume that, at the moment when output is about to reach full capacity, the Government and monetary authorities take steps to restrict demand. Whatever the measures taken,[1] they will serve to check the rise in output. For a time incomes will continue to rise rapidly, so that the rise in prices will continue and may even be accelerated. As, however, output is now rising more slowly than capacity, a new margin of unused resources is created. As this margin increases, the rate of rise in incomes, and with it the rate of rise in prices, begins to slow down. When the proportion of unused capacity has risen to 5 per cent, the Government can afford to relax its restraints and allow output to begin to rise again. Since by this time the rate of rise of incomes will have fallen to 3 per cent a year, a 3 per cent per annum rise in output will be sufficient to restore price stability, which is now, and only now, achieved, and the system will be in long-term equilibrium. If, however, output is allowed to rise by more than 3 per cent, the margin of unused resources will again fall below 5 per cent and the system will again have become fundamentally unstable, though the instability may be con-

---

[1] Other than direct control of wages and other incomes. For discussion of the effectiveness of a policy of controlling wage-rates, see Chapter 6, pp. 99-161, and Chapter 7, pp. 106-109 and 116-117.

cealed for a year or two, while the margin of unused capacity, so painfully created, is being used up.

Problems of a Fluctuating Equilibrium.—If output falls so far that the margin of unused resources becomes greater than is needed in order to equate the rate of growth of incomes with the rate of growth of capacity, the Government's task becomes one of considerable delicacy. On the one hand, it will probably not wish to sacrifice more output than is necessary to prevent a rise in prices; on the other, it is not easy to judge just how much stimulus to give to the economy to bring the margin of unused resources down to the long-term equilibrium ratio, but no further. In practice, it is extremely probable that the Government will overshoot the mark and reduce the margin of unused resources too far. If as soon as it realises what is happening it puts on the brakes again, it will probably overshoot again in the opposite direction. The best we can probably hope for is a series of not too large fluctuations in the amount of productive capacity in use round about the long-term equilibrium level. This will entail periods, mainly while the margin of unused capacity is greater than 5 per cent but falling, when output is rising faster than incomes, and other periods, mainly while the margin of unused capacity is less than 5 per cent but rising, when incomes are rising faster than output. If prices and incomes were equally flexible in both directions this would not matter; for periods of rising prices would be followed by similar periods of falling prices. But if, as is likely in practice, incomes and prices are more flexible upwards than downwards, prices are likely to rise more and fall less than they would if the system behaved symmetrically, so that the long-term trend of prices would be upward. This would mean that, to maintain long-term price stability, we should have to maintain a larger average margin of unused resources than would be necessary if we could hold prices constant.

Effects of Foreign Trade.—Fortunately at this stage we can abandon our assumption of a closed system and invoke the effects of foreign trade. In a completely open system, with transport costs negligible, a faster rise in incomes than in output shows itself, not in higher prices (except in so far as it induces a rise in prices in the world as a whole) but in larger imports, probably smaller exports, and an adverse balance of payments. In an open system, therefore, alternating periods of income rising faster and slower than output would be accompanied, not by rising and falling prices, but by adverse and favourable balances of payments. Since there is not the same tendency for a rise in imports to be irreversible as there is for a rise in prices, a system encountering alternating phases of favourable and unfavourable balances of payments could well be in long-term equilibrium, provided that it had, or could obtain, sufficient foreign exchange reserves to tide itself over the periods of adverse balance. An open system also has what is probably another advantage over a closed system — that governments are quicker to recognise and react to an adverse balance of payments than they are to a rise of prices. Corrective action is therefore likely both to be taken sooner and to be more effectively enforced.

In practice no system is completely open and few, if any, are completely closed. In recent years, however, the reduction in quantitative import restrictions has meant that most systems have become more open than they have been for many years, so that faster rises in incomes than in outputs now tend to be reflected less than formerly in rising prices and more in adverse balances of payments. The change is, on the whole, likely to make it more probable that countries will be able to maintain long-term equilibrium between incomes and output and to avoid inflation.

On the other hand, the more open a system is to the influence of the outside world, the more possible it is that an otherwise stable equilibrium may be disturbed by changes in world price levels. If both import and export prices rise together, there will be a rise in the money incomes of exporters, and perhaps also of makers of goods competing with imports, while real national income will not be increased. The accelerated rise in incomes will bring a rise in prices, though this may be temporarily slowed down by a rise in output above the long-term equilibrium level. Conversely, a fall in both import and export prices will slow down the rise in money incomes without directly slowing down the rise in real national income, so that output will probably decline to below the long-term equilibrium level. The balance of payments will probably become temporarily favourable in the first case and temporarily adverse in the second.

Changes in Terms of Trade.—It is, however, unlikely that prices of imports and exports will rise or fall equally, except perhaps as the result of changes in exchange rates. When world prices rise or fall the changes tend to be greater in prices of raw materials and foodstuffs than of manufactured goods. In the special case of the United Kingdom, a general rise in world prices therefore tends to be accompanied by a worsening of the terms of trade, and a general fall in prices by an improvement. These changes in the terms of trade tend to intensify the effects on the internal situation of the changes in the general level of world prices. A rise in export prices accompanied by a larger rise in import prices both accelerates the rise in money incomes and slows down the rise in real income, thus creating still more excess demand; while a fall in export prices accompanied by a larger fall in import prices slows down the rise in money incomes while accelerating the rise in real income, and may well depress the volume of production to well below the equilibrium level and bring an undesiredly high proportion of unused resources.

While, however, these external influences might well prove unwelcome to a country already in long-term equilibrium, they may, on occasion, come in very useful in helping a country to escape from a position of unbalance. While the rise in import prices in 1950–51 greatly intensified the existing inflationary pressure in the United Kingdom, the two major falls in import prices, in 1951–52 and 1957–58, were of great assistance in arresting inflation.

II

DEVELOPMENTS IN THE UNITED KINGDOM SINCE 1948

Fluctuations in Production.—We are now in a position to begin our examination of economic developments in the United Kingdom since the war. In Chart I on p. 316, and Table I in the Statistical Appendix, is shown a quarterly index, seasonally adjusted, of gross domestic product at 1954 factor cost prices. The figures for 1955 and later years are derived from official quarterly estimates; earlier quarterly estimates have been obtained by breaking down the official annual estimates into

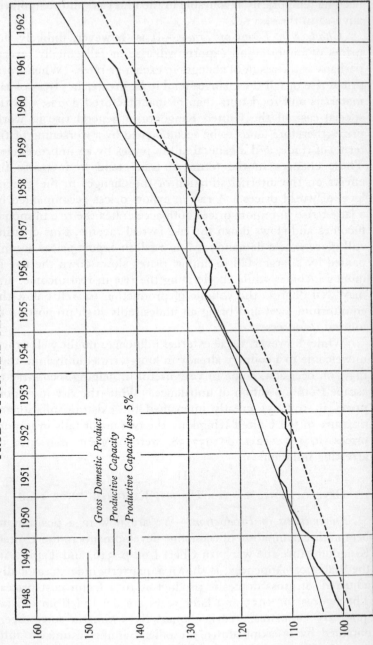

CHART I
PRODUCTION AND PRODUCTIVE CAPACITY

quarters with the help of the index of industrial production. The production curve shows three periods of rising output; from the first quarter of 1948 to the second quarter of 1951; from the second quarter of 1952 to the last quarter of 1955; and from the third quarter of 1958 to the second quarter of 1960. There is also a short period of rising output from the third quarter of 1956 to the second quarter of 1957; and there is a somewhat similar rise in the first half of 1961.

There are similarly three periods of stationary or falling output: from the second quarter of 1951 to the second quarter of 1952; from the last quarter of 1955 to the third quarter of 1958 (interrupted by the minor rise in 1956–57 mentioned above); and from the second quarter to the last quarter of 1960.

Productive Capacity.—The next step is to fit to our output curve another curve to represent the growth of productive capacity. This is defined as the rate at which output can grow with capacity fully employed. This condition would appear to have been satisfied at the 1951 and 1955 output peaks, and we can be reasonably confident that the increase in output between these peaks indicates the actual growth of capacity. Using Table 14 of the 1961 National Income Blue Book, we find that gross domestic product is estimated to have risen from 1951 to 1955 by 11·6 per cent, or at a cumulative rate of about 2·8 per cent a year. If we attempt greater precision by using the quarterly estimates, we find a rise of 12·6 per cent from the second quarter of 1951 to the last quarter of 1955, or an average cumulative rise of just over 2·7 per cent a year.

When we come to the 1960 peak, however, we find that it does not seem to coincide with a period of absolutely full employment. While many industries were fully employed, some, including some makers of consumers' durables, clearly were not. This view is confirmed by the index of unemployment, which never fell during the quarter below 1·5 per cent, as compared with 1·0 per cent at the two earlier peaks. We cannot therefore compare 1960 with 1951 and 1955 to measure the growth of productive capacity. If we wish to extend our observations outside the period 1951–55, we must assume that we can measure the growth of capacity by measuring the growth of output, not only between periods of fully employed capacity, but also between periods in which the proportions of resources in use are similar. This assumption seems reasonable where the percentages of unused capacity are small. Unfortunately, except at points of obviously fully employed capacity, we cannot measure the proportion of capacity in use until we know how much capacity has grown; and we cannot measure the rate of growth in capacity until we know the proportion in use.

Construction of an Index of Productive Capacity : Unemployment Percentages.—In this impasse we are driven to fall back on an outside criterion; and the only one available is the proportion of the labour force currently employed. This criterion is not likely to be a wholly satisfactory one. It is a matter of common observation that when the rise in output is checked, employers tend to retain, at least for some time, a good deal of labour although it is no longer fully employed, so that some of the margin of unused capacity created is in the form of the under-utilisation of labour which is recorded as employed. Conversely, when demand recovers, the first capacity to be re-employed tends to be this unused margin of capacity in the existing labour force. Thus, fluctuations in the proportion of labour employed may be expected to lag behind changes in the proportion of total capacity in use. It is, therefore, unlikely that we can use the unemployment figures as an index of the proportion of total capacity without some reservations. Nevertheless, as it is the only criterion we have, let us test it for the period 1951–55, for which we have a reasonably satisfactory measure of the growth of capacity.

In Table II of the Appendix is set out an index of capacity, rising from 100 in the second quarter of 1951 to 112·6 in the last quarter of 1955, at a cumulative rate of about 2·7 per cent a year. Against this we set an index of gross domestic product at constant prices, also rising from 100 to 112·6, but fluctuating widely in the interim. From these two series we calculate a quarterly index of the proportion of total capacity currently employed. A fourth series gives the seasonally corrected quarterly averages of the percentage of the labour force employed. These last two series are plotted on Chart II (p. 319). Since at both points of fully employed capacity the unemployment percentage was 1 per cent, we have taken 99 per cent as representing full employment.

It is at once clear that the fluctuations in the employment of labour are very much smaller than in the employment of total capacity, and in Chart II the labour employment percentages are given a scale five times as large as that used for the percentages of total capacity employed.[1] On these scales, it would appear that the fit of the two series is unexpectedly good. The period of retention of under-utilised labour in the

CHART II
PERCENTAGES OF CAPACITY AND LABOUR EMPLOYED, 1951-55

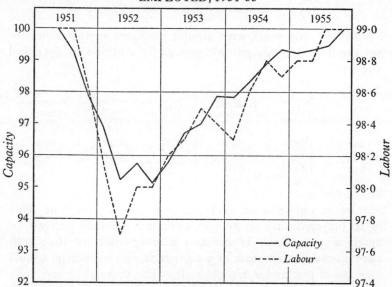

second half of 1951 is brief, and the short-lived discrepancies in the first and second quarters of 1952 and the first quarter of 1954 may well be due to inadequately corrected seasonal movements. The result is sufficiently encouraging to justify the attempt to use this technique for investigating movements in the years before 1951 and after 1955. As a precaution against possible difference in the timing of fluctuations in the employment of labour and capacity, we shall, however, make comparisons only between years in similar positions in the cycle.

[1] The reasons for the much greater fluctuations in the employment of total capacity than of labour include, in addition to changes in the utilisation of employed labour, changes in the length of the working week and in the number of marginal workers entering or leaving the working force.

L 2

Rates of Growth of Capacity.—Let us start by classifying years according to their average percentages of unemployment:

Year	Unemployment Percentage	Year	Unemployment Percentage
1948	1·75	1955	1·10
1949	1·65	1956	1·27
1950	1·42	1957	1·52
1951	1·15	1958	2·17
1952	2·07	1959	2·25
1953	1·65	1960	1·70
1954	1·40		

Taking only years with similar positions in the cycle, we get the following comparable groups (in addition to 1951 and 1955):

	(1)			(2)	
Year	Unemployment Percentage	Production Index	Year	Unemployment Percentage	Production Index
1948	1·75	84·2	1950	1·42	90·9
1949	1·65	87·6	1954	1·40	100·0
1953	1·65	95·8			
1960	1·70	117·7			

Group 2 gives us an aggregate increase over the four years of 10 per cent, and an average cumulative annual increase of nearly 2·5 per cent. In group 1 a comparison of 1949 with 1953 gives a total increase of 9·5 per cent, and an average annual increase of just under 2·4 per cent. The years 1948 and 1960 are not quite comparable with 1949 and 1953 as they stand. We can, however, make them so by allowing 0·5 per cent of output for each 0·1 per cent difference in unemployment. This would make the adjusted index for 1948 84·6 and for 1960 117·9, and gives us the following aggregate increases and annual rates of growth:

Years	Aggregate Increase %	Average Annual Increase (Cumulative)
1948 to 1953	13·4	2·5
1948 to 1960	39·4	2·8
1953 to 1960	23·0	3·0

If we take as our annual rates of growth 2·5 per cent from
1948 to 1953 and 3 per cent from 1953 to 1960 we shall probably not be far out. Before, however, starting to calculate our
index of productive capacity we have one more adjustment to
make. At the end of 1959 many wage awards took the form of
a reduction, usually of two hours, in the length of the standard
working week. In consequence, the average standard week
was reduced, over a wide range of occupations, by about an
hour. Half of this loss was made good by an increase in overtime, but the average length of the week actually worked fell
by half an hour, or rather over 1 per cent, and this fall is still
maintained. It is reasonable to assume that, if the average
number of hours worked a week had remained unchanged,
both capacity and production after the end of 1959 would have
been about 1 per cent higher. To correct for this discontinuous
change, in calculating the rate of growth of capacity we must
add 1 per cent to the gross domestic product for 1960. This
brings the rate of growth of capacity from 1953 to 1959, and
again from 1960 onwards, up to just over 3·1 per cent a year.
The annual rates of growth we shall use for calculating our
index of capacity are therefore 2·5 per cent from 1948 to 1953
and 3·1 per cent for 1953 onwards, with a discontinuous
reduction in capacity of 1 per cent at the end of 1959.

The abrupt increase in the annual rate of growth after 1953
is not, perhaps, a very plausible assumption, though the sharp
rise in industrial fixed investment from 1954 onwards does
lend it some support. One would expect the rise to be a more
gradual one, and in fact there is some evidence that in fact it
was. When we come to Table III we shall see that, although
unemployment in 1956 was much lower than in 1948, 1953,
and 1960, the proportion of capacity in use was very similar.
If we treat 1956 also as a comparable year, we get an annual
rate of increase of 2·9 per cent from 1953 to 1956 and of 3·2
per cent a year from 1956 to 1959 and again from 1960 onwards. The evidence is, however, too slender to provide a
base for the actual construction of our index, and the difference it would have made so far is too small to be of practical
importance. In future years, however, the difference between
a rate of growth of 3·1 per cent a year and one of 3·2 per cent a
year would ultimately become of some significance. Before

that time comes, it is to be hoped that other evidence will become available to confirm or correct the figures used here.

We can now proceed to work out our index of productive capacity, and to fit it to our index of gross domestic product by calculating forward and backward from the two quarters, the second of 1951 and the last of 1955, in which capacity is assumed to have been fully employed. The result is reproduced in Chart I and also in Table I of the Appendix.

Margin of Unused Capacity.—The fitting of the productive capacity curve does a good deal in itself to assist in interpreting the fluctuations of the production index. To get full benefit from it, however, we need a second curve to represent the proportion of capacity which can be used without causing the rate of rise of money incomes to exceed the rate of growth of capacity. The size of the margin of unused capacity needed to secure this objective depends on many factors, and no doubt varies widely from country to country. The factors concerned probably include the following, no doubt among many others.

Among the most important of these factors is certainly the rate of growth of capacity itself. The higher the rate of growth of capacity, the higher the rate of income growth that is consistent with long-term price stability; and since the rate of income growth is assumed to vary inversely with the margin of unused capacity, this means that the higher the rate of growth of capacity the smaller is the margin of unused resources needed to prevent inflation. So far from creating unemployment, a high rate of technical progress makes a low level of unemployment compatible with stable prices.

A second factor is certainly the mobility and adaptability both of employers and employees. If distances between centres of employment are large, if industries are highly concentrated, and if all concerned are reluctant to change their methods of work, occupations, and domiciles, the process of moving capacity from places where it is no longer needed will be slow and the amount of unused capacity will be accordingly large.

Finally, the size of the necessary margin will depend to a considerable extent on the strength and policies of the trade unions. These will be exercised partly through the obstacles they impose on the free movement of labour, and especially of skilled men, from one occupation to another; and partly through the energy and force with which they press their claims for higher wages or other cost-raising benefits. It is possible to make assumptions about the power and policies of unions which would make it necessary, in order to avoid inflation, to maintain an unemployment level of 5 per cent or more.[1] It is unlikely that the five to one ratio between changes in the margin of unused capacity and in the percentage of unemployment continues to hold good indefinitely as unemployment rises (or with 20 per cent unemployment there would be no production at all), but with 5 per cent of unemployment there would certainly be very considerably more than 5 per cent of unused capacity. The recognition of this potential power of the unions to widen the margin of unused capacity needed to prevent inflation to a level which would be politically unacceptable, provides some kind of a bridge between the 'cost-push' and 'demand-pull' theories of inflation. Fortunately, in this country, the historical evidence gives little support to the view that the trade unions have in fact acted in this way.

The Margin of Unused Capacity and the Rate of Income Growth.—To facilitate a judgment of the amount of unused capacity which is needed in this country at the present time in order to maintain long-term equilibrium between rises in incomes and rises in output, estimates of the proportion of capacity employed in each quarter are plotted in Chart III and are set out in Table III of the Appendix. With them, for purposes of comparison, are plotted the proportions of labour employed, on the same scales as in Chart II. The full chart makes it clear that we were fortunate in the closeness of the fit between the unemployment of capacity and the unemployment of labour in the period 1951 and 1955. Both in the years before 1951 and in those after 1955 the similarity of the movements is much less close. While the magnitudes of the movements in the two series maintain the same general relationship, we find that those of the unemployment figures, as would be expected on *a priori* grounds, lag considerably behind those of the capacity utilisation figures, often by several months and

---

[1] See C. D. Finch 'Some Problems of Wages Policy'. (Unpublished London Ph.D. Thesis.)

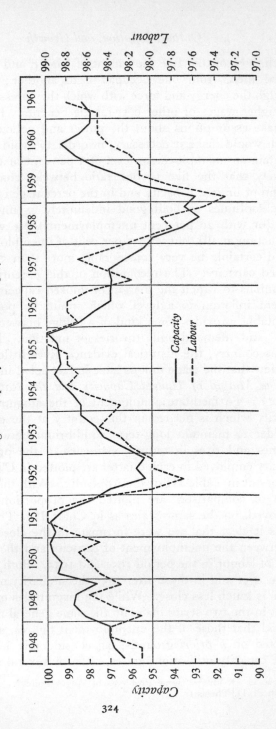

CHART III

A. EMPLOYMENT LEVELS AND CHANGES IN INCOMES AND PRICES

Percentages of Capacity and Labour Employed

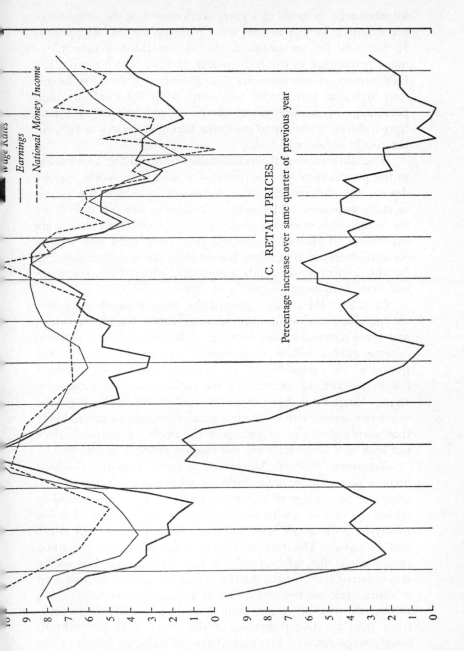

Wage Rates
—— Earnings
---- National Money Income

C. RETAIL PRICES
Percentage increase over same quarter of previous year

sometimes by as much as a year. It is clear that the unemployment figures, by themselves, are of little use for deciding policy. It may well be, for instance, that it was the low unemployment percentage in the last quarter of 1957 which caused the Government to continue its disinflationary policy for longer into 1958 than was strictly necessary, while the relatively high percentage of unemployment in the second half of 1959 may have induced it unduly to postpone taking measures to restrain the rise in incomes and output.

The difference of the relationship between the two curves in the period 1951–55 from what it was in other years may be due to the difference in the industries in which the excess capacity appeared. The 1951–52 recession was felt mainly by the textile industries, especially cotton, which with their long experience of shrinking demand may have been less willing (or able) to retain redundant labour than the rapidly expanding durable consumption goods industries, which were the main sufferers in 1956–57 and again in 1960.

On Chart III are also plotted the percentage changes over the previous twelve months of wage rates, weekly earnings, and gross national money income. The earnings and national income curves follow very similar courses, except for the period of the 'wage-freeze' in 1948–49, and the unexplained fall in the rate of increase of the national money income in 1955. Wage rates, however, move rather differently from the other two series, with wage rates accelerating much more slowly than earnings on the up-swings of the cycle. It certainly does not look as if wage-rates are the leading element in inflation.

Necessary Size of Margin of Unused Capacity.—These income series throw some light on what we can regard as an adequate percentage of unused capacity. The only period in which the rate of rise in national money income slowed down to anything like a safe level was from the middle of 1958 to the end of 1959. The rate of rise in wage-rates also remained round about the safety level for this period. (It should be remembered that in 1959–60 the average length of the standard working week was reduced by about an hour, or over 2 per cent, so that the rise of $3\frac{1}{2}$ per cent in average weekly wage rates from 1959 to 1960 represents a rise of over $5\frac{1}{2}$ per cent in hourly wage-rates.) The rate of rise in earnings fell to safety level in the last quarter of 1958, and rose above it again in the last quarter of 1959.

The other series shown in Chart III is of changes in the retail price index. This series is less significant for our purpose than the income series, for, as we have seen, it is possible to stabilise prices temporarily, even with incomes rising faster than capacity, by allowing the margin of unused capacity to run down. This is what seems to have happened in 1953–54, when the rise in prices was not resumed until the summer of 1954, when the rate of rise in output was slackening with the approach to full capacity; and again in 1959–60, when prices began to rise again only when the rise in output was checked in the second quarter of 1960.

An inspection of Chart III suggests that the only period since the war when the proportion of capacity in use was consistent with long-term price equilibrium was in 1958 and the first half of 1959. Production was below 95 per cent of capacity from the first quarter of 1958 to the second quarter of 1959, below 94 per cent from the second quarter of 1958 to the first quarter of 1959, and below 93 per cent in the third quarter of 1958. The recovery of 1959–60 makes it impossible to say which of these levels would have been just sufficient, if maintained, to ensure long-term price stability without unnecessary loss of output. Economic opinion at the time was unanimously of the view that the level of activity ruling in the second half of 1958 was unnecessarily low, and it is impossible to be sure that it was wrong. It does not, however, seem possible to put the necessary margin of unused capacity at less than 5 per cent, which roughly corresponds to 2 per cent of unemployment, and it may well have been higher, though probably not very much higher. We may probably put it somewhere within the range of 5 to 7 per cent, corresponding to between 2 and $2\frac{1}{2}$ per cent of unemployment. This conclusion is consistent with Professor Phillips' estimate that just over 2 per cent of unemployment is consistent with a rise in wage-rates of $2\frac{1}{2}$ per cent a year.[1] For purposes of policy, it would probably be wise to work on the basis of a 5 per cent margin until this is proved to be inadequate.

It is not always realised that a margin of unused capacity

[1] A. W. Phillips, *op. cit.*

averaging 5 per cent does not involve a large rise over recent
years in the average levels either of unused capacity or of
unemployment. For the five years, 1956 to 1960, the margin
of unused capacity averaged 3·9 per cent and the percentage
of unemployment 1·8. Averages of 5 and 2 per cent would
thus involve a loss of output of only a little over 1 per cent
and a rise in the average number of unemployed of 0·2 per
cent, or 50,000. If the Government's policies were directed to
facilitating the movement to new occupations of those dis-
placed, it could be expected that most of these would be
unemployed for relatively short periods. There is also a case
for more generous unemployment assistance, especially in the
first few weeks of unemployment, for those genuinely seeking
alternative work. It should be remembered that earlier action
to prevent the margin of unused capacity from falling below
the 5 per cent mark would also render it less likely that, from
time to time, it would be forced up, by belated emergency
action, far above it.

The Overstrained Economy.—The addition of a 95 per cent
line to Charts I and III enables us to bring economic developments since the war into much sharper focus. It becomes
clear that the only time in which the economy has been in long-
term equilibrium was in the eighteen months from the end of
1957 to the middle of 1959, although it was also near that
position during the last three quarters of 1952. If this diagnosis
is accepted, the basic cause of Britain's recurrent post-war
difficulties becomes apparent. It also becomes clear that two
periods of price stability, from the beginning of 1953 to the
middle of 1954, and from the middle of 1959 to the second
quarter of 1960, were inevitably temporary, though that of
1959–60 might have been prolonged a little longer, at the cost
of worse trouble later, by allowing output to continue to rise
faster than capacity until it reached the capacity ceiling.

The various measures taken by the Government to check
the over-rapid rise in incomes in 1947–48, 1951–52, and 1955–
1957 have been described in the paper written in 1958 and republished in this volume, on 'Monetary Policy and the Control
of the Post-War British Inflation'. It was there pointed out
that all successful Government interventions had been assisted
by independent changes in the economic situation — in 1951–

1952 both by a fall in import prices and by a spontaneous rise in personal saving, in 1956 by another sudden leap in personal saving (much larger than can be accounted for by the hire purchase restrictions), and in 1957–58 by another fall in import prices. What was not then so obvious was that the margin of unused capacity had already begun to widen, both in 1951 and 1957, well before most of the emergency measures were taken; only in 1955 did the turn come after the Government measures designed to check the rise in incomes.

Recent Developments.—At the end of the paper mentioned above, it was stated that the post-war British inflation was over, and that it would need deliberate action by the Government to re-start it. Whether deliberately or not, the Government duly obliged. In making over-generous tax concessions in the budget of 1959, it may have made the same mistake as the present writer in believing that it was 'doubtful if such financial controls as remain (in 1958) are now having any important effect'. In fact, the removal of restrictions on bank advances permitted them to rise by £1500 millions, or nearly 80 per cent, in less than three years. Although part of this rise was offset by bank sales of securities, which kept the rise in deposits down and the rate of interest up, a mere change in the banks' assets from investments to advances can be expected to have a markedly expansionary effect on incomes. In addition, the removal of hire purchase restrictions gave rise to an orgy of consumer credit expansion. The combined effect of these three relaxations brought a very rapid rise in demand and production. Between the first quarter of 1959 and the second quarter of 1960 output rose by 9 per cent, the equivalent of three years growth of capacity, and the margin of unused capacity is estimated to have fallen from 7 to 1½ per cent.

The Government must be given credit for trying to restrain the rise in incomes at a much earlier stage than in the upswing of 1952–55, and for checking the decline in the unused margin of capacity before it fell to nothing. The methods used, apart from the re-imposition of hire purchase controls, were, however, almost entirely monetary; and as the expansionary measures taken in 1959 had been largely fiscal, the result has been to force long-term interest rates to unprecedented height. While it is easy to understand the difficulty of raising taxes in the 1960 budget, after reducing them so shortly before the 1959 election, it is unfortunate that the policies of expansion and restraint were so asymmetrical. If demand is always to be stimulated by tax reductions, and checked by monetary policy, there is no limit to the rise in interest rates.

The balance between fiscal and monetary policy has been only very partially restored in the emergency measures announced in July 1961. Although a part of the task of checking the excessive rise in money incomes has been entrusted to a rise in indirect taxation, a large, and perhaps the greater, part of the work has again been left to monetary policy.

Criteria for Long-term Price Stabilisation.—It is believed that the use of the technique here suggested, of attempting to stabilise the margin of unused capacity at a level at which money incomes rise at the same rate as capacity, would enable the Government considerably to reduce the magnitude of fluctuations in the growth of output and the level of employment, as well as to prevent or reduce rises in prices and balance-of-payments difficulties. In putting the policy into practice there are, however, two difficulties to be overcome.

The first is that of distinguishing changes in the rate of growth of capacity from changes in the extent of its utilisation. This difficulty is not likely to be insuperable. The rate of growth of capacity changes only slowly over time. Since 1953 it is estimated to have increased only from 2·9 per cent a year to 3·1 per cent a year, or by an average of less than one-twenty-fifth of 1 per cent a year. At this rate, a change in the rate of growth of capacity could go unobserved for several years without distorting the estimates sufficiently to make them seriously misleading for purposes of policy. By the time this distortion became large enough to be significant, it should be possible, by an examination of the full records of previous years (especially of rates of rise in money incomes and the unemployment figures, suitably adjusted for time-lags), to obtain clues to the change in the rate of growth.

The other difficulty, which may in practice prove more serious, is that of obtaining estimates of gross domestic product sufficiently up-to-date to enable policy decisions to be taken in time. Here it can only be hoped that the recent reductions in the delay in publishing official statistics will be continued.

Meanwhile, a reasonable guess can be made by combining the index of industrial production with an extrapolation of the much steadier trend of non-industrial production, which employs about half the working population.

The Growth of Capacity.—The final question we have to consider is that of the relationship between the proportion of capacity in use and the rate of growth of capacity. The problem of price and balance-of-payments equilibrium is in principle quite separate from that of the rate of growth of capacity, though many commentators have tended to confuse them. A country with a 2 per cent per annum rate of growth and a 2 per cent per annum rise in incomes will remain fully competitive with a country with a 5 per cent per annum rate of growth and a 5 per cent per annum rise in incomes. Nevertheless, as we have seen, a high rate of growth of capacity considerably facilitates the maintenance of long-term equilibrium between the growth of incomes and the growth of output. The margins of unused resources and unemployed labour required to prevent incomes from rising by more than 5 per cent a year are considerably smaller than those needed to prevent them rising by more than 2 per cent a year, and the social and political difficulties of maintaining them consequently less. An increase in the rate of growth of capacity will therefore not only increase the rate of growth in the standard of living, but will also facilitate the maintenance of stable prices and an adequate balance of payments.

Conversely, changes in the proportion of capacity employed are probably not without some effect on the rate of growth of capacity. It has here been assumed that the rate of growth of capacity is not affected by small and short-term fluctuations in the proportion of capacity used. This does not, however, mean that permanent changes in the average level of utilisation of capacity might not have some effect on its rate of growth. If a large proportion of capacity remains unused for long periods it may well be that the long-term rate of growth will be slowed down ; though the rapid recovery to its former trend line, after the deep and prolonged depression of the 1930s, of production per head in the United States, suggests that even this cannot be taken for granted. But the permanent maintenance of the small proportion of unused capacity suggested here would be more likely to increase than decrease the rate of growth of capacity.

In conditions of excess demand, with every firm over-booked with orders, there can be no effective competition. Only if at least a few firms in every industry are short of orders and urgently seeking new business does competition become a reality. In its absence, there is no compulsion on the least efficient firms either to improve their efficiency or to go out of business. If, as the result of more effective competition, the rate of progress of the least efficient firms could be brought nearer to that of the most efficient, the resultant increase in the average rate of growth of efficiency might well be substantial.

Other measures to increase the rate of growth of capacity would probably need to be taken over a wide front. More physical investment would, by itself, probably be less effective than is often supposed. The benefits of a large further rise in saving would probably be seen rather in a relief of inflationary pressure and a more favourable balance of payments than in any rapid increase in the rate of growth of capacity. Spectacular increases in rates of growth, obtained from increases in physical investment by themselves, occur only where all the concomitant factors are abundant and the lack of capital presents the only bottleneck. In Britain to-day, the removal of the particular bottleneck of capital shortage would only too probably reveal a whole series of others lying behind it. Meanwhile, some comfort can be derived from the reflection that our present long-term rate of growth in output per head, though probably lower than in some other countries with different conditions and at different stages of development, is perhaps twice what it was either in the inter-war period or in the twenty years preceding 1914. It is probably also slightly higher than the average rate of growth in output per head in the United States during the past century.

STATISTICAL APPENDIX
TABLE I
PRODUCTION AND PRODUCTIVE CAPACITY

Quarter	Gross Domestic Product	Productive Capacity	Productive Capacity less 5%	Quarter	Gross Domestic Product	Productive Capacity	Productive Capacity less 5%
1948				1956			
1	100·0	103·8	98·6	1	125·4	127·4	120·9
2	101·1	104·4	99·2	2	125·4	128·4	121·9
3	101·8	105·0	99·8	3	125·3	129·4	122·8
4	102·5	105·6	100·4	4	126·3	130·4	123·8
1949				1957			
1	104·3	106·2	101·0	1	127·0	131·4	124·8
2	105·5	106·9	101·6	2	128·4	132·4	125·7
3	105·9	107·5	102·2	3	128·1	133·4	126·7
4	105·5	108·2	102·8	4	128·0	134·4	127·7
1950				1958			
1	108·2	108·9	103·4	1	128·2	135·4	128·7
2	108·7	109·6	104·1	2	127·4	136·4	129·6
3	109·9	110·2	104·7	3	127·2	137·4	130·5
4	110·8	110·9	105·3	4	129·1	138·5	131·5
1951				1959			
1	111·1	111·6	106·0	1	129·9	139·5	132·5
2	112·3	112·3	106·7	2	133·5	140·6	133·5
3	112·2	113·0	107·3	3	135·9	141·7	134·5
4	111·2	113·7	107·9	4	138·8	142·8	135·6
1952				1960			
1	111·0	114·4	108·6	1	140·6	143·1	135·9
2	109·8	115·1	109·3	2	141·8	143·4	136·2
3	111·0	115·8	109·9	3	141·7	144·5	137·2
4	111·0	116·5	110·6	4	141·9	145·6	138·2
1953				1961			
1	112·9	117·2	111·3	1	142·6	146·7	139·3
2	114·6	117·9	112·0	2	144·5	147·8	140·4
3	115·8	118·6	112·7	3	(144·6)	148·9	141·4
4	117·6	119·3	113·3	4	(143·2)	150·1	142·5
1954				1962			
1	118·2	120·0	114·0	1		151·2	143·6
2	119·6	120·9	114·8	2		152·4	144·7
3	121·0	121·8	115·7	3		153·5	145·8
4	122·3	122·7	116·6	4		154·7	146·9
1955				1963			
1	122·9	123·6	117·4	1		155·9	148·0
2	124·0	124·5	118·2	2		157·1	149·1
3	125·0	125·5	119·2	3		158·3	150·3
4	126·5	126·5	120·1	4		159·5	151·5

TABLE II

PERCENTAGES OF CAPACITY AND LABOUR
EMPLOYED 1951–55*

Quarter	Output	Capacity	Percentage of Capacity Employed	Percentage of Labour Employed
1951				
2	100·0	100·0	100·0	99·0
3	99·9	100·7	99·2	99·0
4	99·0	101·3	97·8	98·6
1952				
1	98·9	102·0	96·9	98·0
2	97·8	102·7	95·2	97·7
3	98·9	103·4	95·7	98·0
4	98·9	104·1	95·1	98·0
1953				
1	100·5	104·8	95·8	98·2
2	102·0	105·5	96·7	98·3
3	103·1	106·2	97·0	98·5
4	104·7	106·9	97·9	98·4
1954				
1	105·3	107·6	97·8	98·3
2	106·5	108·3	98·3	98·6
3	107·8	109·0	98·9	98·8
4	108·9	109·7	99·3	98·7
1955				
1	109·5	110·4	99·2	98·8
2	110·4	111·2	99·3	98·8
3	111·3	111·9	99·4	99·0
4	112·6	112·6	100·0	99·0

* Table II differs slightly from Table III, since in Table II capacity is assumed to rise continuously at 2·7 per cent a year, while in Table III it is assumed to rise at 2·5 per cent a year until the end of 1953 and at 3·1 per cent a year from the end of 1953 onward.

Table III
EMPLOYMENT OF RESOURCES AND RATES OF CHANGE IN INCOMES

Quarters	Percentages Employed		Percentage Increases over previous 12 Months			
	Capacity	Labour	Weekly Wage Rates	Weekly Earnings	National Money Income	Retail Prices
1948						
1	96·3	98·1	7·8			
2	96·8	98·1	8·1	8·4 ⎫	10·5	
3	97·0	98·4	6·7	⎬		
4	97·0	98·4	6·1	7·7 ⎭		
1949						
1	98·2	98·1	3·8			3·5
2	98·7	98·4	3·2	4·5 ⎫		2·3
3	98·6	98·6	3·2	⎬	6·5	2·8
4	97·6	98·3	2·1	3·6 ⎭		3·5
1950						
1	99·5	98·5	2·2			4·0
2	99·3	98·6	1·7	4·3 ⎫		3·4
3	99·7	98·7	1·0	⎬	5·0	2·8
4	99·9	98·5	3·1	5·3 ⎭		3·9
1951						
1	99·6	98·8	6·8			4·5
2	100·0	99·0	8·1	9·8 ⎫		8·7
3	99·3	99·0	10·0	⎬	9·8	11·9
4	97·8	98·6	10·5	10·7 ⎭		11·6
1952						
1	97·0	98·0	9·2			12·0
2	95·3	97·7	8·3	8·5 ⎫		10·5
3	95·8	98·0	6·9	⎬	9·0	7·8
4	95·4	98·0	6·3	7·5 ⎭		6·5
1953						
1	96·3	98·2	4·5			5·1
2	97·3	98·3	4·6	7·0 ⎫		3·5
3	97·7	98·5	5·0	⎬	6·8	2·6
4	98·6	98·4	3·1	6·0 ⎭		1·3
1954						
1	98·4	98·3	3·0			0·8
2	98·9	98·6	5·3	6·4 ⎫		0·4
3	99·3	98·8	5·3	⎬	6·9	2·6
4	99·6	98·7	4·9	8·1 ⎭		3·5
1955						
1	99·5	98·8	6·0			4·0
2	99·6	98·8	6·5	8·5 ⎫		4·3
3	99·6	99·0	6·2	⎬	6·1	3·5
4	100·0	99·0	7·0	8·7 ⎭		5·5

[Table III continued overleaf

TABLE III (*Continued*)

EMPLOYMENT OF RESOURCES AND RATES OF CHANGE IN INCOMES

Quarters	Percentages Employed		Percentages Increase over previous 12 Months			
	Capacity	Labour	Weekly Wage Rates	Weekly Earnings	National Money Income	Retail Prices
1956						
1	98·4	98·7	8·0		9·2	5·5
2	97·7	98·8	8·6	8·7	10·4	6·2
3	96·9	98·8	8·6		7·8	4·8
4	96·9	98·6	8·1	7·1	8·1	3·6
1957						
1	96·7	98·2	5·2		7·5	4·1
2	96·9	98·5	4·3	3·8	4·7	2·7
3	96·0	98·7	5·4		6·4	4·3
4	95·2	98·5	5·4	5·9	6·0	4·4
1958						
1	94·7	98·1	5·3		6·1	3·5
2	93·4	97·8	2·8	4·1	3·0	4·3
3	92·5	97·9	2·4		3·8	1·9
4	93·2	97·5	3·7	1·2	3·3	2·2
1959						
1	93·1	97·3	3·4		−0·2	2·3
2	94·6	97·7	3·4	3·0	5·2	−0·3
3	96·0	98·0	2·6		3·0	0·7
4	97·2	98·0	1·4	4·3	2·8	0·0
1960						
1	98·2	98·1	1·9*		8·6	−0·3
2	98·9	98·3	2·5*	5·7	7·1	1·1
3	98·0	98·4	2·5*		4·9	1·5
4	97·4	98·4	3·6*	6·6	4·0	1·5
1961						
1	97·2	98·4	4·5*	6·8	6·3	2·2
2	97·7	98·6	4·0*		4·5	3·0
3	97·1	98·6	4·5*	5·5	7·0	4·1
4	(95·5)	98·3	4·3*			4·4

* Between October 1959 and April 1961, the standard working week was reduced by an average of nearly 1½ hours. The increase in *hourly* wage rates from 1959 to 1961 is therefore about 3 per cent greater than the increase in the weekly rates.

Source for Cols. 2-5 and Col. 6: London and Cambridge Economic Service. Figures revised to Feb. 1962.

PRINTED BY R. & R. CLARK, LTD., EDINBURGH